HISTORICISM AND ORGANICISM IN ECONOMICS:
THE EVOLUTION OF THOUGHT

Ecology, Economy & Environment

VOLUME 6

Historicism and Organicism in Economics: The Evolution of Thought

by

Jacob Jan Krabbe

Wageningen Agricultural University,
Wageningen, The Netherlands

KLUWER ACADEMIC PUBLISHERS

DORDRECHT / BOSTON / LONDON

A C.I.P. Catalogue record for this book is available from the Library of Congress

ISBN-13:978-94-010-7256-4 e-ISBN-13:978-94-009-1689-0
DOI: 10.1007/978-94-009-1689-0

Published by Kluwer Academic Publishers,
P.O. Box 17, 3300 AA Dordrecht, The Netherlands.

Kluwer Academic Publishers incorporates
the publishing programmes of
D. Reidel, Martinus Nijhoff, Dr W. Junk and MTP Press.

Sold and distributed in the U.S.A. and Canada
by Kluwer Academic Publishers,
101 Philip Drive, Norwell, MA 02061, U.S.A.

In all other countries, sold and distributed
by Kluwer Academic Publishers Group,
P.O. Box 322, 3300 AH Dordrecht, The Netherlands.

Printed on acid-free paper

With gratitude to my family and friends.

Contents

Preface

This study looks at the roots of German legacy historistic and organistic economic thought, gives a survey of its development and indicates the present-day significance of these ideas. This approach is also of significance for today's institutional economics, and for the field of environmental and resource economics. In this book these fields of study are referred to in various ways.

Essentially, some new ideas appear to be rather old and, what amounts to the same, some old ideas appear to be topical. This is particularly true of the "historical approach" to the economy, with its idea of development. It is also true of the organistic approach, which is largely tied up with it. The point of departure is my study on the German Historical School, published in Dutch in 1983. The scope of the following work, however, is broader, as it also refers to the evolution of historically oriented and organistically oriented economic thought in general. Thus, a number of authors who did not think along the lines of the Historical School are included. For instance, the organically oriented ideas of Menger and Georgescu-Roegen are also examined, as well as the ideas of those who were among the "Institutionalists" and other present-day writers in this field.

This study is supported by various publications by other writers. A great part of the literature under consideration is in German. To make my study as accessible as possible, I have translated crucial passages. This I have done in a way that expresses what, in my opinion, is the quintessence of the statement. For the interested reader, the original texts can be found in the notes, if not in the text itself. It should be noted that I sometimes quote from the English version of books that originally appeared in German. These are the two main works by Carl Menger. In the footnotes I also give translations of French quotations.

A word of thanks should be given to the board of the Wageningen LEB fund for making my work financially possible. The study was stimulated by the Heilbronn symposia on classical German economists, organized by Professor Jürgen G. Backhaus, who also made numerous valuable suggestions. I am also indebted to Professor Warren J. Samuels for his remarks on the outline of my work, to Professor Emeritus Peter Senn, who was good enough to screen the whole text, and to Dr Pierre van Mouche for his constructive comment on my mathematics. Mrs Margery Rigg-Lyall deserves special thanks for her valuable linguistic contribution. However, I bear the responsibility myself for all controversial ideas that may be found in my work.

On a number of occasions I have put forward the scientific ideas and political ideals of "old writers" on socio-economic development, as discussed in this study. I have done so reluctantly because, knowing that these ideas have often been criticized by many authoritative methodologists, I was not sure that this would be welcome. However, I have been delighted to meet numerous colleagues who have already accepted the legacy of these old authors, elaborating their ideas and incorporating them into present-day economic thought.

This book is a report of my reading on the subject. I realize that the choice of writers and ideas contains a personal element and that other choices could be have made equally well. In fact, the field of historistic and organic thought is much broader than discussed in this book. I have confined myself to the "German legacy" and an actualization of these ideas, elaborating on its significance for the interaction between economy and nature, a main point of orientation in classical German as well as in modern economics. My work is meant to be a stimulus for further study on the subject of historicism and organicism.

Heelsum, Netherlands
August, 1995

Jaap Krabbe

Chapter 1
CONCEPT AND ITS MATRIX

In nineteenth-century Germany a special orientation of economic thought developed which has become known as the Historical School. After the Napoleonic conquests, the socio-economic system of what was still an agrarian and feudal society began to develop rapidly. In this cultural climate a historically and organically oriented type of economic thought flourished, which was focussed mainly on economic development. The idea of development was partly formulated in organic terms, which later came to be expressed by the Darwinian term "evolution". The present study is concerned with this way of thought: what it means, what its roots were, and what its significance to economics is.

During the nineteenth century, Adam Smith's message of *laissez faire*, "no government intervention", completed its triumphal march throughout the world. In Germany especially, people were looking for more refined ways of thought that were better tuned to economic reality and topical problems of economic policy. Romanticism became the philosophical basis for a renewed approach. Against this background appeared the works of Wilhelm Roscher, Karl Knies and Bruno Hildebrand, founders of the Historical School. Unlike Karl Marx, they did not radically reject the optimistic liberal economic view of the Classical School. Rather, they relativized the Classical model, focussing their criticism on the following points. A Classical approach like that of David Ricardo was considered specifically individualistic, legitimizing objectionable effects of personal egoism. Further, it was believed that Classical theory wrongly claimed to be applicable to all stages of economic development. The Historical School attempted to avoid such shortcomings by using a methodology which was, at least partly, "organistic".

This current in economic thought became differentiated in the last quarter of the century. On one side, the tradition of "historicism" was continued by the so-called Younger Historical School. On the other side, in the new German Empire shaped by Bismarck, the *Verein für Socialpolitik* was founded, which can be translated as the "Society of Socio-economic Politics", "Society of Social Economics" or "Association for Social and Economic Reform". This society was orientated towards the "social question". The man who played a dominant role on both sides was Gustav Schmoller. In the field of organically oriented economics, however, Schmoller's adversary, Carl Menger, also inherited part of Roscher's legacy, laying the foundation of what I call New Organicism. The impact of the Historical School on economic thought was also considerable in other respects, for instance in the fields of institutional economics, social economics, agricultural economics and environmental and resource economics. There was also a link with modern economic theory through Alfred Marshall, especially as far as the latter was institutionally and evolutionary orientated.

Professor Jan Zuidema elucidated the character of nineteenth-century German economics, which still bore traits of the Cameralist thought of previous centuries, as follows.

> At the universities the future civil servants were educated in law, statistics and economics, among other subjects. That is why so many handbooks on economics with some economic theory, with public finance, with much history and description, were published in Germany in the years after 1800. Economics was an integral part of the *Staatswissenschaften* ["state sciences"]. (J.R. Zuidema, 1988: p. 20.)

Zuidema noticed that in Germany there were Socialists of the Chair long before Schmoller. He said of the historical dimension of German economics that, in the hands of Enlightened philosophers, 'history acquired a new function; working on history was a preparation for social change'.

In this book I first give a survey of the German Historical School, focussing on its historically and organically oriented ideas. The relationship between individual and society and that between man and nature, typical of this approach, are central. Next, I look at the further development of these and similar ideas. I mention epigones like Menger and Georgescu-Roegen, as well as outstanding members of the School of Institutionalists, several related authors, and a few leading environmental and resource economists. I also present some of my own ideas in the field of "organistic" thought.

Enlightenment

The ideas of authors presented in this study do not stand alone, but fit in with certain philosophical movements of their time. My survey begins in the period when the Enlightenment was giving way to Romanticism. One of the early Enlightened thinkers who should be mentioned in this context was John Locke. His ideas are also found in the works of later philosophers like Montesquieu, Hume and Rousseau. In their own works they often gave Locke's ideas an accent not found in the balanced thought of the original writer. They sometimes expanded Locke's ideas by attaching additional meanings to them. This is particularly true for the concept of "nature", which also included society. The Enlightened world of thought was not determined by Locke's ideas alone. Those of Descartes and Newton also played a part. In science, René Descartes pioneered thinking according to "reason", and Isaac Newton gave scientific thought a mechanical dimension, based on a cosmic concept of "nature". Both developed mathematics further for their own scientific purposes. Rational thought, a physics-oriented idea, was applied by philosophers of the Enlightenment to social problems. Society, at least in its ideal form, was conceived of as a "natural" order. Although this concept was rationally founded, many Enlightened thinkers gave it a metaphysical dimension.

The Enlightenment had an ahistorical character, in the sense that writers had no eye for essential changes in the existence of man during the course of time. Thought was banned by the aprioristic idea of a social development from obscure feudalism to a brilliant future, caused by the gradual breaking through of "reason". Here the qualification "ahistorical" should be properly understood. Inherent to Enlightened thought was the idea of progressive development. This includes the evolution from a primitive society with uncomplicated social relationships, little personal freedom and a low level of production to a society with a refined social structure, personal freedom and welfare. Accompanying this was the idea of a development of scientific thought. In the Enlightened approach these two types of development were interrelated, the one conditioning the other.

This type of social progress can be found in the thinking of Montesquieu. His idea of society was not based on Locke's idea of a "social contract". In his work bearing the significant title *De l'esprit des lois*, "The spirit of the law", Montesquieu put his point of departure at an evolving causality in social relationships (Montesquieu, 1748, 1979). In essence, this evolution was thought of as an unfolding of reason in human thinking and behaviour, a process which was also considered a matter of reason. The order that was supposed to come into existence in this way is the "natural order". However, Montesquieu's view was that the picture of real social relations could differ from this image of a social constellation. This was commented on by Althusser.

> Everything goes to show that Montesquieu did not intend to state the "spirit" of laws, *i.e.* the law of laws, without also stating the bad human side of the spirit of laws: the law of their violation, in one and the same principle. (Althusser, 1959, 1972: p. 37.)

Montesquieu presented societies of differing types in which the various social systems were conditioned by factors like geographic structure and, above all, were determined by a certain "spirit". According to Montesquieu, a form of society determined by a certain way of thinking can arise from another form, characterized by a less "enlightened" way of thought. The spirit determining the social organization, as seen by Montesquieu, was described by Aron.

> L'esprit général d'une nation, c'est la manière d'être, d'agir, de penser et de sentir d'une collectivité particulière, telle que l'ont faite la géographie et l'histoire.[1] (Aron, 1967: p. 52.)

However, this development pattern is not a historical picture, in which every stage has its own value. Montesquieu's thought was focussed on a specific social order that was supposed to appear: the "natural order".

Enlightened thought had a political dimension. In France philosophers were critical of the society that then existed, the *ordre positif*, the "positive order". Many laws of the eighteenth-century state were supposed to frustrate reason. They were seen as obstacles to the *ordre naturel*, "natural order". This aspect was developed by the Physiocrats, whose world of ideas was an economically oriented variant of Enlightened philosophy.

Physiocrats

In the seventeenth century, Colbert revised Louis XIV's imperfect fiscal system. However, he was forced to stay within the limits of what was then feasible. Because aristocratic and ecclesiastical properties were untaxed, and because of various municipal privileges, the main tax burden was still borne by the tenant farmers, although it was somewhat lighter than before. The king's expensive wars, however, meant an increase in taxation, and this strengthened the position of exploiting tax-farmers. Further, there was an industrialization policy which concentrated on keeping down the cost of living in manufacturing towns, by forcing down the price of grain. For this purpose and for securing the town food supply, a system of export restrictions on grain was used. This system, which was also established by Colbert, had a negative effect on the income of the farmers. Therefore, in the period preceding the French Revolution, the situation in French agriculture was alarming. Methods of production were traditional, equipment was poor, and productivities of land and labour were therefore at a low level.

At the beginning of the eighteenth century, Boisguillebert pleaded for a tax reform orientated towards an improvement in agriculture, pointing out the advantages of the free trade of grain. Half-way through the century, Gournay propagated a general liberalization of trade for the same purpose. Within this circle of kindred spirits was Turgot, who was to become known as an economist and a statesman. Soon after this, François Quesnay, the court physician, began collaborating with Victor de Mirabeau, in order to shape what they considered the "economic" idea. They called themselves *les économistes*. Thus, the restructuring of French agriculture by way of free trade had already been suggested. Yet, their

---

[1]The general spirit of a nation is the attitudes, actions, thoughts and sentiments of particular groups, such as are formed by geography and history.

ideas differed from those of Gournay which were mainly pragmatically oriented, while Quesnay's were dogmatic (Thurlings, 1978: p. 128).

So, in the Enlightened approach, the world of social phenomena was supposed to be governed by laws that were stamped by *physica*. To the network of interpersonal relationships supposed to form the "natural order" was added the condition of "natural right". This "right" was applied to the head of state as well as to each individual member of society. The Physiocrats, however, focussed their attention on the individualistic aspect of the idea. This was put into words by P.S. Dupont (de Nemours).

> Le Droit naturel de l'homme, dans son sens primitif le plus général, est le droit que l'homme a de faire ce qui lui est avantageux; ou, comme dit l'Auteur [Quesnay] dont je publie aujourd'hui quelques écrits, le droit que l'homme a aux choses propres à sa jouissance.[2] (Dupont, 1768: pp. ij, iij.)

Here "natural right" refers to the right as well as the duty of the individual to take care of himself and his dependants. This typically individualistic approach towards social empiricism has remained a characteristic of Classical and Neo-classical economics.

The name "physiocrats" of the Quesnay school was derived from the word *physiocratie*, the key word in the title of Dupont's work. This name was well chosen. It refers to the most characteristic aspect of this variant of Enlightened thought, the integration of biology into the idea of natural order. For the Physiocrats, this order was not confined to the universe, ruling itself, but was supposed to include the organic nature that serves mankind. Most members of the Classical School, while continuing the Physiocratic tradition in many respects, lost interest in this organic aspect. Nevertheless, it remained an essential part of the thought of the German Historical School.

As a physician, Quesnay was acquainted with the functioning of organisms, and it is in this field that his contribution to economic thinking lays. His idea was that the working of the "laws of nature" is not confined to the sphere of human intercourse, but also includes the biological aspect of agriculture. According to him, only in agriculture could mankind take advantage of *le don gratuit de la nature*, "the Free Gift of Nature". This idea was the point of departure of Quesnay's *tableau économique*. In this circular scheme agriculture is central, which was supposed to be the only form of productive activity.

It is often said that the School of Physiocrats was the first school in economics. This is fully acceptable if Turgot is included (Thurlings, 1978). However, if the school is limited to the intimate circle of Quesnay and his followers, then this statement can be objected to.

---

[2] In its original sense, "natural law" is the right of man to do what is advantageous to him or, according to the author [Quesnay], some of whose writings I herewith publish, the right of man to make choices in line with his own benefit.

Although it is true that the Physiocrats presented a coherent picture of the economy, the most important cohering factor was a metaphysics of a deist nature. Contemporaries called the school *la secte*. What is more tenable is that the Physiocrats laid the scientific foundation of economic liberalism as a political doctrine, although liberalism also has roots in other forms of thought, for example, in Scholasticism. The term *laissez faire*, still used in the same way the Physiocrats used it, has its origins in Mercantilism.

Romanticism: the idea of historicism and organicism

In Enlightened thought there was an individualistic as well as an authoritarian approach to politics. Catherine II of Russia, who encouraged the dispersion of *la lumière*, "the Light", among the Russian nobility, was "enlightened" in the latter sense. How profound the contradiction between the two approaches sometimes was became clear when the Physiocrat P.P. Mercier de La Rivière was received by Catherine. Their ideas differed so much that they appeared to be unable to discuss anything at all. It was into this field of tension that Romanticism arose, forming the basis for a renewed way of thought in "political economy", particularly in nineteenth-century Germany. It is essential for a historical approach to consider gradual changes in human thought and behaviour, in the sense of changes in the image of man and society over the course of time. The Enlightenment had already contributed to this social empirical approach. Romanticism, however, shaped the historical view, putting "historicism" in the centre of the approach.

There are three writers to be mentioned in this study on historicism and organicism as forming the link between Enlightened and Romantic thought: Rousseau, Herder and Kant. All of them took the initiative to "shake off the chains of reason", each in his own way. Jean-Jacques Rousseau should be mentioned for his attention to emotional feelings and the glorification of primitive man. Johann Gottfried *von* Herder should be considered the pioneer of organistic social thought in German Romanticism. Unlike most of the philosophers of the Enlightenment, Herder did not consider a "desirable society" as being part of and determined by (Newtonian) *nature* in all respects. According to his view on cultural development, on the one hand, he ascribed a direct function to human thought and action. On the other hand, he conceived of a harmonious connection between an unfolding culture and (biologically oriented) *nature*. He, and later Roscher, assumed that human existence is rooted in organic nature. Neither saw a sharp boundary between the social and the biological world, and both used the organic metaphor to understand certain social phenomena (Barnard, 1983; Krabbe, 1987: p. 107).

Immanuel Kant, who considered himself a thinker in the tradition of the Enlightenment, was the founder of the idealistically oriented current in Romanticism and, as such, dominated nineteenth-century German philosophy. Kant wanted to find an equilibrium between Cartesian thought and the empirical thought of Bacon, Newton and Hume. In opposition to an idealistic world, the *mundus intelligibilis*, Kant put the *mundus sensibilis*. Knowledge was supposed to be conditioned by aprioristic ideas in the former world, while the object-as-such, called *noumenon*, was located in the latter. In Kant's idealistic world of thought, this object had a transcendental form of appearance, called *phenomenon*. Kant assigned a significant function to the human will. Although he still considered man's behaviour to be in accordance with "natural laws", by stressing the function of the "will" he laid the foundation of a view on human behaviour freed from the rule of natural scientific causality. In Germany Kant's philosophy developed along two streams. In one, the emphasis was placed fully on the idealistic; in the other, the idealistic world of ideas was more or less balanced by an empirical approach.

A remarkable figure in the picture of the extremely idealistic current was the philosopher Schopenhauer. According to him, the world confronting the observer is only *phenomenon*, subjectively perceived in line with Kant. This *phenomenon*, however, is shaped by the *noumenon* of the "eternal will". In contrast to the rosy rational ideals of former times, Schopenhauer's picture of the development of cultures had pessimistic features. This philosophical current, in which Nietzsche should be included, was of less direct importance to the development of historicism and organicism in economic thought. However, it did help to prepare the way for the ideas called philosophy of life, with which the name of Dilthey is associated. This philosophy significantly influenced the "younger" Historical School and was even part of its thought.

Johann Gottlieb Fichte should be considered as part of the other current in German idealism. His ideas are rather close to those of Kant. According to Fichte, reality is "idea", which is related to man, the *ego*. According to his view, the ethical aspect of human existence is the *mundus sensibilis*. He worked this out in a non-individualistic way, which resulted in a typical social utilitarian philosophy. In this sense, he can be seen as one of the founders of socialism. Fichte applied his approach to the field of economic policy in his work on the closed trading country (1800). He categorically rejected *laissez faire*. For him, the ideal social system was an autarchic society in which freedom could be attained by juridical laws, and in which poverty and unemployment would vanish by proper government. This idea had a considerable impact on economic and political thinking in nineteenth-century Germany, in particular on that of the Historical School. Fichte's influence was, indirectly, even greater than that of his contemporary Adam Müller, one of the forerunners of this school.

The philosopher Georg Friedrich Hegel was particularly interested in scientific thought on the social phenomena of his day. In his approach there is an identity between the subject of knowledge and the considering spirit. Unlike previous ideas, he considered "dialectics" to be a way towards knowledge on the basis of the idea that society has a specific development pattern. In this way Hegel made idealistic philosophy suitable for reflecting the dynamics in social empiricism. Reality is idea, and this idea passes into its opposite, to become established at a higher level. Hegel called this process *aufheben*, "elevating" or "lifting". The terms "thesis", "antithesis" and "synthesis" were not used by Hegel himself, but were introduced by Fichte, who elaborated the former's ideas.

Hegel's dialectic approach supported the idea of history being a series of development stages, in which every stage is determined by a certain way of thought (Hegel, 1807). Karl Marx also had a dialectic approach towards socio-economic history. His dialectics was derived from Hegel, but in the context of a "materialistic" philosophy inspired by Ludwig Feuerbach: "one is what one consumes". Members of the early Historical School were also indebted to Hegel, presenting a picture of development in stages in the Hegelian way. Yet their approach was less dogmatic and less radical than that of Marx.

Chapter 2
PREDECESSORS OF GERMAN HISTORICISM

Medieval Scholastic philosophy was superseded by Mercantilism, in which matters of economic policy were seen from the point of view of the sovereign or the state. In the eighteenth century Mercantilism was strongly influenced by the ideas of the Enlightenment. An example of this is the work of the British Mercantilist James Steuart (1767, 1805 I: pp. 2, 7, 199). Mercantilist thought was transformed into the philosophy of the Physiocrats and eventually into that of the mainly British Classical School, the principal heir to the Physiocrats' legacy. The Classicals modified the Physiocratic idea of production and analysed the economic process further. The link between these last two schools was Turgot. This "classical" way of thought was the great antipode of German historicism.

The philosophical background of the early Classical School was put into words by David Hume. Hume tied knowledge to sensible human experiences, called "impressions", thus eliminating metaphysical elements from scientific thought and relating the ideas to empiricism. According to Hume's idea of society, the individual plays a significant constructive role. He said that '[e]very man's interest is peculiar to himself, and the aversions and desires, which result from it, cannot be supposed to affect others in a like degree' (Hume, 1777: pp. 228, 239, 281-82).

According to Hume, reason manifests itself in human "passions", in which "selfish and social sentiments" play a part. He was struck by the uniformity in human behaviour in different times and places. His idea of social development was optimistic, in agreement with the Enlightened idea of progress. Hume said that an individual's respectable endeavour results in "utility", whether directed at wealth or at immaterial well-being. However, his kindred spirit, Adam Smith, separated these two types of human endeavour, dealing with each of them in separate works. Hume's idea of utility had an individualistic as well as a collectivist meaning. Jeremy Bentham elaborated this utility concept in a rationalist and individualistic spirit. His disciple, the late Classical economist John Stuart Mill, wanted to integrate Bentham's utilitarianism into liberal-oriented economics. Nevertheless, this did not affect the Classical School's image, as determined by David Ricardo. Out of the broad field of human motivations, the latter chose the pursuit of gain on which to base a typically economic theory.

The founder of the Classical School, Adam Smith, attracted the attention of the world with his book *An Inquiry into the Nature and Causes of the Wealth of Nations*, mostly referred to as the *Wealth of Nations* (Smith, 1776). His message was that the economic system of his day, with its monopolistic elements of Scholastic and Mercantile origin, should be transformed into a "natural order", in which economic freedom would guarantee everybody's well-being. Smith tied this up with the problem of the division of labour in society and with the range of the interactive community concerned. He assumed that this division was determined by the size of the market, and that the larger the market, the bigger the advantages. Alongside the production factor "labour" Smith put the factor "capital". Ricardo made it clear that a distribution of income is given by the revenues of each of these production factors, together with the revenue of the factor "nature". The view of Smith and his followers in the Classical School was that labour is the elementary standard of value. This idea is also found in Marx, although in a more drastic form.

Sismondi: a philosophical approach

Smith's influence throughout the world was great. Nevertheless, after a time some of his followers became sceptical. One of these was Jean Simonde de Sismondi. Simonde's parents were French, but his family fled to Geneva because of the Revolution. There he was born in 1773. The addition "de Sismondi" refers to an Italian ancestor. In his book *Richesse commerciale*, "Wealth", which appeared in 1803, he fully agreed with the basic ideas of Adam Smith. However, his well-known book *Nouveaux principes d'économie politique*, "New principles of political economy", published in 1819, showed a change in his thought.

> Il n'est aucune branche de l'économie politique qui ne doive être jugée d'après ses rapports avec le bonheur de la masse du peuple.[3] (Sismondi, 1819, 1971: p. 150.)

It was an original idea to judge the significance of all branches of economics in terms of the welfare of the "ordinary man". This idea was also typical of Schmoller's branch of the Historical School. Sismondi's idea of socio-economic science is clearly normative, as expressed by the addition: *'et l'ordre social est toujours mauvais, lorsque la plus grande*

---

[3]There is not a single branch of economics which should not to be judged on its significance for the welfare of the masses.

partie de la population souffre' [4]. Writing about the function of legislation he said: *'Elle soigne les hommes et comme nation, et comme individus'* [5] (Sismondi, 1819: pp. 62, 64). In the last quarter of the nineteenth century, the idea that the social order has to serve the common interest is especially found in the ideas of the *Verein für Socialpolitik*, mentioned above.

Like Werner Sombart in later years, Sismondi paid full attention to the formation of wealth in capitalist society. Sismondi criticized the ideology of *laissez faire*, also in connection with international free trade. He described the way the opening up of new territories for agricultural production meant that, in the traditional production countries, agricultural labourers lost their subsistence (Sismondi, 1819: pp. 202-12). In this way he contributed towards laying the ideological basis for protection, an idea that was also put forward by Friedrich List and later, under certain conditions, by many members of the Historical School. A central idea of this school was that society is not only a conglomerate of individuals, but also an "organic whole". This was in line with Sismondi's ideas.

Müller: a "Romantic" approach

It is already clear that not everyone agreed with Smith's concept of an individualistically oriented natural order. In Great Britain another approach was taken by Edmund Burke, a statesman and philosopher with early Romantic ideas. German thought was influenced by Burke's ideas, as exemplified by the philosopher and politician Adam Müller and his friend, the statesman Friedrich *von* Gentz. Although Müller was an admirer of Smith, he nevertheless rejected the latter's rationalism and individualism. In his work of 1809 Müller presented an advanced form of medieval social thought. Instead of tying up cultural phenomena with the individual, in the way Hume did, he implicated them in the idea of the *Staat.* Müller connected the idea of the German state with the "spirit" of the nation. For him, the state is a whole, formed in the course of time, and has a producing as well as a consuming identity. Production was supposed to be the result of "productive forces" that result, in their turn, from "higher" productive forces. Friedrich List, who was one of his acquaintances, was apparently inspired by this to form his "theory of productive forces".

Adam Müller was considered a conspicuous representative of the "Romantic School" in economics. This term has been borrowed from Roscher, who used it to refer to Müller's historically and organically oriented view on society (Roscher, 1867: pp. 75-105). There are similarities between this view of Müller and that of Fichte, who characterized the national

---

[4]... and the social order is always bad if the largest part of the population suffers.

[5]It serves men, both as a nation and as individuals.

state by saying that: 'It is the state and only the state that unites any number of people into a closed multiplicity, into a whole'[6] (Fichte, 1800: p. 15). Roscher agreed with Müller that society has both historic and organic traits, and attached, indirectly, the label "romantic" to his own approach. However, Roscher was critical of Müller in other aspects, particularly of his lack of clarity in the concepts he used and, further, of his reactionary conservatism. At the beginning of the twentieth century Müller was discovered again by Othmar Spann and, furthermore, by the so-called neo-Romantic School in twentieth-century Austria. Spann said:

> It is easier to blame Müller for his lack of shrewdness in perception than it is to honour him. To do him justice, one should weigh up the profoundness of intuition and the moral power that were necessary to challenge Smith's individualism.[7] (Spann, 1910, 1928: p. 98.)

List, a political approach

The great precursor of the Historical School was Friedrich List, born in the town of Reutlingen in Würtemberg in 1789. He was, however, more than a forerunner, delivering a specific contribution to German historistic thought. During the period of "restoration" after the French Revolution and the Napoleonic wars, List was Professor of Public Administration at the University of Tübingen. As a result of his stand on political liberalism and a customs union between the various German states, to which the influential Metternich was opposed, he was forced to flee, and with the help of Lafayette he settled in the United States. In the New World he became involved in business, and became convinced that young industries in agrarian countries need tariff protection.

It was at this time that List wrote his *Outlines of American political economy*, in which he criticized reflective economics that was based, without question, on *laissez faire*. List commented on the ideas of Adam Smith, which had been put forward in America by Thomas Cooper.

> Indeed, so wrong are these adherents of the Scot's theory, that in spite of the very name they chose to give their science, they will make us believe that there is nothing of politics in political economy. If their science is properly called *political economy*, there must be just as much *politics* in it as *economy*, and if there is no *politics* in it, the science has not got the proper name; it is then nothing else than *economy*. The truth is that the name is right, expressing the very thing these gentlemen mean to treat, but the thing they treat is not

[6]Der Staat allein ist's, der eine unbestimmte Menge Menschen zu einem geschlossnen Ganzen, zu einer Allheit vereinigt.

[7]Es ist leichter, Adam Müllern mangelnde Begriffsschärfe vorzuwerfen als ihn zu würdigen. Man muss die Tiefe der Intuition und die moralische Kraft ermessen, die nötig war, um gegen Smithens Individualismus aufzutreten, wenn man ihn gerecht werden will.

> consonant to the name, they do not treat *political* economy, but *cosmopolitical* economy. (List, 1827: p. 161; italics in original.)

Actually, the contradiction is not as large as these words suggest. List, just as later most of the members of the Historical School were to do, believed that a policy of intervention is complementary to a policy of free trade and that it should not replace it. This interventional policy was focussed towards economic development. In fact, List inserted a motive force into the picture of development: the force of an economic policy orientated towards "intervention". In doing so, he put forward a new idea in economics. Furthermore, List's interpretation of the Enlightened idea of the unfolding natural order, bound to *laissez faire*, can also be found in the Classicals he criticized. In the time of Schmoller, the idea of intervention acquired a social dimension, by referring to the "social question".

The contradiction was mainly in List's nationally determined approach, in which the Classicals were blamed for "cosmopolitism". List put into words the nucleus of his thought.

> I would name nationality as my system's most characteristic distinction. My entire premise is based on the nature of nationality as an intermediate stage between individuality and humanity.[8] (List, 1841, 1877: p. xxxiii.)

He wanted to show that welfare is the result of a policy orientated towards vital national units. According to him, any policy that does not take account of nationally determined potentials in the field of production will lead to poverty and international dependency. He was of the opinion that the German policy of his day bore this hallmark. The founding of the *Zollverein*, the "customs union", between the German states, and the building of new infrastructure, particularly railways, were to improve prospects. After his return to Germany, List vigorously propagated these ideas.

Special attention should be given to his "scheme of stages". List distinguished five stages in the development of society. Two primitive periods, indicated as "wildness" and "herd state", are followed by *Agrikulturstand*, "state of agriculture", *Agrikulturmanufakturstand*, "state of agriculture and manufacture", and *Agrikulturmanufacturhandelsstand*, "state of agriculture, manufacture and trade". It seems as if these stages do not refer to successive periods that are clearly defined, but rather to stages that merge into each other (List, 1841: pp. 11, 155). In his lectures, Professor Thurlings stressed that what is typical of this scheme of stages is the way List indicated how each stage arose from the previous

---

[8] Als charakteristischen Unterschied des von mir aufgestellten Systems bezeichne ich die Nationalität. Auf die Natur der Nationalität als des Mittelgliedes zwischen Individualität und Menschheit ist mein ganzes Gebäude gegründet.

one. This aspect is less clear in the "stage theories" of the Historical School proper, in which the emphasis lies on the description and characterization of the various stages. According to List, in the "state of agriculture" the right policy is good government with free trade. In this way the natural development opportunities are able to be utilized as best as possible. In the fourth and in the last stages, however, the right policy was considered to be a system of protecting import duties on industrial products, meant as "educative protection". These tariffs should not be so high that international competition is entirely eliminated. Agricultural production would not need such protection, for it would follow in industry's wake.

I have already pointed out that List borrowed Müller's idea of the state as a historically shaped organ holding productive forces. Gide and Rist criticized the lack of clarity of List's idea of these forces. They noticed that it apparently included: *'liberté de penser et liberté de conscience, liberté de la presse, jury, publicité de la justice, contrôle de l'administration, gouvernement parlementaire'* [9] (Gide and Rist, 1920: pp. 319-20). In this connection they noted:

> Mais, de toutes les forces productives d'une nation, aucune n'est à ses yeux plus fécondante que l'industrie manufacturière. Les manufactures développent d'abord au suprême degré les forces morales de la nation.[10] (Gide and Rist, 1920: p. 321.)

Allowing "productive forces" be manifest in society is, according to List, the creation of a national social order in which production is maximized in all material and immaterial aspects.

List seized every opportunity to present his philosophy of productive forces as an alternative to that of the school of Adam Smith and Jean-Baptiste Say, which he called a theory of exchange values. However, if one wants to rate List's thought at its true value, it is better to see it as complementary to Classical thought. He placed the economic order and its development within the scope of economics, and rationally criticized the principle of *laissez faire*. Further, he focussed on the problem of improvement of production techniques. List can thus be considered an early representative of development economics.

---

[9][F]reedom of thought, freedom of conscience, liberty of the press, trial by jury, publicity of justice, control of administration, and parliamentary government (Gide and Rist, 1947).

[10]But of all the productive forces of a nation none, according to List, can equal manufactures, for manufactures develop the moral forces of a nation to a superlative degree (Gide and Rist, 1947: p. 282).

Chapter 3
PHENOMENON "HISTORICAL SCHOOL"

Before looking at the typical ideas of various members in the school of which some fore-runners have already been mentioned, I want to look for a moment at the phenomenon of the Historical School as such, for questions arise about what the concept of "school" here is and how this school should be described.

Idea of the Historical School

In any discussion of German historicism, the question should be posed whether, in this connection, we can actually speak of a "school". If Joseph Schumpeter's socially oriented criterion is used then several problems arise. This concept of school was defined and applied in his book *History of economic analysis*. Schumpeter said that schools are social realities.

> They have their structures - relations between leaders and followers - their flags, their battle cries, their moods, their all-too-human interests. Their antagonisms come within the general sociology of group antagonisms and of party warfare. (Schumpeter, 1954: p. 815.)

This characterization is fully applicable to the German Historical School. However, it is not clear how kindred spirits like Knies, Bücher and Inama-Sternegg, who worked rather separately, should be placed. Without wishing to seem to be contradicting Schumpeter, I opt for the paradigm idea of T.S. Kuhn as the main criterion for identification of a current in science such as "the Historical School". In this it is the issue of which relations are considered to be of interest, which way of analysing is considered appropriate and what normative significance is assigned to it (Kuhn, 1962).

It is not that the Historical School is characterized by a uniform paradigm. As will later become clear, the members of the school did not agree on all points, and principal questions were mostly answered in a nuanced way. Nevertheless, a heterogenous paradigm[11] did serve as a binding element. This does not mean that thought within the school differed entirely from that in other schools. So, the ideas of some authors, *e.g.* Roscher and Bücher, are related to Classical thought. Some of the later members of the school advocated the marginal utility theory.

I limit the Historical School to economists, in fact to socially oriented economists. This means that, for instance, the philosopher and historian Wilhelm Dilthey is excluded, however important he may have been for the ideas of the branch that was dominated by his kindred spirit, Gustav Schmoller. According to my view, the most typical characteristic of the Historical School is economic historicism, which partly coincides with organicism, the other subject of this study. In this context historicism means that the scientific observer has a good eye for the changing picture of society; that he puts socio-economic development in the centre of his economic philosophy. This idea is not the same as the concept of historicism introduced into economics by Karl Popper (1957), which refers primarily to predictability on the basis of development patterns of society. This was rightly criticized by Popper. However, I want to relate the concept of historicism to the econometrist Robert Solow's point, which he made when discussing the division of labour between economic history and economics.

> [E]conomic history can offer the economist a sense of the variety and flexibility of social arrangements and thus, in particular, a shot at understanding a little better the interaction of economic behavior and other social institutions. (Solow, 1985: p. 328.)

Although the form of historicism mentioned by Popper is also found in the Historical School, it is the other concept that was dominant. By stressing the typical concept of economics rather than the aspect of personal leadership in practising science, I present the Historical School as the school of the spectacular pioneer Wilhelm Roscher and not primarily that of Gustav Schmoller, however influential the latter may have been in the personal field.

In using the term paradigm, I also refer to the ideological background of the Historical School. If, in a political treatise, Inama used the expression *nosse rem publicam* (borrowed from Scholasticism) to mean "the people's sake", he did not see the "righteous price" in an order supposed to be wished by God, nor the realization of the "natural order" by the way of *laissez faire*. The interest of the people was, according to him and his companions in the School, a just and also purposeful remuneration of the efforts of the common man. In this connection, I want to mention the religious motivation of most of

---

[11]It is remarkable that in a similar context the term *Paradigma* (paradigm) had already been used by Roscher, an immortal in the history of economic thought.

the members of the School. Of course, their view on society was not based on ecclesiastical doctrine, as it had been for the Scholastics, and religious considerations played no part in explaining social phenomena, as it had for the deistic Physiocrats. To understand the religious motivation in the Historical School, it must be remembered that the School's idea of society had a significant idealistic component. It is the idea that society is shaped by the people that are part of it, according to their ideas about how society should be organized. According to this view, the most essential contribution to the construction of society is the formation of "good" ideas about its organization. In the Historical School, during times of strong religious contrasts, thinkers of various confessions agreed with the old prayer *Veni Creator Spiritus*.

The *prima facie* subject "the Historical School" cannot be separated from the political problems with which the members of the school were engaged at that time. Economic development and later also "social reform" were considered political challenges. However, to deepen the study subject, another step can be taken, at least if the interest of the reader in the subject, just as mine, is also determined by both the scientific and the political problems of today. It can be said of any significant study on the evolution of historicism and organicism that, in the last instance, the subject matter is formed by topical scientific and practical problems.

Points of departure in depicting the School

The main characteristics of the Historical School are: the picture of socio-economic development of man and society, the organic aspects of it, the character of causality in economics, the ethical aspects of economic thought, the integration of statistics into economics, and the anticipation of modern macro-economic ideas. I do not want to treat these aspects as separate themes; they are too linked for that. It is my intention to present the significant author's ideas in their mutual relationship, and in doing so, to refer to ideas of other writers, both within and outside the School.

The writers of the Historical School focussed on the developing relation between the individual and society, a relationship which was understood in such a way that qualities of the first determine the character of the last, and *vice versa*. This brought with it the question of "holistic forces", which are causal relationships within social life that are not imputed to independent individuals, because they are assumed to be characteristic of society as a whole. List's "productive forces" can serve as an example of this. Another holistic concept characteristic of the Historical School is Müller's idea of the "national spirit", in which individual members of society are supposed to participate.

The Historical School was occupied with the development of the institutional structure of production and consumption. Socio-economic development, the phenomenon on which the ideas of the school were oriented, was thought of in different ways. Most members characterized this development with the help of the concept of development stages, called *Entwicklungsstufen* or simply *Stufen*. Yet, one scheme of stages often differed profoundly from another. Investigation of the development pattern of economies brought with it the problem of causality in economics, something with which the members of the school had to wrestle. Roscher still approached it in terms of natural science, partly bearing Herder's signature. Knies, however, criticized him for this, referring to the function of human freedom in the process of societal development. A generation later, Schmoller saw the economic system as an interaction between human spirit and nature. In the spiritual sphere, causality was supposed to be approached by using the method of the social sciences. In the sphere of nature, the approach should be the natural science method. An important element in the methodology of the "younger" Historical School is *Verstehen*, "understanding", which means the investigator has to imagine himself at the place and time of the situation being studied.

The members of the Historical School were convinced that Classical thought should be either supplemented or replaced by a historically oriented approach. Some of them put so much emphasis on the historistic principle, that it typified their entire thought. This gave historicism an epistemological trait. It was especially Schmoller and his followers who insisted that the "being" can only be understood in its process of "becoming". Knapp's "state theory of money" can serve as an example of this approach. Moreover, all members of the school had an organically oriented idea of society, in one form or another. The way they made the idea concrete, however, differed from one to the other. A significant idea was that of the *Staat*, which some of them understood idealistically, in the Kantian tradition. Others, like Schmoller and his followers, were inspired by Dilthey's philosophy of *life*, and approached society mainly on this basis. Carl Menger, founder of the Austrian School, introduced a typical "organistic" approach, thus, in a way, following in Roscher's footsteps.

The Historical School should not be seen as a typical example of the normative practice of science. It is true that Schmoller's thought had a normative feature, but this can also be said of most of his fellow authors in other schools. Taking the Historical School as a whole, the opposite could also be maintained. I confine myself to the statement that although the school subjected the question of the rationale of value judgements in economics to thorough investigation, nevertheless different conclusions were reached. Most members of the Historical School agreed with Wilhelm Roscher that economics focusses on *das Sein*, "being" ("is"), rather than on *das Sollen*, "urging" ("should"). This means that they were in line with David Hume's view 'that one can never derive "ought" propositions from "is" propositions' (Arrow, 1994: p. 1). Nevertheless, it should be admitted that, for example, Schmoller's thought had a normative feature. This, however, was not meant to detract from Roscher's principle. Rather, it was an implication of his typical economic philosophy since, according to him, political statements are primarily the result of ideas that arise in cultural life and that can be perceived by the investigator. In the Historical School there were sharp differences of opinion about the ethical content of economic thought. The normative approaches of people like Cohn and Held clashed with the "value free" approaches of Max Weber and Sombart.

Shaping the picture of developing thought

In this study the centre of attention is the German Historical School. The question, however, on the basis of the criteria mentioned in the previous section is, who can be seen as significant representatives of this school and, further, how they can be logically classified. My solution is an opportunist one, focussing on the aims of this study. This implies that, from other points of view, other pictures might be just as good, if not better.

The general view is that Roscher, Knies and Hildebrand represented the "older" Historical School. They laid the foundations of the school as a whole, and also that of institutionally and organically oriented thought in economics. Further, in this study I discuss the "second generation" of the School. However, before turning to the main members, Gustav Schmoller and his followers, I want to look at two different positions. First, those of Bücher and Philippovich, independent writers in the "younger" Historical School: following in Roscher's footsteps, they both aimed at integrating historistic thought into a broader field of economic thinking. Bücher orientated his specific ideas towards Classical thought, while Philippovich orientated his thought towards marginal utility theory.

Second, I look at the organistic ideas of Menger, even though I do not consider him to have been a member of the School, since his historistic ideas were not central to his thought. There was a strong controversy on the point of historicism between him and his contemporary Schmoller, which became known as the *Methodenstreit*, the "struggle of method". Schmoller and a great number of like-minded thinkers formed the Younger Historical School proper. A main element in their thought was social reform. For the sake of clarity, I make a distinction between "reformers", characterized by their political stand, and "fundamentalists", who aimed at providing "theories" for this. The group of reformers, Conrad, Cohn and Brentano, was rather heterogenous. The group of fundamentalists, Held, Inama, Knapp, however, was more homogenous. No discussion of the integration of statistics into economics is complete without mention of Ernst Engel. Although he cannot be placed in the Historical School, he nevertheless influenced the School's ideas of social statistics and social problems in general.

Even today, historicism and organicism still form only an undercurrent in economic science, although this world of thought put its stamp on economics. So too did historistically oriented writers like Werner Sombart and Max Weber, whose ideas I discuss as well. The ideas can be found in "mainstream economics", and particularly in various branches of modern Institutionalism. I place Georgescu-Roegen's "bioeconomics" in line with Menger's New Organicism. Present-day environmental systems theory is also reminiscent of old forms of organistic economic thought.

Chapter 4
THE "OLDER" HISTORICAL SCHOOL

I fully agree with the idea that Roscher was the founder of the Historical School. He was the dominating personality in the "older" School and was also acknowledged as such by his contemporaries, including his kindred spirits, Knies and Hildebrand. Their ideas can be considered to complement those of Roscher, and therefore they can be seen as co-founders alongside him.

Roscher, founder of economic historicism and organicism

Wilhelm Georg Friedrich Roscher was born in Hannover in 1817 into a family of prominent public functionaries. He studied history and public administration at Göttingen and Berlin. He was a pupil of the outstanding historian Leopold Ranke who, relying on original historical documents, converted Hegelian history into a non-aprioristic one. Roscher became Professor of History and "State Sciences" at Göttingen and afterwards at the University of Leipzig.

It was Roscher's aim to correct and amplify contemporary Classical theory, the merits of which he recognized. He wanted to integrate the Classical view into a picture of society which was shaped by a new way of thought, characterized by him as the historical or the historico-physiological approach. This task he fulfilled in a creative manner. Nevertheless, his approach did have some weak spots. The weakest point probably was his methodical dualism. On the one hand, in presenting subjects from Classical theory like value, production and income, Roscher used Classical deductive reasoning which had originated in the Enlightenment. On the other hand, in dealing with the history of society and the development of institutions, Roscher adopted Herder's organistic ideas and, to a lesser degree, idealistic ideas which had originated in Hegel. It should be remembered, however, that half-way through the nineteenth century eclecticism had become a significant cultural phenomenon. Thus, on this point Roscher's thought bore the hallmark of his time.

According to Roscher, all cultures are characterized by analogous stages of rise, flourishing and decay, which were also considered the development pattern of mankind as a whole. This idea fitted into nineteenth-century German thought on social development. However, he did not share the idea of philosophers like Fichte that it is a task of science to design an ideal society and to indicate what policy would lead to the realization of this ideal (Fichte, 1800: pp. 11, 12). In his frequently reprinted *Grundlagen der Nationalökonomie*, "Foundations of social (national) economics", (from now on referred to as *Grundlagen*), Roscher made the well-known distinction between "what is" and "what should be" to which I have already referred (*Grundlagen,* 1854, 1868: §22, p. 42). Relying on Hume, he wanted to express the idea that, in economics, only the former is under discussion, the latter supposedly belonging to a world of thought that was indicated as *Praxis*, "practice". It is doubtful, however, whether Roscher himself fully succeeded in shaping such a value-free science, particularly when he spoke, in organic terms, of the diagnosis and the therapeutics of social ailments (Roscher, 1849, 1878: pp. 357-493; *Grundlagen*: §217, p. 462n; Krabbe, 1995).

Roscher's approach

In Roscher's view, a national society is considered to be an organism in which households function as mutually dependent parts. This approach claimed that an insight could be gained into the functioning, and the rise and decay of both the whole and its parts, the specific organs. This process was supposed to be in accordance with "laws" which were not considered to differ essentially from those of biology. Hence, his use of the adjective "physiological". Roscher's presentations on this theme were numerous but, unfortunately, his concept remains vague.

Roscher rightly maintained that economics is focussed on economic behaviour. He said that this behaviour is according to a plan in which the economic principle manifests itself: achieving the most with the least sacrifice. Economic behaviour is executed by individual households as well as by society as a whole. According to him, the plan aspect of the national economy reveals itself in the economic order (*Grundlagen*: §12, p. 22). The maintaining of it should be the subject of a separate, practically oriented science, which he called *Polizeiwissenschaft*, "science of control" (literally "the science of policing").

According to Roscher, self-interest functions as a strong constructive power in society. However, he wanted to relate this motivation to ethical considerations, culminating in "an aspiring for the kingdom of God" (Roscher, 1863, 1878: pp. 51-86). He believed that the increase of economic freedom and individual freedom in general is characteristic of a "rising" culture. A tendency to curtail this freedom, finding expression in the restrictions of communism on the one hand and extreme competition on the other, was considered typical of cultural "decline".

It is not easy to summarize what Roscher understood by the "historical" or "historico-physiological" method, which he believed should be followed in economics. To begin with, it must be said that this approach was tied to the aprioristic idea that in the economies of all cultures there is an analogous development governed by "general laws of life", indicated as *Naturgesetze*, "laws of nature". For Roscher, the validity of universal laws of socio-economic development was assumed as a matter of course. However, his attempt to support this idea with historical observations is not convincing. His kindred spirit, Karl Knies, rightly asked which part should be assigned to the free will of man in the process of social development.

Roscher held that in the development of any culture three stages can be distinguished: youth, maturity and old age, according to the development of the individual man. These *Stufen*, "development stages", were not supposed to appear in identical forms, but in analogous shapes. Roscher characterized the three stages by the position of specific production factors. In the first, nature dominates, since 'forest, waters and pasture nurture a small population almost gratuitously' *(Wald, Gewässer und Weide nähren eine dünne Bevölkerung fast freiwillig)* (*Grundlagen*: §47, p. 88). In the second, the labour factor is of crucial importance. The stage of old age was thought to be dominated by the capital factor, which in antiquity was supposed to have been mainly invested in slaves. There was little support for this scheme of stages. There was some from Knies, who called the first stage of social development *Naturalwirthschaft*, "natural economy" (Knies, 1853: p. 262). The second stage, however, was characterized by Knies as *Geldwirthschaft*, "money economy". To this, Hildebrand added a third stage, typified as *Kreditwirthschaft*, "credit economy". For Roscher, the economic *Praxis* was the field of political application as well as the "proof" of his theoretical picture (Backhaus, 1992: p. 114).

Roscher had already mentioned the principle of substituting production factors that remain comparatively cheap for those that become more expensive (*Grundlagen*: §198, p. 421). It was on this principle that he based his idea of the intensification of land use in the course of time. It must be said that his laws of social development are not realistic. However, his method of "analogy" was developed by Max Weber to that of "ideal types". Furthermore, Roscher's attention to causality and interdependency in economic analysis should be appreciated.

Specific ideas in Roscher

Roscher's main criticism of Adam Smith and, particularly, David Ricardo was that he considered their theory only applicable to a distinct stage in social development. He further maintained that in Classical thought self-interest had been emphasized too much, at the cost of social duties and specific social functions. Apart from this, he appreciated the Classical theory and integrated it into his organistic approach. Roscher adopted Smith's principle of division of labour, and even gave it a function in his philosophy of social development. In his book on agricultural economics he dealt with the genesis of the national state.

> This general law of development can above all be traced back to the great principle of division of labour that almost always rises and falls with culture.[12] (Roscher, 1859, 1885: p. 7.)

Roscher approached the ideas needs, production and exchange from the concept of a "natural" economic planning.

> I understand economy as the planning activity of man, in order to satisfy his needs by obtainable goods. ... The more numerous the needs of men are and the more various their abilities, the more natural the exchange is.[13] (*Grundlagen*: §2, p. 3.)

In defining productivity, Roscher formulated the economic principle.

> [A]n application of production factors is the most productive that satisfies society's greatest needs with the smallest expenditure of means.[14] (*Grundlagen*: §55, p. 103.)

Roscher was ahead of his time when he considered production to be the transformation of means resulting in satisfaction of needs. According to Roscher, "value" depends upon the good's significance to the user. On this point Roscher was close to the School of Marginal Utility. Therefore, as C. Brinkmann rightly noticed, it is not surprising that in 1871 Carl Menger dedicated his epochmaking work to Roscher (Brinkmann, 1956: p. 41). Another motive might have been that his student Menger felt a certain affinity with Roscher's organically oriented approach.

---

[12]Diess allgemeine Entwicklungsgesetz kann zunächst schon auf das grosse Princip der Arbeitsgliederung zurückgeführt werden, die ja fast in allen Dingen mit der Kultur selber steigt und sinkt.

[13]Unter Wirthschaft verstehen wir die planmässige Thätigkeit des Menschen, um seinen Bedarf an äusseren Gütern zu befriedigen. ... Je zahlreicher die Bedürfnisse der Menschen, je verschiedenartiger ihre Fähigkeiten sind, desto natürlicher der Tausch.

[14][D]iejenige Anwendung der Productionsfactoren [ist] die productivste, welche das grösste Bedürfniss der Volkswirthschaft mit dem kleinsten Aufwande von Mitteln befriedigt.

Roscher did not consider his ideas to be in conflict with Classical market-oriented theory. He held that under conditions of full competition and mobility of production factors, ratios of prices are in proportion to those of production costs. Here he was anticipating the idea of general economic equilibrium (*Grundlagen*: §§107, 112, pp. 205, 212). He also adopted Ricardo's rent idea.

> Whoever produces under comparatively favourable circumstances receives an extra profit through the equal market price of what for him is a cheap good, which is larger accordingly as circumstances become more favourable.[15] (*Grundlagen*: p. 210.)

With this he noted that a rent refers to land by differences in fertility and location. He added that a rent could also have other causes. As an example he mentioned production secrets. This idea is an early form of Alfred Marshall's quasi-rent concept (Marshall, 1890, 1925: p. 424).

More ideas of modern macro-economic thought can be perceived in Roscher's works, as, for example, the concept of the identity of production with income. Here he relied on J.B. Say's *lois des débouchés*. In his *Traité d'économie politique*, Say dealt with the means by which productive contributions are remunerated to men.

> Ces moyens, en quoi consistent-ils? En d'autres valeurs, d'autres produits, fruits de leur industrie, de leurs capitaux, de leurs terres.[16] (Say, 1803, 1841: p. 183.)

Roscher said literally that "turnout (output) is income". He used the concept of "the pure income of the nation", a concept that is close to the present-day idea of the total amount of value added (*Grundlagen*: §§144-46, pp. 300-04). He also mentioned the objective and the subjective approaches for measuring it.

> Its calculation can be based on either the goods obtained or the personal remunerations received.[17] (*Grundlagen*: §146, p. 303.)

Roscher said that the main characteristic of capital is its productive capacity. It was also typified by the fact that the savers concerned have to forego consumption. The latter

---

[15]Wer unter günstigeren Umständen producirt, der empfängt in dem gleichen Preise des für ihn doch wohlfeilern Gutes einen überschüssigen Gewinn, um so grösser, je mehr seine Verhältnisse den ungünstigen überlegen.

[16]What do these means consist of? Of other values, other products, the fruits of their labour, of their capital and their land.

[17]Um dasselbe zu berechnen, können wir entweder von den eingenommenen Gütern, oder von den einnehmenden Personen ausgehen.

consideration referred to the abstinence idea, introduced into economics by the Classical economist, Nassau Senior. This idea also borders upon the thought of the later Marginal Utility School. The idea was expressed in Roscher's rhetorical question, in discussing the formation of capital.

> Who would ever save, which implies giving up present pleasure, if he is not sure of getting pleasure in the future?[18] (*Grundlagen*: §77, p. 143.)

Roscher's well-known example of capital formation was the story of a primitive fisherman who is saving on energy in order to invest it in a boat and nets. This example was preceded by remarks on the interest on capital, which Roscher said depends 'on real productivity of capital and on real sacrifice, which is the abstinence of the utility it has to him'[19]. Roscher's judgement on the social significance of saving, as well as of squandering, is double-edged. He appraised saving positively if the savings were not hoarded. He appraised squandering negatively for being in conflict with the economic principle. However, he judged squandering positively for its contribution to *die Nachfrage nach Waaren*, "the demand for goods" (*Grundlagen*: §§218-19, p. 463).

In his treatise on business cycles Roscher attributed slumps to systematic deregulation of the monetary system. He said that money offers the opportunity to delay decisions on buying, which Say's law does not take into account. Roscher understood that credit institutions also play a part. Furthermore, he recommended employment projects in times of crisis.

> As it is clear that sales crises almost regularly reappear at certain intervals of time, the crisis could preferably be postponed by such government projects.[20] (Roscher, 1849, 1878: pp. 380, 474.)

Early variants of Keynesian thought can also be found in works by other writers of the Historical School, like Lujo Brentano.

---

[18]Wer möchte sparen, d.h. also dem gegenwärtigen Genusse entsagen, wenn er des zukünftigen Genusses nicht sicher wäre?

[19]... auf der wirklichen Productivität der Kapitalien, und auf dem wirklichen Opfer, das in der Enthaltung von ihrem Selbstgenusse liegt.

[20]Wo man beobachtet hat, dass Absatzkrisen fast regelmässig in gewissen Zwischenräumen wiederkehren, da könnte man solche Staatsarbeiten ganz vorzugsweise auf die Krisis versparen.

Knies' historistic method

Karl Knies was born in Marburg, in 1821. He was an economist with historical, philosophical and monetary interests. Politically he was a liberal. Knies was appointed to a chair in Kassel, but had to leave it at the restoration of absolutism. Then, for some time, he lectured in Schaffhausen. Afterwards he was appointed to a chair in Freiburg (Breisgau), and at last in Heidelberg, where he lectured in "state sciences" for the rest of his career. Karl Knies was a pupil of Bruno Hildebrand. Nevertheless, because there was a significant complementarity between the historistic ideas of Roscher and Knies, I want to discuss him first. Knies elaborated and amended Roscher's original, but rather superficial ideas about a historical approach to the economy. He gave a methodological profundity to Roscher's historicism. The most outstanding feature of Hildebrand's work, on the other hand, is his political engagement, which puts him closer to Schmoller than to Roscher.

Knies' methodological book *Die politische Oekonomie vom Standpunkte der geschichtlichen Methode*, "Political Economy from the point of view of the historical method", to which I refer in this section under *Methode*, appeared in 1853. Unfortunately, the work is rather abstruse and also otherwise not easily accessible. In the book a number of methodological themes were presented in varying form and context, in almost endless repetition. The second edition appeared in the years 1881 and 1883, under the modified title *Die politische Oekonomie vom geschichtlichen Standpunkt*, "Political Economy from the historical point of view". This modification, added to the fact that in Knies' monetary works from 1873 to 1879 few historistic ideas are found, caused H.W. Spiegel to make the statement that, at last, Knies acknowledged that a historico-economic method does not exist (Spiegel, 1971: pp. 423-24). Although I do not go as far as this, it is clear that, after a lapse of years, he wanted to put his earlier work into perspective. However, it must be realized that in Knies' encyclopedic work on "money and credit", ideas are found which are fundamental to Knapp's "state theory of money", to be discussed in Chapter 8.

The point of departure of Knies' methodological work is the abstract subject matter of economics, the economic aspect of human behaviour. According to this approach, economics is a science in which 'at all discussions of questions about the world of material goods, one always has to do with a human being, with an intellect and with an intellectually motivated personality as well'[21] (*Methode*: p. 355). Knies related economic causality to a man acting in freedom. His idea of human behaviour, however, is not purely individualistic. He had in mind a "national man", whose behaviour is determined by the *Volks-*

[21]... es doch bei aller Behandlung von Fragen aus der sachlichen Güterwelt immer wieder mit dem Menschen, mit einer geistigen und von geistigen Triebfedern bewegten Persönlichkeit zu thun hat.

geist, "spirit of the nation". In Knies' approach, this "national man" should be placed into a historical context, in a holistic way.

> [A] nation is something other than an accidental aggregate of individuals. Its historical existence includes various living spheres through which the same spirit is blowing, enclosing all individuality in a unifying frame, through which this whole develops into a coherent movement.[22] (*Methode*: p. 109.)

The central idea of Knies' "historical method" was the changing image of man, which is the typical feature of historicism. Knies did not concentrate on *homo oeconomicus* as such, but on the whole man who was considered nationally oriented.

> [T]he economic phenomena of national life are historically inseparably bound to the collective existence of nations.[23] (*Methode*: p. 248.)

Thus in Knies' view, economics is focussed on the economic aspect of the development of national cultures. So, in his approach, many cultural phenomena are drawn into the scope of economics.

> It is certainly the "rule" that in man political, religious and ethical motives are functioning which look to assert themselves in all fields, for his personal life is a unity.[24] (*Methode*: p. 242.)

This broad concept of the economic field of study was typical of the entire Historical School. This approach contrasts with mainstream economics, originating in Classical thought, which focusses primarily on the empirical subject matter of economics and thus on phenomena which are typically economic.

Knies' historical method was rooted in Hegel's holistic approach towards social development. Knies rejected the idea that society is governed by "natural science laws", which was still the customary approach in his time. He assumed that human behaviour gives causality a specific character. It was on this that he based Roscher's idea that

---

[22] [W]ie von einem einheitlichen Kern aus umfasst das geschichtliche Dasein eines Volkes die verschiedenen Lebenskreise, und gerade deshalb, weil durch alle diese ein einheitlicher Geist weht und alles Einzelne, von einem gemeinsamen Kreisring umschlossen, in einer Gesammtbewegung sich entwickelt, ist ein Volk etwas Anderes als eine beliebige Summe von einzelnen Individuen.

[23] [D]ie wirthschaftlichen Manifestationen des Volkslebens zeigen sich geschichtlich untrennbar verbunden mit dem gesammten Dasein der Völker.

[24] Die "Regel" ist sicherlich, dass in dem Menschen politische, religiöse, ethische Triebfedern wirksam sind, und sie wegen der Einheit seines persönlichen Lebens auf allen Gebieten Geltung zu verschaffen suchen.

economic method should not deal with "identical" phenomena but with "analogous" phenomena. He spoke of the analogy of causal forces in social life, and the *Analogie der Entwicklung*, "analogy of social development" (*Methode*: pp. 346-47). It was not Knies' intention to deny the right of existence of Ricardo's theory. He agreed that this deductive system is empirically oriented. However, just like Roscher, he considered it a hardly realistic reflection of reality and, as far as he considered it realistically at all, only applicable to a certain stage of social development (*Methode*: pp. 19, 339, 340). Like Roscher, alongside the "theory" of economics Knies placed the scientific "praxis", orientated towards real socio-economic situations that were thought to be historically grown (*Methode*: p. 35). According to my view, this *Praxis* is the essence of Knies' historicism. It means that on the one hand, the researcher looks for analogies and, on the other, for unique aspects of situations to be investigated. These two poles of thought are also characteristic of the Historical School as a whole.

Knies wanted to complement the deductive approach of Classical design with an inductive approach, to give theory an empirical basis.

> From whichever point of view economic theory might be considered, it should always be recognized as an indispensable condition, that it is based on facts of historical life, whereby theory must be determined without being in conflict with any veracity.[25] (*Methode*: p. 333.)

Yet, Knies cannot be called a typical empiricist. Rather, he was an idealist. Hegel's idea of social development according to "reason" and "necessity" was presented by Knies in the form of a development with momenta of freedom as well as of necessity. By freedom he meant "the human ability to shape existence in space and time". Knies' methodological work was focussed towards the determination of laws of development. However impressive his system of ideas might be, on this point the mountain brought forth a mouse. His concept of development laws was as vague as Roscher's. Yet, on the point of the characteristics of socio-economic development, it makes sense to ponder his ideas.

* *

[25]Von welchem Punkte aus man deshalb auch die Theorie über die ökonomischen Dinge betrachten mag, immer wird man es als eine unerlässliche Bedingung erkennen, sich den Thatsachen des geschichtlichen Lebens hinzugeben, sie als das Fundament anzunehmen, wodurch sich die Theorie bestimmen lassen muss und gegen welche sie keine Wahrheit beanspruchen kann.

Like Sismondi, Knies distinguished between an individual and a collective man.

> [T]he personal element in the economy is not only related to man as an individual, but it also includes man in his relations to society and state, for personal manifestations in these spheres should not be considered merely the sum of manifestations of isolated individual existence.[26] (*Methode*: p. 244.)

With this he formulated the main criterion of holism in social thought. Knies said that in social development the influence of the individual man is easily overrated.

> [E]ven the greatest personalities in history are excellent bearers of movements of their time and of ideological currents, or, in such an individual the character of his people is, as it were, condensed and becomes manifest.[27] (*Methode*: p. 283.)

In society the relationship between the influences of *objective Mächte*, "objectivated ideal forces" and typically individualistic human behaviour is, according to Knies, subject to alteration. He stated that in medieval times it was "ideal forces" that dominated social life, while in the Renaissance it was individualism that became the most important causal factor (*Methode*: p. 108).

Knies put forward a number of principles of socio-economic development. The principle that economic and cultural developments are bound together has already been mentioned. Another principle is that in society everything is related to and consistent with everything else, a structure of social phenomena which is subject to systematic change. Further, Knies believed that the process of socio-economic development takes on typical shapes, from stage to stage (*Methode*: pp. 112, 249). As I have already mentioned, Knies' scheme of stages was inspired by Roscher. In Knies' development scheme Roscher's phase of "natural economy" is followed by a phase typified as "money economy". Here, the term "money" refers to gold and silver coin. Roscher's idea that the various development stages are characterized by certain levels in the division of labour was adopted by Knies.

---

[26][D]ass das personale Element in der Volkswirthschaft nicht bloss auf die Menschen als Individuen zu beziehen ist, sondern auch die Menschen in ihrem geselligen und staatlichen Verband umfasst, weil die Manifestation der personalen Welt in demselben nicht als eine blosse Summe von Manifestationen des isolirten individuellen Lebens angesehen werden kann.

[27][G]erade die gewaltigsten Persönlichkeiten in der Geschichte sind auserlesene Träger von Zeitrichtungen und Ideenströmungen, oder es tritt einmal in dem Einzelnen gleichsam condensirt der Charakter seines Volkes auf.

> It is the division of labour which introduces the structural diversification of economic activities and develops, it further, forming production sectors, splitting them up, and regrouping them.[28] (*Methode*: p. 265.)

However, Knies did not succeed in making it clear how causality functions in this development.

Knies had two objectives for the position of ethics in economics. On the one hand, he aimed at value-free fundamental economic thought, resulting in a "merely descriptive economic theory". On the other hand, in the field of economic policy, he wanted to eliminate political apriorisms like the Classical idea that economic liberalism is "good" because of its nature. However, he did not support the opposite either. Yet he rejected the idea that the individual's aim for self-interest necessarily leads towards *das Gemeinwohl*, "general good", towards welfare for all.

Hildebrand's "political" economics

Bruno Hildebrand was a historically oriented economist, who became particularly known for his studies on the ideas of early socialists. He was born at Naumburg in Thuringia in 1812. Hildebrand was professor in Breslau and then in Marburg, where he was dismissed for liberal political activities. He then became professor in Zürich and Berne. In Switzerland he was promoter of a railway and initiator of a statistical office in the capital. He eventually returned to Germany, where he was appointed to a chair in Jena. He also established an office of statistics in Thuringia. Hildebrand's main work was *Die Nationalökonomie der Gegenwart und Zukunft*, "Political economy of the present and the future" (1848), in which he analysed the works of French and German socialists who preceded Marx. I refer to this book as *Zukunft*. His intention to follow it up with a study on the "historical method" was not carried out. However, the book (to which I will refer in particular) together with some later smaller publications offer sufficient insight into Hildebrand's methodological ideas. It is on these that I shall focus.

Like Roscher and Knies, Hildebrand dealt with the question of the ethical dimension of economic thought. Ideas about socio-economic reform were examined systematically. The title of his book refers to his ideas of the present and the past.

---

[28]Die Arbeitstheilung ist es, welche die ständische Gliederung in die ökonomischen Thätigkeiten einführt und immer weiter führt, die grossen Erwerbszweige im Allgemeinen sondert, sie im Detail spaltet und hinwiederum gruppirt.

> Every present generation and every acting statesman should interweave the past and the present, bearing them both equally in mind.[29] (*Zukunft*: p. 47.)

Placing this in the context of social reform, the writer considered it obvious that: 'this social fermentation process is necessarily followed by a similar process within science'[30] (*Zukunft*: p. 4). With this Hildebrand consciously took a step in the direction of engaged economics. Yet, it should not be concluded from these statements that he wanted to subject economics to all kinds of normative thinking about the organization of the state. He was well aware of the methodological difficulties in this field. Therefore, he was rather reserved about the feasibility of using normative thought on economic questions. This became clear when he put forward the scientific criticism to which socialist ideas should be submitted. According to Hildebrand this criticism should be focussed on the socialists' judgement about the topical, historically determined social situations, on the ideals, outlined by the socialists, at which mankind should aim and, lastly, on the socialists' judgement about the economic approach. He commented on this three-point criticism.

> Although, strictly speaking, here [in Hildebrand's methodologically oriented study] only the last criticism is relevant, the three elements of their [the old socialist's] thought are so coherent that splitting off one consideration from the others appears not to be permissible.[31] (*Zukunft*: p. 109.)

In a publication on statistics, he typified traditional economic thought as clearly value-loaded.

> [T]he Physiocrats as well as Adam Smith based most of their economic and political statements on philosophical premises, namely on theorems of the ethics of their day.[32] (Hildebrand, 1866: p. 2.)

Hildebrand did not oppose economics being subjected to value judgements in specific cases. However, he rejected the idea of the tacit use of ethical considerations in economic

---

[29]Jede gegenwärtige Generation, jeder handelnde Staatsmann hat immer die Vergangenheit und die Zukunft in einander zu weben und beides gleichmässig im Auge zu behalten.

[30]... dieser Gährungsprocess im Volke auch einen innern in der Wissenschaft zur Folge hat.

[31]Obgleich, streng genommen, nur diese ihre letztere Kritik hierher gehört, so stehen doch alle drei Bestandtheile ihrer Lehren in so engem Zusammenhange ..., dass eine Losreissung des einen von den übrigen unstatthaft erscheinen muss.

[32][D]ie Physiokraten sowohl als auch Adam Smith leiteten den grössten Theil ihrer volks- und staatswirthschaftlichen Sätze aus philosophischen Prämissen, namentlich aus Lehrsätzen der damals herrschenden Ethik ab.

thought. Of the three "founders" of the Historical School, he was the only one who was a member of the *Verein für Socialpolitik*. This was in line with his idea that there should be a close relationship between economics and politics.

Like Roscher and Knies, Hildebrand maintained that aiming towards self-interest does not necessarily lead with necessity to general welfare. He even believed that Smith's thought was based on an immoral foundation. When he discussed causality in Classical thought, Hildebrand called this approach "pseudo scientific". According to him the quintessence of economic causality is that any social situation arises from the previous one. He considered the socialists' approach to be as ahistorical as that of the Classicals. Against the idea of economic individualism he put the idea of the *Staatswirth*, the "economic leader of the state", who had to reconstruct society if necessary, and control its development (*Zukunft*: pp. 29-41, 263, 282).

> [T]here is no definition of it [the state], but only a living idea which is dynamic and not acquired but has to be experienced.[33] (*Zukunft*: p. 47.)

Yet, Hildebrand's interest in the "state" did not prevent him from noticing that 'all mankind's civilization arises from individuality' *(alle Civilisation der Menschheit entspringt aus den Individualitäten)* (*Zukunft*: p. 271).

* *

Hildebrand conceived of three stages in social development, based on Hegel and Fichte's idealistic pattern of thesis, antithesis and synthesis.

> What in the natural economy is chained together by personal sensual ties and, in the money economy, is loosened from one another, in the credit economy is linked up again by spiritual and ethical ties.[34] (*Zukunft*: pp. 278-79.)

This scheme of stages was orientated towards that of Proudhon, in which he distinguished two elements of truth. The first is the idea that economic life is governed by laws of development, on which, he said, economics should be focussed. The other is the idea 'that every economic institution, every form in which the economic life of the nation is enfolding itself, has only a relative justification and can be disastrous as well as benefi-

---

[33][E]s gibt von ihm keinen Begriff, sondern nur eine lebendige Idee, die selbst beweglich ist und nicht erlernt, sondern erlebt werden muss.

[34]Was in der Naturalwirthschaft durch äusserliche, sinnliche Bande an einander gefesselt, von der Geldwirthschaft aber von einander gelöst wird, das verbindet die Creditwirthschaft wieder durch geistige und sittliche Bande.

cial'[35] (*Zukunft*: p. 325). Another point of similarity was formed by the seventh stage of Proudhon's eight-stage development scheme, which was characterized as the stage of credit. Hildebrand shared Proudhon's positive judgement on the institutions that were supposed to be typical of the "credit economy". In this connection he mentioned the bill of exchange, the loan on security and the mortgage, and furthermore the deposit bank, the discount house and the central bank.

In a separate publication Hildebrand elaborated on this scheme of stages. His criterion for the classification of development stages was the institutional context of the exchange of goods (Hildebrand, 1864). In this approach the stages pass over into one another gradually. When speaking about the "natural economy", Hildebrand had the agrarian medieval society in mind, organized according to the feudal system. He said that in the towns of that period, nevertheless, an early form of money economy had existed. He noticed that in this type of economy rents and taxes were paid in kind, and that large payments were in the form of transfers of property rights to land. This natural economy was to be replaced by money economy, which originated in the medieval towns. In the money economy, Hildebrand said, the accumulation of capital became possible. It was stimulated by an increase of its productivity, which was facilitated by the formation of national states. For, with the help of money, production for the market replaced traditional production for self-support. Hildebrand considered Mercantilist and Physiocratic thought to be typical of the transition period. However, he considered Smith's theory to be *Geldwirthschaft*, "money economy", *in optimum forma* (*Zukunft*: pp. 14, 276).

Hildebrand's judgement of the "money economy" was both positive and negative. He appraised the rise of production, which he supposed to be typical of this stage, as positive. His judgement was negative if this stage was characterized by "industrial slavery", which was much worse 'than the personal slavery of Antiquity and the Middle Ages' (*Zukunft*: pp. 118, 277). Unlike former times, he believed, the entrepreneur had no practical interest in the well-being of the worker's families. The integral commercialization of social life broke down traditional coherences without replacing them with something else. This idea is found again in the works of Adolf Held and Georg Knapp, of the "younger" Historical School and, in a way, in Max Weber's thought.

According to Hildebrand, unrestrained competition is socially destructive. However, the lack of credit institutions is the root of all evil, and he considered this lack to be typical of the stage of the money economy. As already pointed out, he considered the third

[35]... dass jede ökonomische Institution, jede Form, in welcher sich das wirthschaftliche Völkerleben entfaltet, nur eine relative Berechtigung hat, und eben so unheilvoll, wie segensreich wirken kann.

stage a synthesis. Like Marx, who asserted that all social defects would vanish by abolishing private property, Hildebrand believed that the creation of appropriate credit institutions would guarantee a flourishing economy and a harmonious society.

> As coinage, if fully adopted, separates people from one another, so the payment instrument of credit ties them up, mutually committing them and creating a series of associations, rooting them in reciprocal trust on the one hand and evoking conflicting interests between such associations on the other.[36] (Hildebrand, 1864: p. 19.)

Hildebrand rightly noticed that the granting of credits increases the demand for goods, stimulates capital formation and improves the efficiency of the economic process. He held that the society which is to be designed by economic politics should be based on both ethical and practical principles. Sometimes, he said, a policy of international free trade is best suited for this. Under other circumstances, a policy of protection should be adopted (*Zukunft*: p. 90).

[36]Während das Metallgeld nach vollzogenem Umsatz die Menschen sofort wieder von einander löst, knüpft das Zahlmittel des Credits die Menschen an einander, verpflichtet sie gegenseitig und erzeugt eine Reihe von Associationen, die einerseits in dem gegenseitigen Vertrauen wurzeln, anderseits wieder ein gegenseitiges Interesse an einander hervorrufen.

Chapter 5
INDEPENDENTS IN THE SCHOOL'S SECOND GENERATION

Two outstanding members of the second generation of the Historical School I call "independents": Karl Bücher and Eugen Philippovich. The arguments for this I mentioned in the last section of Chapter 3. On the one hand, just like Schmoller, these members accepted Roscher's patrimony. On the other hand, in various respects they distanced themselves from Schmoller and his disciples. Like Roscher, they aimed at a synthesis with deductive economics. Schmoller, however, was inclined to stress the methodological contrast that had developed between the Classicals and the founders of the Historical School.

Bücher's historically oriented approach

Karl Bücher was born near Wiesbaden in 1847. He studied "state sciences" and history in Bonn and Göttingen. He held chairs at various universities including those at Basel and Leipzig. His principle work, issued in 1893 in two parts, to which I refer under *Entstehung* I or II, was *Die Entstehung der Volkswirtschaft*, "The genesis of the national economy", later translated under the felicitous Darwinian title "Industrial evolution". German social policy of Bücher's day can be seen as an omen of the modern welfare state. Bücher, however, saw similarities with forms of government care in former cultures. This marks him as a conservative socialist (of Lutheran signature).

In 1914, an economic textbook was published by Bücher, Schumpeter and Wieser. None of these writers was among Schmoller's intimate circle. Bücher wrote the first contribution, under the title *Volkswirtschaftliche Entwicklungsstufen*, "Economic development stages", in which he indicated what, in his opinion, the relationship is between this typical field of study and economics in general.

> A fortunate destiny gave man a needy nature and an unlimited urge to develop himself. The former continually drives him towards new enjoyments. The latter demands more and more perfect means for his development.[37] (Bücher, 1914: p. 2.)

Thus, Bücher said that man has a natural inclination to develop his needs and, consistent with this, to develop his ability to satisfy them. He assigned an "economic nature" to man. This was the core of his historicism. The principle served as a matrix for Darwinian ideas in his thought. In Bücher's view, the economic nature of man is subject to development. Among primitive man this was integrated in playing and in religious activities. In contrast, Bücher said, most modern people experience labour as a nuisance. He noticed that 'the game is older than labour, art older than production oriented on utility'[38] (*Entstehung* I: p. 29).

According to Bücher, the economy is formed by the behaviour of people according to the economic principle of achieving the greatest satisfaction of needs by the smallest sacrifice possible. He focussed on systematic modifications to the behavioural facets of cultural change. In this historical process of gradual change he saw a number of stages. So, his philosophy of development stages was primarily a historic characterization of economic development, and no stereotypical historistic scheme. The main criterion of Bücher's division into *Stufen* was the spatial dimension of the relationship between producer and consumer. The stage of self-sufficiency was called *Hauswirtschaft*, "home economy". Roman *latifundia* and medieval courts served as examples. The next stage was characterized by an economic system of "town and district" (with direct exchange and *Kundenproduktion*, "production on order"), called *Stadtwirtschaft*, "town economy". The last stage was that of production for the market, called *Volkswirtschaft,* "national economy".

Bücher's development scheme, which includes an initial stadium, was supposed to be applicable to European societies. Like Roscher, he assigned a crucial role in the process of economic development to the evolution of the division of labour. In connection with this historical process he spoke of *Gesetzmässigkeit der Entwicklung*, "causality of development" (*Entstehung* I: p. 158). To be able to judge this idea one must bear in mind that Bücher did not ascribe a predicting property to economics. The next development stage was, in principle, considered to be unknown. This agrees with the historical element in his thought, since this is also the stance of most historians.

---

[37]Ein gütiges Geschick hat in den Menschen eine bedürftige Natur und einen unbegrenzten Drang zur Fortentwicklung gelegt. Jene treibt zu stets neuem Genuss, dieser verlangt immer mehr und immer vollkommener Mittel zu seiner Entfaltung.

[38][D]as Spiel ist älter als die Arbeit, die Kunst älter als die Nutzproduktion.

Bücher said that in the three development stages of home economy, town economy and national economy, especially in the last, man would be characterized as *der Kulturmensch*, "the cultured man". According to his view, there were a few preceding stages, in the beginning of which man was to be typified as *der Urmensch*, "the primordial man". Although Bücher assigned to the latter an "economic nature", the behaviour of the primordial man was supposed to be, in a sense, comparable with that of animals. In this connection he said: 'The urge for self-preservation and satisfaction is the agent of development'[39] (*Entstehung* I: pp. 13, 27). According to Bücher's view, primordial man developed gradually into cultured man, who keeps stocks and meets his needs with the help of appliances and tools, curbing the powers of nature. The family developed into a production and consumption household, and some forms of exchange appeared. Bücher criticized the judgement of his day which blamed primitive man for unethical conduct. He was of the opinion that primordial man's efforts deserve full admiration.

> Above all, his way of working ensures the man of nature a great deal of joy in living and an everlasting cheerfulness, for which he should be envied by the European, troubled by labour and worry.[40] (*Entstehung* I: p. 81.)

Bücher perceived several tendencies in this socio-economic evolution. The production and consumption unit, which initially coincided, diverged in the course of development. In the second stage there were still direct relations between the two types of households. In the last stage, however, separation became almost total. In the course of this development process, products lost their personal characteristics and evolved to market goods. According to this view, the social unity involved in production and consumption developed from a circle of relations through a regional community into a national society.

Bücher presented a remarkable philosophy on the rise of the European town. According to him, the town was initially a stronghold, intended to function as a refuge for the farmers of the region, who had certain duties in maintaining and defending the fortress. He held that this group of people evolved to that of privileged citizens. According to him, it is possible to draw an analogy between the organization of these towns and that of the medieval courts, characterized by statute labour. Both communities, he said, were strictly regulated, and both were directed towards self-support.

---

[39]Der Trieb der Selbsterhaltung und Selbstbefriedigung ist das Agens der Entwicklung.

[40]Und vor allem seine Art zu wirtschaften sichert dem Naturmenschen ein Mass von Lebensfreude und immerwährender Heiterkeit, um das der arbeitgeplagte und sorgengedrückte Europäer ihn beneiden muss.

Bücher related the transformation of the old civic economy into a national economy to the rise of national states in the sixteenth century, which, in Germany, was only completed in the nineteenth century. He considered Mercantilist thought typical of the period of transition. He mentioned the fact that in medieval urban economies some developments anticipated a national economy, and contributed towards shaping the transformation process. Further, he mentioned the lifting of the ban on interest, which facilitated the accumulation and mobility of capital. He noticed the changing structure of trade currents between the various town districts.

Bücher noticed that, in this process of socio-economic development, money evolved to a dominating force.

> The home economy was, in essence, an economy of nature. Money, if it appeared, served both consumption and the accumulation of wealth. The town economy was based on transactions in ready cash. The national economy is largely a credit economy, in which money serves as a means for the circulation of goods and for the formation of income.[41] (Bücher, 1914: p. 17.)

This description shows that he had adopted Hildebrand's idea of the credit economy. Bücher was also influenced by Johann Rodbertus, initiator of reformational socialism in Germany. The latter's ideas that in a capitalist society labour becomes merchandise and capital goes its own way in an unwanted manner can be found in his works. Further, he linked up with Rodbertus' studies on Roman antiquity, his concept of the home economy referring to the *oikos* of Rodbertus.

Typical of the national economy, Bücher noticed, is the production of merchandise for the market.

> If in the home and town economies the only goods brought in from abroad were "merchandise" which filled gaps in domestic production, then almost everything that was produced in a division of labour system became merchandise. Thereby trade changed fundamentally, becoming a general liquidation institution for all produce.[42] (*Entstehung* I: pp. 139, 134.)

---

[41]Die Hauswirtschaft ist wesentlich Naturalwirtschaft; Geld, wo es auftritt, dient zugleich dem unmittelbaren Gebrauche und der Schatzbildung; die Stadtwirtschaft hängt am Bargeschäft; die Volkswirtschaft ist in weitem Masse Kreditwirtschaft; Geld is Umlaufs- und Erwerbsmittel.

[42]Wenn in der Haus- und Stadtwirtschaft nur diejenigen Güter den Warencharacter annahmen, die aus der Fremde zugeführt wurden, um Lücken der Eigenproduktion auszufüllen, so wird nun fast alles Ware, was in einer arbeitsteilig gewordenen Produktion erzeugt wird. Und damit ändert der Handel vollständig seine Natur. Er wird zur allgemeinen Liquidationsanstalt für die gesamte Produktion.

Bücher was critical of the dominating role acquired by capital in the society of his day. According to him, the entrepreneur became subservient to capital, directed towards the highest returns. He said that all social classes have to pay toll to this fictitious capital.

> What is most alarming of this whole [capitalist] system is that its supporters are everywhere and nowhere, exercising their power, not personally and directly, but through those that are pushed forward, to bear the whole odium of the situation.[43] (*Entstehung* I: p. 146.)

Bücher criticized the Classical approach on the one hand and praised it on the other. His criticism focussed on what he considered the neglect of the historical aspect of economic thought.

> Adam Smith assigns to man a natural inclination towards an inherent desire for exchange, and considers even the division of labour a consequence of this. Ricardo considers the hunter and the fisherman as two types of capitalist entrepreneurs, paying wages and making capital returns. He elaborates the rise and decline of their production costs and the prices of their produce. And to also mention an outstanding German of this school, Thünen, in constructing his "isolated state", relies entirely on these presuppositions about the exchange economy.[44] (*Entstehung* I: p. 90.)

Nevertheless, Bücher considered the Classical way of abstraction to be essential to economics.

> For, in order to approach the complicated causation of exchange processes in society, there is, in fact, no other method of research but isolated abstraction and logical deduction.[45] (*Entstehung* I: p. 159.)

Amongst the many thinkers who influenced Bücher, such as Roscher and Marx, the philosopher and historian Wilhelm Dilthey should also be mentioned. In his comment on

---

[43]Gerade das ist das Unheimliche dieses ganzen Systems, dass seine Träger überall und nirgends sind, dass sie regelmässig ihre Herrschaft nicht persönlich und unmittelbar, sondern durch vorgeschobene Personen ausüben, die das ganze Odium dieses Zustandes auf sich zu nehmen haben.

[44]Adam Smith lässt dem Menschen von Natur eine Neigung zum Tausche angeboren sein und betrachtet selbst die Arbeitsteilung erst als deren Folge. Ricardo behandelt den Jäger und Fischer der Urzeit wie zwei kapitalistische Unternehmer. Er lässt sie Arbeitslohn zahlen und Kapitalprofit machen; er erörtert das Steigen und Fallen ihrer Produktionskosten und des Preises ihrer Produkte. Um auch einen hervorragenden Deutschen dieser Richtung zu nennen, so geht Thünen bei seiner Konstruktion des isolierten Staates ganz von den Voraussetzungen der Verkehrswirtschaft aus.

[45]Denn es gibt in der Tat keine andere Forschungsmethode, mit welcher man der komplizierten Verursachung der Verkehrsvorgänge nahe kommen kann, als die isolierende Abstraktion und die logische Deduktion.

Dilthey, H.P. Rickman noticed that the Historical School: 'maintained that everything including laws, religions and even human nature was a product of history and subject to historical change. Every phenomenon could therefore only be understood in terms of its historical setting' (Rickman, 1976: p. 157). This not only fully accounts for the ideas of Dilthey's kindred spirit, Schmoller, but also for those of Bücher, one of Schmoller's antagonists in the *Methodenstreit*, already mentioned.

* *

Of the many subjects Bücher discussed in his works, two should be mentioned here: his study on the nature of the division of labour and that on consumption. Linking up with Roscher's view on the first, Bücher put the principle of the "community" of labour opposite that of the "division" of labour. He made it clear that the division of tasks implies that a form of cooperation exists, and that the study on the organization of labour should therefore not be focussed on the division aspect only. He went so far as to refer to List's idea of the harmony of "productive forces". By doing so he said, however, that he did not want to come into conflict with Smith's idea of "cooperation".

In his remarkable work *Arbeit und Rhythmus*, "Labour and rhythm", which includes the scores of old labour songs, Bücher divided labour into primitive people's *Bedarfsarbeit*, "needs-oriented labour", and modern society's *Erwerbsarbeit*, "income-oriented labour" (Bücher, 1896, 1902: p. 9). This distinction was also made by Werner Sombart, who incorporated it into his scheme of stages. Bücher had a negative judgement of the labour climate in the factories of his time, just like other members of the Historical School, such as Adolf Held. Bücher noticed that salutary rhythmic labour had been replaced by labour with machines that produced objectional noise, so that the songs of labour ceased.

> The labouring man is no longer master of his own movements. The tool, initially his servant and reinforced limb has become his master, dictating the measure of his movements. The tempo and duration of his work is withdrawn from his own control. He is chained to the dead, yet lively mechanism.[46] (Bücher, 1896, 1902: p. 419.)

Bücher should be considered one of the founders of consumer theory. He presented a picture of the relation between income and consumptive use, and perceived the significance of consumption for macro-economic demand. Consumption, he said, keeps the econ-

[46]Der arbeitende Mensch ist nicht mehr Herr seiner Bewegungen, das Werkzeug sein Diener, sein verstärktes Körperglied, sondern das Werkzeug ist Herr über ihn geworden; es diktiert ihm das Mass seiner Bewegungen; das Tempo und die Dauer seiner Arbeit ist seinem Willen entzogen; er ist an den toten und doch so lebendigen Mechanismus gefesselt.

omy running (1893, 1925: p. 339). He proposed an increase of this demand by increasing wages in times of depression.

Philippovich's idealistically oriented approach

Eugen Philippovich *von* Philippsberg was born in Vienna in 1858. He lectured in economics at the University of Freiburg "in Breisgau". He then became a professor in Vienna, where he remained until his death in 1917. He was searching for an economic system between extreme economic liberalism and a system of centralized production. He took an active part in the *Verein für Socialpolitik*, where he proved to be a critical thinker, and critical also of the typical ideas of this circle. Philippovich looked for a synthesis of the ideas of the Historical School on the one hand and those of the School of Marginal Utility, particularly those of Menger, on the other. Although he was closest to the former, methodologically he stood nearer to Menger. Compared with Roscher and Bücher, who were primarily empirically oriented, Philippovich was significantly influenced by German idealism, in particular by his neo-Kantian contemporaries Wilhelm Windelband and Heinrich Rickert.

Philippovich assumed that, in the course of time, people's ideas develop through experiencing the advantages and disadvantages of economic political principles and, in connection with this, through the influence of "creative spirits". New ideas, he said, result in new economic relationships. He therefore assigned a function to ideas in the causality of the process of socio-economic development. This "idealistic" attitude to social development is also found later in Sombart. In his textbook *Grundriss der politischen Oekonomie*, "Outline" or "Ground plan" of Political Economy, of 1893, to which I refer under *Oekonomie* I and II, Philippovich commented on causality in social development.

> Regularities that can be observed in economic empiricism might lead us to perceive economic changes as a necessary result of certain initial conditions. These changes in the organization of economic activities of men, however, like all historical life, rest largely upon consciously planned interventions by men themselves in the development process.[47] (*Oekonomie* I, 1893, 1923a: p. 42.)

[47]Regelmässigkeiten, die wir in der empirischen Volkswirtschaft beobachten, können uns dazu führen, Veränderungen in ihr als ein notwendiges Produkt bestimmter Voraussetzungen zu verstehen. Diese Veränderungen in der Organisation der menschlichen Wirtschaft beruhen aber, wie alles geschichtliche Leben, zu einem grossen Teile auf einem planvollen, bewussten Eingreifen des Menschen selbst in den Entwicklungsgang.

This formulation left room for other causes of economic change besides these human considerations. A two-fold view on causality is found in the opening of Philippovich's book *La politique agraire*, "Agricultural politics".

> Il est certain, par example, que le développement de notre état économique résulte du concours de forces qui diffèrent entre elles par leur nature, par leur puissance, par leur direction, mais il est certain aussi que le résultat définitif de la volonté et de l'influence des individus sur l'économie n'est pas une quantité négligeable. (Philippovich, 1904: p. 1.)[48]

"Freedom" has, according to Philippovich, both an individual and a collective aspect.

> In society freedom can, in fact, only exist if the individual is given the opportunity of contributing to the corporative [*read:* institutional] and political systems of control.[49] (*Oekonomie* II: p. 4.)

In the economic system, he distinguished *das gemeinwirtschaftliche Organisationsprincip*, 'the collective economic principle of order', from *das privatwirtschaftliche Organisations-princip*, 'the private economic principle of order'. The latter he also called *das Verkehrswirtschaftliche Princip*, "the economic exchange principle" or "market principle". By the former he was not only referring to central government, but also to lower authorities and to the various agencies authorized to decide on socio-economic matters. Thus, Philippovich's approach had both an individual dimension and an institutional one. An interesting element in this picture of development is his view on capital formation. He said that railways built in the nineteenth century were financed by production increases and savings, which were realized in society by economic activities resulting from this innovation. So, he said, the railways paid for themselves, through the issue of shares and bonds. According to him, modern industry is financed in the same way (Philippovich, 1905: p. 24).

Some remarks should be made about Philippovich's methodological ideas. He said that there is complementarity between "induction", orientated on facts, and "deduction", consisting of logical reasoning only. Like Menger, he identified "theory" with deductive patterns of thought. On the question of the practical aspects of economic thought, Philippovich trod in the footsteps of Roscher, who made a principal distinction between

---

[48]It is certain, for example, that the development of our social economic state is the result of a concurrence of forces which differ from each other in nature, force and direction. However, it is also certain that the ultimate result of the will and the influence of individuals on the economy cannot be neglected.

[49]Die Freiheit wird in der Gesellschaft tatsächlich nur darin bestehen können, dass den einzelnen die Möglichkeit gegeben wird, an den korporativen und politischen Zwangordnungen mitzuwirken.

analytical and political economic thought. Accordingly, Philippovich's textbook of 1893 is divided into two parts, entitled "general economics" and "economic policy", respectively. His "idealism", however, with its inherent danger that the border between these two fields of thought is unclear, placed him close to Schmoller on this point. The works of both writers have a slight normative tendency, in the sense that science was supposed to include statements about what is "good" or "sound" in the organization of society. This, however, also accounts for all organistic economic thought, especially for the Roscher and Bücher types.

Philippovich noticed that in many cases not everyone benefits from an economic political measure and that the interests of some could even be damaged. As an example he mentioned the introduction of an import duty. He considered it a task of economics to describe the pros and cons of such a measure as objectively as possible. Yet, he said, the choice is often culturally determined.

> Economics alone is not sufficiently capable of evaluating economic facts from a cultural point of view. For this, such facts should also be placed in relation to other cultural values, to law and ethics, and this needs a socio-philosophic basis.[50] (*Oekonomie* II: p. 8.)

* *

There is a scheme of stages to be found in Philippovich's thought. Unlike Bücher's thought, however, it is not a dominating element in his thinking. It principally serves to clarify his institutional ideas. His division of development into stages was meant as a synthesis of the ideas of Bücher and Schmoller on the same point. Bücher's approach was orientated to the evolving characteristics of production and consumption, while Schmoller's was focussed on the changing political system which was supposed to determine the economic system. However, physical and biological conditions also played a significant part in Schmoller's approach.

Like Bücher, Philippovich distinguished two main stages, the *geschlossene Hauswirtschaft*, "closed home economy", and the *Verkehrswirtschaft*, "market economy". He divided the latter phase into 'the period of locally bound trade, denoted "town economy", the period in which trade was bound to the functioning of the state, and that of free trade,

[50]Die Volkswirtschaftslehre allein reicht nicht mehr aus für eine Wertung wirtschaftlicher Tatsachen vom kulturellen Standpunkt aus. Eine solche ist nur möglich, wenn wir sie in Beziehung setzen zu anderen Kulturwerten, zum Recht, zur Ethik und wird daher sozialphilosophische Unterlagen haben.

typical of the developed economy'[51]. In contrast to Bücher, Philippovich's development pattern ends with the stage of the *Weltwirtschaft*, "world economy", in which the economies of the national states, with their autarchic aims, are replaced by a mondial system of free trade. This last idea deviated from the main stream of the Historical School.

For Philippovich, as has already been pointed out, a crucial role in the process of economic development is played by commonly accepted ideas of the best organization of production in society. He elaborated on this subject in two publications, dated 1910 and 1914. The first, dealing with liberalism, was praised by Hayek (Hayek, 1933, 1949: p. 116). Philippovich was of the opinion that "ideas" have not always determined economic life. In the Middle Ages, he said, this was not the case, because the Scholastics did not create an economic system.

> This phenomenon has only been able to be seen since the time of the rise of the authority of the state that is capable of influencing the physical, judicial and economic aspects of social life in a unifying, steady and purposeful way.[52] (Philippovich, 1914, 1924: p. 12.)

Philippovich remarked that Mercantilist thought formed the foundation of centralized government policy in the period of transition from a medieval economy to the times of economic liberalism. He assigned a pragmatic social involvement to Mercantilism: the more prosperous and cultivated the individuals, the better the interests of the state are served. As an example he mentioned Colbertism. According to Philippovich, the idea of the welfare state also stems from the Mercantilist world of thought, in particular from the British philosophical and political thinking of that era. In this view, welfare policy is based on the twofold idea that, on the one hand, private households are functionally united in a national household and, on the other, government is responsible for the well-being of the members of society as well as for a proper functioning of the various socio-economic institutions.

Cameralism, the typical German variant of Mercantilist thought, was characterized by Philippovich as a science.

---

[51]... die Periode des lokal gebundenen Verkehrs (Stadtwirtschaft), des staatlich gebundenen Verkehrs, und des freien Verkehrs (entwickelte Volkswirtschaft).

[52]Diese Erscheinung beobachten wir erst seit der Zeit des Entstehens einer Staatsgewalt, welche imstande ist, die physische, rechtliche und wirtschaftliche Seite des Gemeinschaftslebens ... einheitlich, gleichmässig und zielbewusst zu beeinflussen.

> [T]his was mainly aimed at the education of functionaries entering the administration of the princely *camera*, the central place for the management of finance, forestry, domains and mining.[53] (Philippovich, 1914, 1924: p. 132; my italics.)

One of the writers of this school that he mentioned was Hörnigk, author of a book bearing the intriguing title *Oesterreich über alles*, "Austria above all", which referred to the national interest dominating private interests. Philippovich noticed that in Mercantilism and Cameralism individual interests were subservient to the system of the state. However, he said, after the Renaissance there was a current which demanded more room for the individual; there was a tendency towards the emancipation of the individual man. He noticed that the Physiocrats, and in their footsteps the writers of the Classical School, elaborated the economic component of this idea. Philippovich described how economic liberalism in nineteenth-century Germany was part of a political struggle to allow individual men to show themselves in social intercourse. His basic idea was that the state is not strong enough to give the individual sufficient help. People are supposed to help themselves, and the state must create favourable conditions for this to happen.

Philippovich's judgement of liberalism had both a light side and a dark side. The judgement was favourable if he considered the broad opportunities for the manifestation of the individual personality, especially if this increased production and "enfolded" needs. The judgement was less favourable if he noticed that traditional social relationships were vanishing and that the market was penetrating into all parts of economic life, so that 'the price becomes the destiny of man'.

> Economic individualism (liberalism) brought about not only a change of living conditions, but also a change of the ideal of life, which at present is more than ever directed towards the ordering of the material foundations of our existence.[54] (Philippovich, 1910: p. 20.)

Philippovich considered the consumers' cooperative, the producers' cooperative of the Owen type, and Raiffeisen's agrarian credit cooperative to be the conservatives' and socialists' answer to economic liberalism. Like Hildebrand, he studied the socialist world of ideas. Unlike Hildebrand, he did not restrict himself to the ideas of the early socialists. He also discussed the ideas of Rodbertus, Marx and Engels. According to him, socialist

---

[53][D]ie nach ihrem Hauptzweck, die in die Verwaltung der fürstlichen "Kammer", der Zentralstelle für die Verwaltung der Finanzen, der Forsten, Domänen, Bergwerke, eintretenden Beamten, über die Aufgaben ihrer Aemter zu unterrichten.

[54]Der wirtschaftliche Individualismus (Liberalismus) hat nich bloss eine Aenderung des äusseren Lebensbedingungen, sondern auch eine Aenderung des Lebensideals bewirkt, das heute mehr denn je auf die Ordnung der materiellen Grundlagen unseres Daseins gerichtet is.

thought is in line with the critical ideas about private property and equality of the Scholastics and humanists like Thomas More, and of the Utopists of later times.

Philippovich described the world of ideas of the German "social reform" as it took shape in the second part of the nineteenth century. He characterized these ideas by using the organic metaphor.

> In Germany these ideas were inherently linked with an idea which in this country has never entirely disappeared. The idea is that society should have an organic articulation (in contrast to the atomism implied by the liberal principle) and that the state must take up its responsibility if the individual man cannot help himself any more.[55] (Philippovich, 1910: p. 74.)

According to him, the most important elements in *Sozialpolitik* are the organization of the work force, the assurance of sufficient wages, and the legal protection of the labourer. The protection of other social groups falls also within the scope of "social policy". He noticed that this policy is not orientated towards the interests of the "state" with its "enlightened functionaries", but towards the needs of "society". Into this context he put the establishing of the *Verein für Socialpolitik.*

> The need for social reforms had already been pronounced earlier by conservative parties. However, interest in it had also arisen in liberal circles.[56] [... In liberal circles] the promotion of social reforms meant the rejection of the extreme basic optimism of individualism, that a natural harmony will arise if everything is left to itself.[57] (Philippovich, 1914, 1924: p. 178.)

It is interesting to see how Philippovich conceived of economic policy. For him it was primarily the forming of an idea about what is desirable in social life and the way in which these objectives should be realized. For this, he said, it is necessary to have an insight into the causalities of a developing society. He considered economic politics an applied interdisciplinary science. He recognized that it is not always possible to support practical aims by arguments of pure economics only, especially if the balancing of specific interests of different individuals is under discussion.

---

[55]Innerlich knüpfen sie in Deutschland an den hier niemals ganz verdrängten Gedanken an, dass die Gesellschaft eine organische Gliederung aufweisen müsse im Gegensatz zu der Atomatisierung, welche das liberale Prinzip verlangte, und dass dem Staate positive Aufgaben zustehen müssten, dort wo der Einzelne sich nicht mehr selbst helfen kann.

[56]Die Notwendigkeit sozialer Reformen war schon vorher von den konservativen Parteien betont worden. Aber auch in den liberalen Kreisen war das Verständnis dafür erwacht.

[57]Die Vertretung sozialer Reformen bedeutete hier nur Ablehnung des grundsätzlichen Optimismus des extremen Individualismus, dass eine natürliche Harmonie sich einstellen werde, wenn alles sich selbst überlassen bliebe.

Chapter 6
MENGER'S NEW ORGANICISM

Carl Menger, originally *von* Menger, was born in 1840, at "Neu Sanden", in what was then Austrian Galicia. He studied law in Vienna, Prague and Cracow. After serving the Austrian court and government, he was appointed to a chair at the University of Vienna, where he lectured in economics. Menger became famous as the founder of the Austrian branch of the School of Marginal Utility. Discovering a "protoneoclassical" tradition in nineteenth-century German economic thought, Streissler suggested that Menger's 'formulation of marginal productivity in marginal utility terms and its application to all factor remunerations in exactly the same manner' should be placed against this background (Streissler, 1990: p. 59). Menger also became well-known as a methodologist who allowed space for organically oriented ideas. I focus on him in the last function. In this connection I use the term "new organicism", considering it, on the one hand, a modern version of Wilhelm Roscher's organicism, drastically transformed, and, on the other, an entirely new approach. The term is reminiscent of Francis Bacon's *Novum organum*, characterized by empiricism and inductive logic. I have pointed out elsewhere, when discussing this issue (1993a), that I do not consider this problematic since Menger himself approvingly referred to this work.

Jan Zuidema stressed the significance of causality and time in Menger's work. He distinguished three causality patterns in it: the causation of value, the causality in "roundabout" production, and a vague historical causality, which referred to the institutional context of the economic process (J.R. Zuidema, 1988). It is this historical causality that is of most interest within the scope of my study.

"Dualistic" economics

Carl Menger did not agree with the idea that the social sciences should be distinguished, in principle, from natural sciences. This idea had been put forward by neo-Kantians like Windelband, and adherents of the philosophy of life, represented by Dilthey and Schmoller. Menger even strongly opposed this type of methodical dualism. In adopting a homogenous method in economics, he was in line with Roscher's thought, although he rejected Roscher's idea that socio-economic development is determined by "laws of nature". Menger criticized Roscher for aprioristic thinking in the field of the development of society. He also refuted Schmoller's idea that in economics technological and natural causes, on the one hand, and psychological and ethical causes, on the other, should both be studied in their own right, in order to discover their economic relevance. According to Menger, the difference between the various fields of study lies not in methodical principles, but in the typical points of view of the various sciences. He stated that in economics this viewpoint is the "necessitous nature of man" (Krabbe, 1988). However, I hope to make it clear that there is another form of dualism to be found in Menger's economics.

Many of Menger's methodological ideas were set down in his *Untersuchungen über die Methode der Socialwissenschaften, und der politischen Oekonomie insbesondere*, published in 1883. In 1985 an English version of this appeared, edited by L. Schneider and translated by F.J. Noch, under the title *Investigations into the method of the social sciences with special reference to economics*. I refer to this version under *Investigations*.[58]

Menger made a distinction between a mechanistic and an organistic approach. In contrast to the mechanical system, the organic system was characterized as being a "higher whole".

> Not only *organisms*, but also *mechanisms*, show a purposefulness of their parts with respect to the whole, and not only in the former, but also in the latter, the normal function of the unit is conditioned by the normal condition of the parts. The organism is distinguished from the mechanism by the fact that on the one hand it is not, like the latter, a product of human calculation but of a natural process. On the other hand its individual part (each organ) is conditioned not only in its normal *function*, but also in its normal *nature* by the connection of the parts to form a higher unit (the organism in its totality) and by the normal nature of the other parts (the organs). This is by no means the case with a mechanism. (*Investigations*: p. 132n; italics in original translation.)

According to Menger, the proper approach for studying the core of economics is the mechanistic one, resulting in a "theory" of utility and prices. This theory was supposed to have an "atomistic" and an "exact" character. In Menger's view, theory is oriented towards the behaviour of individual members of society, who are all assumed to maximize their personal utility. Nevertheless, when dealing with the economic system as a whole, including its institutional aspects as well as the development of it, he adopted a partly organically oriented approach, calling it "realistic economics" and assigning to it both an "empirical" nature and a "descriptive" one. He placed the word "organistic" between inverted commas in order to stress the organic metaphor's limited significance in the

---

[58]References to the pages of Menger's original works can be found in Krabbe, 1988 and 1993a.

context of economics. He had strong objections to Roscher's organistic idea of the state (Milford, 1990: p. 219).

Menger assumed that his "organistic" approach did not conflict with an atomistic price analysis. His consumer-oriented valuation system was not based on individuals' rational considerations only, but also on impulses and inclinations (*Investigations*: p. 87). For him, man's needs are caused by a combination of biological, instinctive and psychological factors. He spoke of a "harmony" in the satisfaction of human needs, and in the structure of wants and the packages of consumption goods, from an individual as well as from a social point of view. Schmoller's idea of harmony was in the concept of the interaction between "nature" and "culture", and therefore is of a different kind. (Krabbe, 1988; see also the study on Menger's methodology by Hutchison, 1953, 1962: pp. 145-152.) Menger had profound objections to the approach of most of the members of the Historical School. These objections found expression in his position in the *Methodenstreit* with Schmoller. Above all, Menger rejected the idea that economics is a philosophy of development orientated towards the science of history, an approach he called *Historismus*, to be translated as either "historism" or "historicism" (Menger, 1884).

Menger's organistic principles

Carl Menger used Roscher's expression "physiology and anatomy of wants", but he assigned a specific meaning to the term. He stated that wants and their counterparts in the sphere of goods form a "higher whole", which he considered an "indivisible whole". He maintained that a "philosophy of analogy" between organisms and social complexes can, to a certain extent, be fruitful. According to his view, components of the institutional structure can serve the functioning and the development of the social whole in a significant way, mentioning the institutional determinants of prices of goods, interest, land rents and profits as examples. However, Menger made it clear that in economics such holistic phenomena must not be studied by using a biological method, but by applying a specific social science method. For him, "development of wants" is a part of both institutional development and technological development (Krabbe, 1993a).

The *Methodenstreit* can be placed in the antithesis between thought in the Platonic tradition and thought in the Aristotelian tradition. The Historical School was strongly influenced by the former, through nineteenth-century German philosophers who had a Platonic interpretation of Kantian idealism (Krabbe, 1991). However, there were also other influences, especially on organically oriented thinking in the School, like those of Herder and Dilthey. Menger, on the other hand, was influenced by the Aristotelian approach of the Classicals, a stream of thought which was based partly on Bacon. Menger's organically oriented ideas were thus conditioned by an "essentialist" approach of Aristotelian stamp. This form of essentialism differed fundamentally from that of most of the members of the Historical School, in which the "essence" of social phenomena was supposed to be in a historical process of coming into existence, expressed by the proposition "being is becoming".

E.E. Berns (1989) elucidated the Aristotelian aspect of Menger's *discourse* (the conceptual framework of his work), in which he was partly relying on Hutchison (1978, 1981). According to Berns, Menger was influenced by the phenomenological philosopher Franz Brentano (brother of the economist, Lujo Brentano). Franz Brentano, wanting an "empirical psychology", 'worked explicitly for a renaissance of Aristotelian realism'. Discussing Menger's concept of causality in his theory of value, Berns noticed: 'The "ultimate cause" to which all economic phenomena must be reduced ... has a goal-oriented structure and functions as a final cause *(causa finalis)*' (Berns, 1989: p. 95). Menger's "organistic" ideas, however, refer not to the sphere of exact laws, to which he assigned this form of causality, but to the empirical-realistic sphere, in which time has to play a specific part and, therefore, in which teleology is of a special nature. Berns discussed Menger's concept of history, with reference to the formation of institutions.

> The beginning and the end points of this conception are liberal: a subjective value theory on the one hand and the idea of a rational society on the other hand. In between, however, lies an historical world in which institutions are still the unintended consequences of the interaction of individuals. These spontaneously developed institutions must be treated with respect because they, as long as the time is not yet ripe, cannot be completely understood and because they witness the direction of history as a process of progress of the understanding of the nature of things and of human nature. (Berns, 1989: p. 104.)

In his discussion on "parallelisms"[59] in the patterns of historical causality, Menger referred to thought in the Historical School.

> But what a methodological error it is to confuse these [parallelisms] with the laws which teach us how supply and demand or the quantity of means of circulation influence the price of goods, how the distance of pieces of land from the market and their differential fertility influence ground rent, how the greater or lesser thriftiness or the more or less active business spirits of the inhabitants of a land influence the rate of interest in it. These are laws which after all cannot reasonably be designated *in toto* as parallelisms of the historical development of the economy! (*Investigations*: p. 120.)

He then compared his view on the function of historical thought in economics with Darwin's approach in the field of natural science research, noticing some similarity.

---

[59]On "parallelism" see also Menger, 1884, 1966: p. 48.

Organistic ideas in Menger

More should be said about Menger's organically oriented ideas, including his idea of harmony between wants and means. Most of these ideas are found in his epoch-making work *Grundsätze der Volkswirthschaftslehre*, published in 1871, and translated and edited by J. Dingwall and B.F. Hoselitz under the title *Principles of economics* (1950). I refer to this translation under *Principles*. Carl Menger's approach is based on the idea that wants must be seen in their relation to "properties" of scarce things: private and public goods. He said that it does not matter whether these properties are real, or imaginative and only assigned to goods. He noted that scarcity can be artificial, for example, by monopolizing the supply of goods that were formerly free available (*Principles*: pp. 53-4, 104). Another principle of Menger's thought is that satisfaction of wants must be put into a causal context, which is bound to an interval of time. He noticed that causality could contain an element of uncertainty. He also mentioned that, in consumer decisions, expected incomes play a part. Further, in his thought ideas can be found that anticipate the principles of time preference and "roundaboutness", later elaborated and introduced into economic theory by Böhm-Bawerk (*Principles*: pp. 51, 67, 69-71, 82-4, 152-55, 162-63).

Menger's concept of wants has a typically organic dimension since he stated that wants arise partly from *Trieben*, inclinations in human nature (Menger, 1883: p. 78). In this context he put forward the idea of a hierarchy of the wants that are subject to development. He maintained that although total human wants are unlimited, specific wants are satisfiable. Thus, after certain wants are satisfied, others will arise (*Principles*: pp. 94-8).

> [T]he concept of infinity is applicable only to unlimited progress in the development of human needs, but not to the quantities of goods necessary for the satisfaction of these needs [specific wants] during a given period of time. (*Principles*: p. 83.)

Another organistic trait in his thought was the idea that the social pattern of wants and its counterpart in the sphere of goods form an "indivisible unit" (*Investigations*: pp. 130, 139, 194).

> The theory that "organisms" are indivisible units and their functions are vital expressions of these structures in their totality does not establish an objection to the exact (the atomistic!) orientation of theoretical research either in the realm of natural or of so-called social organisms. (*Investigations*: p. 139.)

Menger presented a harmonious picture of wants and means, the corner stone of which was the idea of complementarity. He made it clear that the direct or indirect utility of goods also depends upon the quantities of other goods available. The idea of complementarity refers to the structure of wants of individuals, as well as to that of society as a whole. He believed that these structures of wants are mirrored by the composition of consumption packages of families, as well as by the total package of means applied in society (*Principles*: pp. 56, 59-60, 75-6, 96-7, 162-63). Menger held that the development of society's institutional structure has an impact on the structure of theory. He believed that disturbance of the social process of satisfaction of wants could cause a catastrophe (*Principles*: pp. 51-2, 82-3, 154; *Investigations*: p. 104).

> Human life is a process in which the course of future development is always influenced by previous development. It is a process that cannot be continued once it has been interrupted, and that cannot be completely rehabilitated once it has become seriously disordered. (*Principles*: p. 154.)

Nature in early Austrian thought

In the course of economic development the relationship between man and nature becomes ever more complex. It was the merit of the early "Austrians", particularly Böhm, to be fully aware of this, expressing economic growth in terms of the extension of production routes. In this connection, it should be realized that Austrian economics was typically anthropocentric, mainly in the individualistic sense of the term. The point of departure of economic reasoning is man. This implies that, on the one hand, the distance from the economic agent "nature" becomes ever greater and "roundabouts" take ever more time. On the other hand, man himself was considered part of nature. As such, his wants and pursuits are partly determined by it, and nature is always close to him.

In the opening words of his *Positive Theorie des Kapitales*, Eugen *von* Böhm-Bawerk (1888, 1921) formulated the Austrian attitude towards nature and natural sciences. For him, production is the result of cooperation between men and nature. In this field of study, economics and natural sciences should be "compatible". He said that in economic theory statements must "not conflict with natural science" *(nie antinaturwissenschaftlich; nicht naturwidrig)*; what is false in the latter is also false in the unity of all knowledge (p. 4). According to him, economics and sciences of nature are border fields of study, differing in principle. He said that, although production is "entirely in the ban of natural sciences", these fields of study must not be identified with one another (p. 6). According to his view, this is also true for the science of psychology. Thus, Böhm disagreed with Schmoller's idea that economics is, in essence, applied ethics and psychology. On the point of the relationship between natural sciences and economics, Böhm's approach was similar to Menger's.

Early Austrian economics contained an idea of social ordering reminiscent of the Physiocrat's perception of the Enlightened natural order idea. In this connection I refer to Friedrich *von* Wieser. His idea of nature, used in his term "the natural value" *(der natür-*

liche Werth), refers to a social order created not by "the Creator" nor by "nature", but by "needy men". The idea of the "needy man" is also found among Historical School members like Bücher. Wieser placed a "natural" approach towards economic phenomena alongside an "empirical" approach. The latter dealt with the way in which the principle of ordering is realized. Like the Physiocrat interpretation, Wieser's order concept was partly organically oriented. He believed that economic ordering according to human nature might include "the assumption of a coherence of all that lives" *(die Ahnung eines Zusammenhanges alles Lebens)* which, however, does not stand in the way of valuation on the basis of marginal utility. The antipole of the Physiocrat's idea of natural order was the *ordre positif*, of Mercantilist signature. That of Wieser's order was the "communist state" (Wieser, 1889: pp. 19, 60).

In Menger's approach there was a balance between a "historical" and institutional approach, on the one hand, and a theory of prices, quantities, and factors of an individualistic nature determining them, on the other. Böhm focussed fully on the latter. Another member of the early Austrian School, Emil Sax, put emphasis on the former. Menger was closer to the Historical School than Böhm, but Sax was closer to it than Menger. Sax had a partly organically oriented concept of the economy, in which "living nature" plays a rather important part. He elaborated Menger's idea of natural inclinations in the patterns of wants for goods. Further, some of Schmoller's wisdom about the relationship between humanity and nature is also to be found in Sax (1884).

Austrian scholars agreed that the role of capital becomes ever more important in a developing economy. However, they did not go so far that nature disappears entirely from sight, as it does in the theories of many later representatives of Classical types of economics, fully orientated towards the market process. The Austrian conceptual structure is such that nature is always in the picture, as capital was not considered an original production agent, but was supposed to be derived from the original agents labour and nature. This is also the approach that was taken by Walther Eucken and John Stuart Mill. It is in contrast to Schmoller's approach in which capital is complementary to nature, having the character of synthetic nature. This does not mean that Austrian economists always gave nature the attention it deserved. Wicksell criticized Böhm-Bawerk on this point (R.P. Zuidema, 1970: p. 95).

Like David Ricardo, who projected Adam Smith's ideas into an abstract and consistent model, Böhm made a similar transformation of Menger's ideas. The advantage of such creative transformations is that some of the original ideas are pictured more clearly. A disadvantage is that other ideas are underexposed or vanish from the picture altogether. This was the fate of Menger's view on the organic facets of wants. Another of Menger's ideas not found in Böhm is that of the harmony in individual and social satisfaction of wants, an idea which, in the last resort, was orientated towards land, natural resources, and other environmental factors.

The Austrians rightly thought economics as primarily a valuation system which includes the valuation of nature. Menger replaced the Ricardonian rent idea by the valuation of components of nature according to the principle of marginal utility, through *Zurechnung*, "imputation" or "assignment". Menger considered that, if the scarcity condition is not fulfilled, nature does not have the character of an economic agent, and that it should be considered an economic good if it appears to be "scarce". He made it clear that as a result of economic development, non-economic elements of nature can become economic production agents. One of his examples was that of clean water. It can be said that he had a clear view on the idea of "new scarcity". In Menger's approach, if the total demand by individual users at zero price is greater that the quantities available, scarcity is determined by the fact that consumers are willing to pay for it. I have already made it clear that, according to him, it does not matter whether this demand is based on a misconception by consumers, or whether the scarcity is artificially created by specific institutions.

In a way, Schumpeter can be considered to have stood partly in the Austrian tradition, although he wanted to include supply functions in the economic valuation system. He called the principle of marginal utility "the organon of pure economics". Unlike Menger, he was reluctant to identify scarcity with price, confining himself to the statement that "indices of economic significance" and "exchange values" are acquired from the same principle (Schumpeter, 1954: p. 913). Menger's rigorous link between scarcity and prices has been accepted by economists for a long time. Nowadays, however, they realize that elements of nature which bear no price at all nevertheless have an "intrinsic" value, which might have economic significance. This type of scarcity remained beyond Menger's scope. Later this idea was put forward by Georgescu-Roegen and by Goudzwaard (1970). Discussing differences in Menger's approach on the one hand and the approaches of authors like Hayek and Mises on the other, Shearmur pleaded for strengthening biologically oriented thinking in Neo-Austrian economics (Shearmur, 1990: p. 199).

In Austrian thought the economic system is ordered by consumers and entrepreneurs. According to Menger, this results spontaneously in a harmonious picture. This might be true if people live close to nature, as happens in less developed societies. However, in modern economies, which become ever more complicated, in the process of which the gap between man and natural resources is steadily increasing, this should be doubted. In fact, to these two ordering factors, a third one should be added: environmental policy. This policy must be based on two pillars: the insight offered by environmental sciences, and the system of political decisions, according to scientific data and priorities of original and authorized decision makers in society, in which due attention is given to cost and benefit considerations. This also counts for John Gowdy's idea of "de-development". Gowdy (1994: p. 52) posited that, in order to preserve nature, what we need is not a steady-state (Daly, 1991, 1993), but a "declining state", compatible with long-term sustainable development. There is no reason to assert that such a "declining" economy becomes less complicated, bringing the production agent Nature closer to consumers.

In his book *The coal question*, Carl Menger's congenial spirit William Stanley Jevons discussed the subject of the exhaustion of nature. Wondering what should be done when the coal stocks were exhausted, he argued that it is impossible for an economy to keep on growing because of the limited resources. Jevons saw that substitution of comparatively scarce resources and technological innovations could provide relief (Heijman, 1991: p. 18). Nevertheless, his conclusion for the Britons was: "We have to make a momentous choice between brief greatness and longer continued mediocrity" (Jevons, 1866: p. 376). Later, Nicholas Georgescu-Roegen was to come to a similar conclusion for mankind as a whole.

> [T]he higher the degree of economic development, the greater must be de annual depletion [of nature] and, hence, the shorter becomes the expected life of the human species. (Georgescu-Roegen, 1970, 1976: p. 59.)

Chapter 7
SCHMOLLER, FOUNDER OF THE "YOUNGER" HISTORICAL SCHOOL

Gustav Schmoller, later *von* Schmoller, was born in Heilbronn in the German state of Wurtemberg, in 1838. He studied *Staatswissenschaften*, "public administration", in Tübingen. In the Germany of that time, this branch of studies still bore the stamp of Cameralist thought. As a professor he lectured on this subject at the Universities of Halle, Strasbourg and, finally, Berlin. He was the main initiator and, for a long time, chairman of the *Verein für Socialpolitik*, founded in 1872, in which he was a propulsive force behind studies in socio-economics and German economic history. For Schmoller, economic history and history of economic thought were strongly linked. He was the dominant figure in what was called the Younger Historical School, in which he had many disciples. He also became influential at the Emperor's court in Berlin. In this position he promoted the study of economics in Prussia and the newly established Empire according to his own ideas, which were in part also those of Bismarck.

Schmoller was an idealist, in the sense that he assumed that ideas arising in society form the basis of its organization. This is seen in his interest in institutional phenomena and their analysis. The holistic idea of *Volksgeist*, put forward earlier by Adam Müller, can also be found in Schmoller. In this, however, he was referring especially to his kindred spirit, Wilhelm Dilthey. Schmoller's main publication was his bipartite work *Grundriss der allgemeinen Volkswirtschaftslehre*, "Outline of national economics", to which I refer under *Grundriss* I (1900, 1908) and *Grundriss* II (1900, 1923).

Alongside his "idealistic" approach, Schmoller put forward the idea that the economic process forms "part of the great process of nature", controlled by "laws of nature" (*Grundriss* I: p. 127). He believed, however, that these laws only form conditions for what is going on in the sphere that he considered typically economic.

> Economic production consists always of an active intervention by man in the great, ever continuing process of nature. It should be shaped in such a way that the forces of nature are the least harmful and the most beneficial for him.[60] (*Grundriss* I: p. 3.)

He approached the complex phenomenon of economy and nature in a way that can be seen as an early form of economic systems theory. In Roscher's economic system, nature had been fully integrated. Schmoller replaced this unified system by an "ordered" one, with subsystems, each of which should be analysed by a method adjusted to the phenomena under investigation (Krabbe, 1993a).

His concept of economics

In his definition of *Volkswirtschaft*, "national economy", Schmoller referred to the idea of *Wirtschaften*, "economizing". According to him and his followers in the Historical School, economizing is not production of material goods only, but also includes working for 'higher, non-economic purposes'. In the national economy people are bound together by similar *(einheitliche)* ideas, morals and laws (*Grundriss* I: pp. 3, 5). According to Schmoller, competition often has destructive effects. He criticized the Classicals for being unaware of this aspect.

> [T]he relentless, free, individualistic battle of competition appeared the only ideal. In their *theory*, limits set by morals, customs and law were overlooked, although in fact they never disappeared.[61] (*Grundriss* I: p. 66; my italics.)

Schmoller stated that moral conduct coincides with efficient behaviour. The essence of his historicism is found in the statement that the ethical judgement is "a developing datum" *(ein Werdendes)* (*Grundriss* I: p. 434). Developing morals result in ever new or renewed institutions. For him, "institutions" was an idealistic term, referring to ideas such as property, marriage, slavery. "Institutes" are the institution's counterparts in the sphere of social empiricism. Matrimony is an institution, the family is an institute; private enterprise is an institution, the company is an institute (*Grundriss* I: p. 61). Certain institutions and their corresponding institutes were typical of certain stages of socio-economic develop-

---

[60]Die wirtschaftliche Produktion besteht stets in einem aktiven Eingreifen des Menschen in den grossen, nie ruhenden Naturprozess; er soll so gestaltet werden, dass die Kräfte der Natur dem Menschen am wenigstens schaden, ihm am meisten nützen.

[61][D]er rücksichtslose, freie, individuelle Konkurrenzkampf erschien als das einzige Ideal; seine Schranken durch Moral, Sitte und Recht, die niemals in der Wirklichkeit verschwanden, übersah man in der Theorie.

ment. Institutions are understood as crystallizations of the economic ideas of that time and place (*Grundriss* I: p. 99).

According to Schmoller, the economy consists of both ethical and natural elements. Economics, however, was supposed to focus on the first. As a consequence, he believed that the economic system must be able to bear the test of justice.

> The ... optimistic idea which denies all exploitation by [the system of] free market intercourse ignores the elementary psychic fact that every formation of value, as well as every other social fact, is subject to be judged according to whether it complies with moral ideals, benefitting the whole as well as the parts.[62] (*Grundriss* II: p. 122.)

This placed him in the field of politically committed economics. Nevertheless, he agreed with Roscher that economics is focussed on *Sein* ("is") and not on *Sollen* ("should"). According to Schmoller's view, these two ideas on the point of the political orientation of economic thought fit in with one another because political ideas alive in society are considered observable data. However, he did not pay enough attention to the fact that in society various ideas are normally evident about the policy to be followed, out of which choices must be made in the policy-making process.

No justice is done to Schmoller if his approach is typified as being "inductive" only, and as little is done to Menger if his method is characterized as being only "deductive". Schmoller made a plea for the *primacy* of induction in an epistemological process, that coincides with the development of the socio-economic field of study. In the first development stage, "intuition" was also supposed to play a part. When social economics was fully developed, thought was considered entirely deductive. According to him, induction is the preparation of conclusions out of singular observations to underlying causalities.

> The putting together of various observations and comparing them, the attempt to provide total images for extensive domains of economic life in a tentative way, is a principle way of bringing unification to the chaos of dispersed singularities. It also contains the initial impetuses for inductive conclusions, since the main aim of all description is to prepare induction, which is the conclusion from singularities to the fundamental law. However, as such it is not yet induction, and even serves deduction and its ever renewed verification of facts.[63] (*Grundriss* I: p. 102.)

---

[62]Die ... optimistische Auffassung, welche alle Ausbeutung durch den freien Marktverkehr leugnet, ... übersieht die elementare psychische Tatsache, dass jede Wertbildung so gut wie jede andere gesellschaftliche Tatsache dem Urteil unterliegt, ob sie den sittlichen Idealen entspreche, heilsam fürs Ganze und alle Teile wirke.

[63]Die Zusammenfassung mehrerer Beobachtungen und ihre Vergleichung, der Versuch, so ausprobierend Gesamtvorstellungen über grössere Gebiete des volkswirtschaftlichen Lebens zu schaffen, ist ein Hauptmittel, in das Chaos zerstreuter Einzelheiten Einheit zu bringen. Es liegt

Schmoller held that "indisputable truths" *(feststehende Wahrheiten)* are found through observation, definition and classification of ideas, by finding typical phenomena and causal relationships. This method of "abstraction" was supposed to develop an outline of a certain economic situation, determined by time and place (*Grundriss* I: pp. 101, 111; Schmoller, 1897). He believed that investigation along the lines of induction and deduction leads to an insight into causality in socio-economic life, by way of observation of 'regularly and typical repeating series of phenomena' *(regelmässig und typisch sich wiederholenden Erscheinungsreihen)* (*Grundriss* I: p. 109).

His methodical "dualism"

I have already mentioned that Schmoller was of the opinion that economic reality has two facets, which should be scientifically examined in two fundamentally different ways. The first aspect, indicated by him as the world of phenomena that are typically economic, concerns the ethically and physiologically based behaviour of man in socio-economic intercourse. The other aspect is formed by the world of capital and nature. He saw the latter world of phenomena as an integral part of the economy. The use of capital as well as nature was considered to be essential to man the producer. According to Schmoller, knowledge about the first aspect should be gained from the social (mental) sciences, including economics in the narrow sense of the word, whereas knowledge about the second aspect must be gained from the natural sciences, and should be utilized in economics, in the broad sense of the term.

I have already pointed out that, in a way, Schmoller was a follower of Roscher. He adopted Roscher's distinction between "internal" and "external" nature, the first term referring to the fact that, in a certain respect, man himself forms part of nature. He also shared Roscher's interest in the function of nature in production: the sequence of the components of economic life mentioned in Schmoller's phrase "land, people and techniques" *(Land, Leute und Technik)* testifies to this. Although his disagreement with Classical thought was considerably stronger than that of Roscher, Schmoller respected Roscher because, as he said, the latter's work was governed by a spirit other than that of the liberal Classics. Further, he referred with approval to the basic idea of development that can be found in Roscher's words. Schmoller's work also contains variants of Roscher's "organic metaphor" (*Grundriss* I: pp. 93, 119, 126-27).

---

darin auch der Ansatz zu induktiven Schlüssen, wie alle Beschreibung ihren Hauptzweck darin hat, die Induktion, d.h. den Schluss vom einzelnen auf das zu Grunde liegende Gesetz vorzubereiten; aber sie ist an sich noch nicht Induktion und dient ebenso der Deduktion und ihrer stets erneuten Prüfung an den Thatsachen.

It should by now be clear that, unlike Karl Bücher, Schmoller did not integrally maintain Roscher's way of thinking in terms of "sciences of nature". In fact, Schmoller was strongly influenced by Dilthey's "philosophy of life", in which economics is part of the *Geisteswissenschaften*, the "mental sciences" or "humanistic sciences", and his idea of "economic life" must be placed against the background of this philosophy.[64] The adoption of this methodological principle meant that he narrowed the proper subject matter of economics to "the ethico-mental sphere". Yet, the works of Schmoller testify *de facto* to a much broader view on economics, as well as to the acknowledgement that the sciences of nature contribute to it. Schmoller said that human existence is determined by "external" nature. He assumed that during the process of social development, the economy becomes less and less dependent on nature. The current environmental crisis, however, challenges the validity of this idea (*Grundriss* I: pp. 146, 229).

Thus, as well as a narrow approach, Schmoller also had a broad concept of the scope of economics.

> National economy can be seen as a system of moral as well as natural forces. It is both, at the same time, according to the point of view considered.[65] (*Grundriss* I: p. 59.)

When the character of causality in the economy (thus broadly conceived of) was discussed, he spoke of all economic phenomena being determined by two factors: physical and biological causes on the one hand and psychogenic and moral causes on the other. In this holistic approach, "natural" and "mental-historical" causes interact, "nature" and "culture" are intertwined. On the basis of each of these two points of view, he concluded that the researcher is confronted with "typical series and forms" *(typischen Reihen und Formen)*. The synthesis was a "historico-economic philosophy" which has links with ethics and sociology on the one hand and with natural sciences on the other. Schmoller believed that although the "mechanistic" causality of physics differs from the "psychogenic" causality, they are, nevertheless, "parallel" (*Grundriss* I: pp. 105-07, 125, 139).

The idea of development was always in Schmoller's thought. He considered it to be applicable to the economy in its broadest sense, including the natural sphere as well as the mental sphere. Schmoller linked up with Darwin's ideas on analogies between biological and social life. However, he warned against drawing premature conclusions based on inad-

---

[64]When discussing the influence of German idealism on Schmoller's thought, Athanasios Giouras mentioned Fichte in particular (Giouras, 1994: pp. 9-13). Dilthey's influence is discussed by Schefold (1989).

[65]Man kann die Volkswirtschaft als ein System natürlicher, wie als ein System sittlicher Kräfte betrachten; sie ist beides zugleich, je nach dem Standpunkte der Betrachtung.

equate organic analogies. He also cautioned against a misunderstanding in extrapolating the Darwinian idea of selection in the struggle for life into the social system. Schmoller believed that the principle cannot be applied to the conflict in society between the rich and the poor, but to the tendency to abolish obsolete institutions and to create new ones: the tendency to control rivalry and competition in society, that is, to correct the evil in it and make the most of its benefits. For him, this meant an important role for the government (*Grundriss* I: pp. 64*ff*, 106, 123). Schmoller was sympathetic to the analogy between the division of labour and biological life, referring to the ideas of men like Herbert Spencer and Karl Bücher. Nevertheless, he had reservations about their approach in terms of natural sciences. Schmoller himself pointed to the renewing effect of the succession of generations on the shaping of economic life (*Grundriss* I: pp. 161, 346).

Today, Samuelson (1993), Simon (1993), and Bergstrom and Stark (1993) have all discussed the function of altruism in evolving economies. Their ideas support Schmoller's stand on this point. Simon said:

> [T]here is a need for economics based upon the facts of history and political and social life. Such an economics will have little to say a priori but will reason from numerous painfully gathered facts. It will have the merit of describing the world in which we actually live. Altruism, especially altruism derived from group and organizational loyalties, will play a major role in it. (Simon, 1993: p. 160.)

His economic systems theory

Schmoller's "dualistic" picture can be differentiated further in the context of a systems theory approach. This involves envisaging the economy as a system of systems. These systems, which can be perceived in his works, are the "mental" economic system, the system of technological thought, and the system of the environment, consisting of capital and nature. He considered the *Geisteswissenschaften* to be suitable for the investigation of the former subsystem, and the natural sciences to be of overriding importance in the explanation of the latter two subsystems. However, there was supposed to be such a degree of interdependence between the three subsystems that the various approaches were attuned to each other. These three systems are described below, and the entire assembly, seen as a whole, is also characterized. Further, there is a brief explanation of how Schmoller's systems theory functions in his evolutionary approach.

"Mental" or decision sphere. Economic decision-making takes place in the "mental" sphere. Decision-making was rightly seen by Schmoller as the nub of the domain of economic events. His basic idea of this world of phenomena was that social systems in

general, and systems of social choice in particular, are implications of moral systems. Institutions are precipitations of moral life. Thus, according to him, the mental sphere consists of three subsystems, the foundation of which is formed by the ethical system in society (D_1 in Figure 1). Schmoller assumed that the ethical considerations of the various members of society fit into this system in a harmonious way. He paid little attention to ethical contradictions between individuals (*Grundriss* I: p. 70).

According to Schmoller, a harmonious ethical system determines a system of institutions, given the framework of physical circumstances: the environment. This system of institutions (D_2) is the second subsystem in the mental sphere. For him, an institution is 'a partial factor of ordering in social life, serving specific aims and focussed on an independent development of it'[66]. This should be envisaged as consisting of customs, rules and laws. Institutions relating to different areas of social life were considered to be complementary. This system crystallizes out as a system of "institutes", also indicated as "social organisms". He noticed that man participates in various institutes. The system of institutes (D_3) is the third subsystem in the "mental" or decision sphere (*Grundriss* I: p. 61).

The mental subsystem is related to the other two subsystems in various ways. Schmoller said that a new ethical order is necessary for utilizing new techniques. He remarked that man's attitude is influenced by the machine, and considered this effect sometimes to be negative. However, he added, negative effects can also be observed in old forms of production (*Grundriss* I: pp. 226*ff*).

Technological sphere. Schmoller placed capital in the sphere of nature. The know-how needed to utilize both capital and nature he called technology, which he defined as methods to master mankind's several tasks. The idea refers to "techno-economic" capabilities of man to utilize nature with the help of material auxiliaries. The present-day economist, Arnold Heertje (1973: p. 165) has distinguished two conceptions of technological knowledge, a narrow one and a broad one. Both refer to objective knowledge. The second concept, however, includes all conditions of production that are not typically economic. Schmoller's idea of technology should be placed into the latter category. Schmoller thought of a system of technological knowledge that was divided into two subsystems. He held that technology is, in a sense, a practical application of natural sciences. He spoke of

[66]... eine partielle, bestimmten Zwecken dienende, zu einer selbständigen Entwickelung gelangte Ordnung des Gemeinschaftslebens.

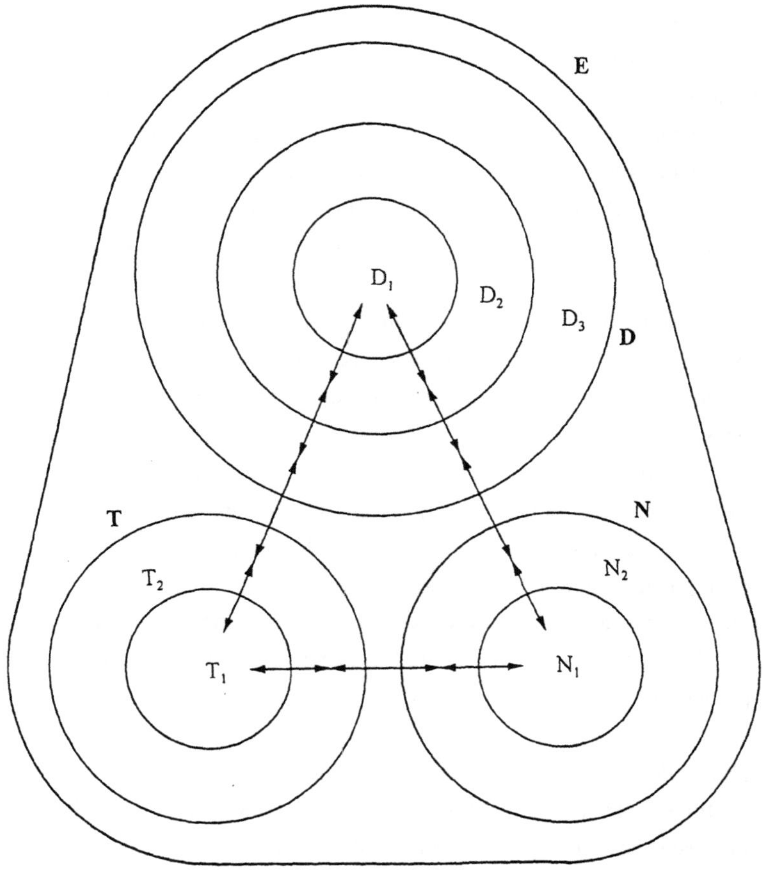

E: entire socio-economic system

D: decision system
D_1: ethical subsystem
D_2: subsystem of institutions
D_3: subsystem of institutes

T: technological system
T_1: subsystem of basic technological knowledge
T_2: subsystem of applied knowledge

N: system of capital and nature
N_1: geographical subsystem
N_2: subsystem of machinery and artifacts

arrows: interactions between subsystems

Figure 1: Schmoller's economic system of systems

a 'rationalization of all economic processes, which is supported by knowledge of nature'[67]. According to his view, techniques are methods whereby "external nature" is made subservient to mankind. For Schmoller the main sources of life on earth were heat and light (*Grundriss* I: pp. 190, 220).

Schmoller put forward his idea that in the Renaissance the basis was laid for the natural sciences that were to find their application in industrialized production a few centuries later. He stated that a system of fundamental scientific knowledge (T_1 in Figure 1), the first subsystem in the technological sphere, forms the basis of a system of practical knowledge (T_2), the second subsystem in this sphere. The idea is found again in the ideas of Schumpeter, who distinguished between "invention" and "innovation". Schmoller's terms were "science" and "praxis". Some of Schmoller's ideas, such as that technology includes the use of technological means to rid the economic process of nature's evil effects fit well into present-day environmental economics (*Grundriss* I: pp. 191, 212).

Schmoller's "structure and process analysis" was discussed by Karl-Heinz Schmidt.

> According to Schmoller's approach, "technological progress" is an endogenous factor with respect to social-economic development. Technology is interpreted as an intermediate link between two groups of factors, natural resources and the moral, cultural and institutional situation. (Schmidt, 1993-94: p. 391.)

Schmoller made it clear that technological progress not only makes it possible to increase the standard of living, but also to achieve a steady growth of an active population. However, he also stressed the restrictions placed on opportunities for technological progress, referring to Liebig for the limited opportunities for production growth in agriculture. Speaking in general, he described technological progress as shifting the limits to production set by nature. The technological system is not only typified by interdependency with the system of capital and nature, but also by interactions with the "mental" system. Schmoller noted that in the search for ways of earning a living, there is coherence between the system of practical knowledge and the ethical system. He also pointed out that technology has an impact on the process of social differentiation and, further, on the organization and location of production (*Grundriss* I: pp. 139, 223, 230).

Schmoller linked technological development with the extension of the production route, in its geographical sense. This idea does not coincide with Böhm-Bawerk's roundabout idea, which is related to the lengthening of the production route in terms of time. According to Schmoller, there is a relationship between the technique of production

[67]... auf Naturerkenntniss gestützten Rationalisierung aller Wirtschaftsprozesse.

and the institutional structure. In controlling nature, progress calls for new institutions, in accordance with "eternal moral ideals" *(ewige sittliche Ideale)* (*Grundriss* I: p. 228).

Sphere of capital and nature. According to Schmoller, the sphere of capital and nature is also composed of subsystems. A system of a set of compound machines (N_2 in Figure 1) is connected with the geographical structure (N_1), placing the physical component of economic life into a specific subsystem. He remarked that economic activity is concentrated near systems of waterways. He elucidated the significance of the climate and the fertility of the soil for the economy, as well as that of the condition of the flora and fauna. Like Menger, he noticed that nature only needs to be paid for if the land is appropriated. Unlike Menger, he believed that the facts of "external nature" must be approached according to the method of the natural sciences. Yet, Schmoller considered nature to be also of interest to the humanistic sciences, as it plays a part in the economic scene as a whole. He stated that it was acknowledged in methodology that natural and mental causes mingle, so that there is interdependency between the spheres of Political Economy, nature and technology (*Grundriss* I: pp. 133-139).

Schmoller was aware of the pollution caused by the economic process, and of the problem of the exhaustion of mines. He ascribed pollution mainly to the use of the steam engine, speculating that "clean" production would be possible in the future by the application of better kinds of power generation, so that the dirty period would be comparatively short. Nowadays, the same speculation is sometimes made about nuclear power plants (*Grundriss* I: p. 215).

Unity of the socio-economic body. I have interpreted Schmoller's idea of the economy as a system of subsystems. Organistic systems theory, however, also contains a specifically holistic approach, in which typical properties can be perceived that are not derived from properties of elements of the system as a whole. According to Schmoller, the characteristics of the whole correspond with the functioning of the subsystems described. Therefore, the subsystems concerned were perceived as components of economic life, being the economy in its broadest sense. In Schmoller's view, this economic life forms a whole. The term he used is "the social body". To him, the idea of "social and economic unity", idealistically perceived, and the idea of "development", mentioned above, were points of departure. He held that this developing unity could be interpreted optimistically as well as pessimistically. He reckoned Charles Fourier and Werner Sombart to the optimists, and Sismondi and Marx to the pessimists (*Grundriss* I: pp. 64, 227).

I have already made it clear that Schmoller thought of the economy as a *Grundriss*, an "outline" or "ground plan", of economic phenomena. He noticed that attention should be paid in comparative studies to natural and physical differences, to the structure and the size of capital, and to the structure of the whole of societal institutions and institutes *(Grundriss* I: pp. 64, 123*ff)*. He said that geographical circumstances give a certain direction to economic development, since they impose impediments to production as well as offering opportunities for it. To what extent these are surmounted and utilized, respectively, depends on the level of technology, morals, and other socio-economic factors. He saw economic life as 'the spirit triumphing over nature' *(ein Sieg des Geistes über die Natur)* (*Grundriss* I: pp. 130, 139).

Schmoller was of the opinion that the analysis of the process of development should not be focussed merely on the evolution of the socio-economic whole. He assumed that the evolution of its components and subcomponents, as shown in Figure 1, should at first be studied separately. Then, at a later stage of investigation, the latter pictures could be integrated into an image of the developing whole. An outstanding element in his organicism was the stimulation of *Produktivkräfte*, "productive forces", which is reminiscent of the ideas of Friedrich List. Schmoller perceived the national state organistically, as increasing the productivity of production factors by a more efficient utilization of natural resources, capital formation, better technologies and, above all, a better organization of socio-economic life. On the last of these, he spoke of *Kollektivkräfte*, "collective forces". He was not dogmatic about "protection" or "free trade", but believed that the right answer 'depends first of all upon a right perception and valuation of domestic economic forces and foreign counter forces'[68] (*Grundriss* II: p. 741).

His picture of development

Schmoller's picture of development was characterized by an evolution from a "low" to a "high" culture. He opposed the idea that in the course of this process man liberates himself from nature, saying that man will always remain a parasite of the earth.

> Higher culture and techniques do not loosen man from nature. Rather, they bind him closer to it and help him to control it, if he understands it, making its laws and limitations subservient to him.[69] (*Grundriss* I: p. 140.)

---

[68]... hängt in erster Linie von der richtigen Schätzung und Erfassung der heimischen Kräfte und der auswärtigen Gegenkräfte ab.

[69]Der Mensch löst sich mit höherer Kultur und Technik nicht von der Natur los, sondern verbindet sich inniger mit ihr, beherrscht sie, indem er sie versteht, aber auch ihren Gesetzen, ihren Schranken sich unterordnet.

According to Schmoller, "cultural development" has both a technological and an institutional aspect, resulting in two criteria on the basis of which the various development stages were characterized: the level of technology used and the level of organization of the process of production and consumption. On the basis of the first criterion he put forward the following development scheme. The initial stage was that of winning food *(Nahrungsgewinnung)*, in which man provided for himself by searching and appropriating. This stage turned into that of systematic hunting and fishing, followed by that of primitive agriculture, without cattle or plough. This *Stufe* he called hoe cultivation *(Hackbau)*. The next phase was that of fully developed agriculture and cattle breeding. This was followed by an ordered technological development which focussed on the utilization of waterpower and milling, production of iron and the utilization of fire in general, "trade technology", and finally, transportation technology. Here, he was referring particularly to developments in early Europe. This development results in the engineering age *(Maschinenzeitalter)* of European and American signature (*Grundriss* I: pp. 196-212). Schmoller was optimistic about prospects for population growth. He saw many opportunities for absorbing it, such as transmigration and "condensation of population" *(Verdichtung der Bevölkerung) (Grundriss* I: pp. 183*ff*). He was thinking of industrialization, which offers employment for many and raises the standard of living for all.

If Schmoller, however, applied the criterion of the organization of the socio-economic process, the chronological division he presented was 'village, town, regional and national economy' *(Dorf-, Stadt-, Territorial-, Volkswirtschaft)* (*Grundriss* I: p. 105). In this picture division of labour functions as the main cause of economic progress. According to Schmoller, any modification of the division of labour should be subjected to an ethical judgement, since not all social change is progress.

> Like all human activity, the division of labour advances by trial and error, by partial shaping and ordering. Then, from time to time the ruthless conflicts of interests partly mark it with their ugly stamp. If there is no counterbalance, whole social classes are shrivelled and crippled by it, through one-sided physical or mental labour.[70] (*Grundriss* I: p. 392.)

The economic historian Harold Wright made it clear that Schmoller used "stages" as parts of a frame of reference for describing and categorizing the changes in technology, such as methods of deeper mining, and the responses of people and institutions, such as the changes in mining policy by the German states' (Wright, 1993-94: p. 107).

---

[70]Die Arbeitsteilung schreitet, wie alles Menschliche, durch tastende Versuche, durch einseitige Gestaltungen und Ordnungen vorwärts. Die harten Interessenkämpfe drücken auf ihr erst zeitweise einen hässlichen Stempel auf; ganze Gesellschaftsgruppen sind durch sie, durch eine zu einseitige körperliche oder geistige Arbeit ohne Gegengewicht verkümmert oder verkrüppelt worden.

According to Schmoller, the division of labour is not the only factor which determines social classes. He also assigned a role to class-consciousness. Alongside *Nationalgeist*, the "spirit of the nation" as a whole, he placed *Klassengeist*, the "class spirit" of specific groups (*Grundriss* I: p. 429). Income policy formed an important element in his thought. The income distribution is not only to be determined by the market mechanism, but also by the economy's institutional framework. He considered the creation of the right institutes in this field to be an important element of economic policy. In this he was thinking more of the guaranteeing of a minimum income rather than of lessening income inequalities as such.

According to Schmoller, the phenomenon of the business cycle is characteristic of a capital-intensive economy in a process of growth and transformation. He assumed that under these circumstances cyclical over-investment can easily occur, caused by monetary disturbances and speculation. Trade cycle policy should be focussed on these causes and must include a price policy. He said: 'A proper, right and just price level is also always the best regulator of economic life'[71] (*Grundriss* II: p. 559). Schmoller's ideas about socio-economic development have a teleological component. He considered this element characteristic for all scientific thought. He believed that this point of departure leads to the acceptance of the existence of the 'aims of God, and those of history and creating nature' *(Zwecken der Gottheit, der Geschichte, der schaffenden Natur)* (*Grundriss* I: p. 112).

Jürgen Backhaus explained the present-day interest in Schmoller by the latter's attention to public administration and institutional matters in general, by his interdisciplinary approach, and by the role played by technology in his picture of economic development (Backhaus, 1989b: pp. 34-36). At a symposium on Gustav Schmoller in Heilbronn, 1988, the economic methodologist A.W. Coats discussed the accomplishment of historical-oriented approaches in disciplines such as economics. He concluded that Schmoller would have welcomed recent efforts to break out of the confines of conventional static equilibrium theorizing.

> [E]fforts to develop evolutionary or process-type theories would undoubtedly have earned his [Schmoller's] approval, so too would the current efforts to extend the orthodox boundaries of economics so as to take account of relevant but neglected non-economic influences. (Coats, 1993-94: p. 257.)

At the end of this discussion on Schmoller's ideas, I want to quote Peter Senn, who examined Schmoller's influence on economists in the Anglo-Saxon world.

---

[71]Ein richtiger, billiger, gerechter Wert ist stets auch der beste Regulator des wirtschaftlichen Lebens.

Scholars who do not even know who Schmoller was are building upon foundations that Schmoller helped to lay. The web of economic knowledge is extremely complex. So is its diffusion. However it happened, Schmoller's work is now part of that web. (Senn, 1993-94: p. 315.)

Chapter 8
SCHMOLLER'S FOLLOWERS IN THE "YOUNGER" SCHOOL

Until the beginning of the twentieth century, Schmoller's "younger" Historical School was an important movement in German "political economy" and socio-economic history. Of the many authors in this field I want to mention a few who are of special significance to historistic and organistic thought: Conrad, Cohn, (Lujo) Brentano and, further, Held, Inama, Knapp. The first three I characterize as "reformers", since they had a militant attitude towards socio-economic reform. The last three I see as "fundamentalists", for they concentrated mainly on principles of this way of thought. However, the cynical description "Socialists of the Chair" referred to all of them. This name was adopted from the critical publication *Kathedersozialismus*, written by the nineteenth century liberal, Heinrich Oppenheim.

Reformers

The orientation of the three writers whom I call reformers was rather divergent. Johannes Conrad's ideas were orientated towards those of Hildebrand and Roscher, founders of the Historical School. Gustav Cohn, however, presented a late variant of Enlightened utilitarian thought, whereas Lujo Brentano was a typical progressive political thinker for the beginning of twentieth century, anticipating ideas of the modern welfare state. Nevertheless, all of them were founders of the *Verein für Socialpolitik*, and all took an active part in it.

Conrad

The first author I want to look at is the economist and statistician, Johannes Ernst Conrad. He was born in 1839 in rural West Prussia, the son of a landowner. He received a practical agricultural education on the family estate. He read natural and state sciences in Berlin and Jena, and studied for his doctoral degree under Bruno Hildebrand. Later, he took over Hildebrand's *Jahrbücher für Nationalökonomie und Statistik*, which series became known as *Conrad's Jahrbücher*. He was appointed to the chair of *Staatswissenschaften* at Halle which became vacant after Schmoller's departure.

Conrad's main publication is his voluminous work *Grundriss zum Studium der Politischen Oekonomie*, "Outline for the study of economics". His historistic point of view was put forward in the first part, entitled *Nationalökonomie*. He stated that, in contrast to animals, man has the ability to modify his abilities and, by this, his way of living. According to Conrad's view, the history of the development of necessities coincides with the history of the economy, in which picture technological development also plays a part (Conrad, 1896, 1900: p. 21). However, Conrad warned against putting too much emphasis on the historistic principle in economics, considering it not strong enough to support a typically historistic variant of economics. He said that deduction and induction must complement each other, and supported a method of "isolating abstraction", similar to Thünen's way of thinking. The nature of production is, according to Conrad, an increase in value, which is generally the result of human activity in relation to nature.

> I come to the conclusion that natural conditions have a strong influence on the shaping of the national economy, setting certain limits to economic development. However, the higher the level of culture, the broader man's scope of opportunities is, making him more independent of nature in his endeavour to create a life and activities.[72] (Conrad, 1896, 1900: p. 31.)

The fourth part of Conrad's *Outline* is a treatise on statistics. Conrad considered this field of study a *Staatswissensschaft*, "state sciences" or "public administration", economics focussing on qualitative aspects, and statistics on quantitative aspects of the same subject: socio-economic empiricism. He distinguished history and statistics, the one supposedly referring to society as a whole, and the other to components of social life.

> The first deals with facts about acting man, investigating his *motives*, in a psychological way. The last deals with the *consequences* of this acting, in a specific one-sided way, ignoring psychological considerations.[73] (Conrad, 1896, 1902: p. 6; italics in original.)

---

[72]Wir kommen zu dem Ergebnis, dass zwar die natürlichen Verhältnisse einen grossen Einfluss auf die Gestaltung der Volkswirtschaft ausüben und der wirtschaftlichen Entwickelung gewisse Grenzen ziehen, dass aber, je höher die Kulturstufe ist, um so weiter sich auch der Spielraum gestaltet und der Mensch sich um so unabhängiger von ihnen sein Leben und seine Thätigkeit zu schaffen vermag.

[73]Die erstere betrachtet den handelnden Menschen, seine Thaten, untersucht seine *Motive*, sie hat psychologisch zu Werke zu gehen, die letztere beachtet nur die *Resultate* des Handelns in bestimmter einseitiger Weise; die psychologischen Momente liegen ihr fern.

There are two different ways of thought here: a primarily idealistic approach with intuitive aspects, and a mainly empirical, econometric approach. Referring to Ernst Engel, Conrad spoke of the heuristic-technical task of statistics (p. 5) on which "comparative statistics" should be based. To be able to formulate causalities in social life, the statistician has to eliminate "coincidences" by using a sort of probability calculus.

* *

Conrad first presented himself as a reformer in the first chapter of his *Outline* where, following in Hildebrand's footsteps, he paid attention to the ideas of social critics. However, it was in the second part, entitled *Volkswirtschaftspolitik*, "economic politics", that he showed himself to be the complete reformer. This part was reprinted many times as *Leitfaden zum Studium der Volkswirtschaftspolitik*, "Guideline to studies on economic politics". In Conrad's view, Economic Politics is a "practical" science, based on "theoretical" economics, the latter being supposed to describe "causalities" in socio-economic life. The subject of the science of economic policy is the set of aims of the government, representing society. It is a normative field of studies, in which social objectives are formulated, and an indication is given how these are to be realized. A description of the history of branches of agriculture and industry was also supposed to be part of this science, as it might be of importance for the shaping of institutions in these fields.

Conrad's "economic politics" was an applied type of welfare theory. The task of government is 'the furtherance of general welfare' *(die Förderung des allgemeinen Wohlstandes)* (Conrad, 1901, 1914: p. 1). Sometimes this should have the character of advancement of the welfare of individuals but, at other times, individual interests must be subordinated to those of society as a whole. According to Conrad, social policy ought to be focussed on the development of the pattern of social necessities on the one hand and on an increase of production on the other. This means that wealth should be rightly distributed. He rejected nineteenth-century economic liberalism, referring to the "social question", put forward in the Germany of his time.

> In the economic struggle for life it is especially the weak parties that should be protected against arbitrary exploitation by the strong since, in a situation of economic freedom, parties do not confront each other with equal force.[74] (Conrad, 1901, 1914: pp. 2-3.)

[74]Besonders hat er den Schwächeren in dem wirtschaftlichen Kampfe um das Dasein gegen die willkürliche Ausbeutung durch den Stärkeren zu schützen. Denn in dem Zustande wirtschaftlicher Freiheit stehen sich die Parteien nicht mit gleicher Macht gegenüber.

Conrad saw poverty as a relative notion. It is the situation of those who are not in a position to live according to the level of cultural development. He supported education and a number of social provisions, and advocated a policy tuned to opportunities for earning a living. He assumed that this could be reached by increasing the productivity of low income groups and, adopting Malthus' idea, by limiting the opportunities for marriage for people with insufficient income.

Cohn

The second author I call a reformer was the Prussian economist, Gustav Cohn, born in 1840. He became a pragmatic utilitarianist, orientated towards socio-economic reform. For several years, he lectured at the Technological Universities of Riga and Zürich. In 1884 he was appointed to a chair at the University of Göttingen. In fact, Cohn's historicism was closer to the ideas of Montesquieu than to those of, say, Bücher. I see him as a late star of the Enlightenment, shining with a new radiance in the Historical School. If Cohn did not label the Middle Ages as obscure, it was because he perceived ideas in medieval thought that he considered applicable to the society of his own time. Further, he did not agree that the natural science method was suitable for socio-economic studies, considering the appropriate method an ethically oriented one.

Cohn's historicism was primarily a method for creating an image of present society. He considered this method to be characteristic of the *Geisteswissenschaften*, saying that social facts can only be understood in the context of historical development (Cohn, 1885: p. 7). This approach was inspired by Dilthey's philosophy of life, which Cohn developed towards an economic-oriented philosophy of that type. He posited that all science arises from "life" and is used in the service of life as well. He called this the anthropological principle by which, he said, economics is characterized. Cohn's historicism was a kind of organicism, for it had a Darwinian evolutionary character.

> All study on the development of primitive people, ..., confirms the insight that the moral world develops gradually from elements of nature, just as nature itself shows an evolution from lower to higher, in which man is the crown of creation.[75] (Cohn, 1885: p. 214.)

---

[75]Alle auf die Anfänge zurückgehende Beobachtung der Völker, ..., bestätigt die Einsicht, dass die sittliche Welt durch einen langsamen Stufengang sich auf den Elementen der Natur aufbaut, wie diese Natur selber eine Entwicklung vom Niederen zum Höheren darstellt, in welcher der Mensch die Krone der Schöpfung ist.

He was here discussing 'the historical world that shapes itself, pursuing its own purposes'[76] (Cohn, 1885: p. 32).

Cohn's view on the ethical content of economic thought was determined by his basic view on science. He assumed there are two types of science, according to whether the subject matter is governed by "spirit" or by "nature", which are both "rays of the same light", all contributing to insight into "eternal truths". He put forward the idea that demarcation of various fields of study is only a matter of a practical division of labour and not a principal one. He believed that this implies that economics and ethics coincide. Unlike Schmoller, Cohn radically rejected Roscher's antithesis between "is" and "should". He was criticized by other members of the school for mixing these two fields of thought, as was Adolf Held, whose ideas I discuss below.

Cohn did not consider "labour" a sacrifice in the production process, but an activity which gives meaning to the life of the working man. According to his view, the essence of economic policy is the furtherance of a culture with ever better conditions of existence for all.

> How can the possessions of some be justified against the lack of possessions of others, if not by its significance to the progressive culture of mankind?[77] (Cohn, 1905: p. 7.)

He strongly supported the study on questions put forward by the movement of the Socialists of the Chair which was taking shape in the *Verein*.

> It was a standing up for sensible reforms of working class conditions - reforms which fasten onto modern ideas about the shape of labour relations: legal protection of labour, social insurance, coalition rights, trade unions, and housing reform. Further questions concerned tax reform and the nationalization of railways.[78] (Cohn, 1905: p. 227.)

Brentano

The last "reformer" I want to look at is Lujo Brentano. His first name was a contraction of Ludwig-Joseph. He was born in Aschaffenburg in 1844, into a family of prominent intel-

---

[76]... die historische, sich selbst gestaltende Welt, welche ihren eigenen Zwecken nachgeht.

[77]Wie lässt sich die Thatsache des Besitzes der Einen gegenüber der Besitzlosigkeit der Andern sonst rechtfertigen, wenn nicht durch ihre Bedeutung für die fortschreitende Cultur der Menschheit?

[78]Es war ein Eintreten für besonnene Reformen in der Lage der arbeitenden Klassen - Reformen, welche an die moderne Gestalt des Arbeitsverhältnisses anknüpfen - Arbeiterschutzgesetzgebung, Arbeiterversicherung, Koalitionsrecht, Gewerkvereine, Wohnungsreform. Dann kamen die Fragen der Steuerreform, der Eisenbahnverstaatlichung hinzu.

lectuals and artists. He studied law and economics, writing a doctor's thesis on Thünen's theory. He held chairs at various German universities. According to himself, the periods he spent at Breslau, Strasbourg, Leipzig and Munich were important in forming his ideas. In his early years as a scientist, he accompanied Ernst Engel on a study tour to England. He was the youngest member of the *Verein* at the time of its foundation.

> The young scholars who joined together in it [the *Verein*] formed a lasting bond of friendship, and none of them ever doubted that the strongest impetus was given to it by the youngest member.[79] (Knapp, 1915: p. 48.)

According to Brentano, scientific criticism and social criticism are in line with one another, but do not coincide. He summarized the task of science with the term *rerum cognoscere causas*. The scientist ought to distance himself from political and ethical considerations, including his own, and focus on "causalities". Brentano's own achievements in this fundamental field should be mentioned, in particular his contributions to consumer theory, the idea of labour productivity, and utilitarianism. His most significant activity, however, was in the applied field: his support for the trade union movement.

Brentano was a liberal. As a confirmed free-trader he opposed Bismarck's protectionism. He also disagreed with Schmoller's authoritarian bureaucratic views on the organization of society, although their ideas were, in many respects, similar. Yet, he strongly opposed the ultra liberal Manchester School, which showed no interest in market-oriented institutional reform. On this point he shared the opinion of his contemporaries in the Historical School, who all condemned *Manchestertum*, "Manchesterism". Like the other members of the School, he rejected the atomistic concept of society, which he saw as a degeneration of an earlier form of it. According to him, labour unions would restore the bond between people which had been lost, and would fulfil a function comparable to that of the medieval guilds. As an author, he started his career in 1871 with *Die Arbeitergilden der Gegenwart*, "Contemporary labour guilds". It is a study on the nineteenth-century British economy.

Brentano's method of investigation was related to his concept of society and its development. He rejected the idea of a natural order and opted for what he called a historico-empirical approach. This implied that society should be seen in all its institutional diversity.

---

[79]Die jungen Gelehrten, die daran teilnahmen, haben sich in einen dauernden Freundesbund vereinigt, und keiner von ihnen hat je bezweifelt, dass der mächtigste Anstoss dazu von dem jüngsten ausgegangen ist.

> Individuals living in a certain area all are influenced in a similar way by common descendent, language, morals, taste, history, laws, and government institutions. Being bound together as a distinct nation, as a whole, they are to be distinguished from other, comparable groups. This is also true of the national economy[80]. (Brentano, 1924: p. 100.)

He rejected the socialist ideal image of society in which, he said, everything is directed from a central point, an idea that he attributed to Rodbertus. He considered it a form of aprioristic thinking about social problems.

Historicism, the idea of changing man, had an important place in Brentano's thought. Dilthey and Brentano knew each other, and it may be presumed that they influenced one another. The most outstanding trait in Brentano's historicism was the idea that two opposite ideas can be found in the course of Europe's history: a development from a communal way of life to an individualistic one, and a development in the opposite direction. The first tendency was a development from many-sided production by relatives and their servants, to specialized production units and comparatively small living units, in which economic intercourse became ever more intensive and the market ever more important.

> So the development of the economic unit was from the whole to the singular, and not the opposite. The individual production unit is not at the beginning, but at the end of present development where, however, it is not independent and left to itself, but is limited, protected and stimulated by the overall coordinating economic unit of the state.[81] (Brentano, 1923: p. 267.)

The relativization at the end of this citation refers to the opposite tendency. The original family unit became more and more integrated in ever larger and stronger social structures. First, manors, guilds and towns; later, the all-embracing state. Brentano considered the contemporary economic situation to have been the result of the past and the forerunner of the future.

---

[80]Wie die einzelnen Menschen durch ein bestimmtes Territorium, auf dem sie wohnen, durch gemeinsame Abstammung, Sprache, Sitte, Geschmack, Geschichte, Gesetze, Staatsanstalten in gleicher Weise beeinflusst werden und dadurch als ein Ganzes, als ein Volk, von anderen ähnlichen Gruppen sich unterscheiden, so auch ihre Volkswirtschaft.

[81]So ging die Entwicklung der Wirtschaftseinheit vom Ganzen zum Einzelnen, nicht umgekehrt. Das Individuum als Wirtschaftseinheit steht nicht am Anfang, sondern am Ende der bisherigen Entwicklung, indes nicht unabhängig und nicht sich selbst überlassen, sondern beschränkt, geschützt, gefördert durch die sich darüber erhebende Wirtschaftseinheit des Staats.

> It is the task of theory to study the past and the present in order to foresee development in the future and thereby to open the way to "praxis".[82] (Brentano, 1924: pp. 101-2.)

What is striking about this formulation is that the term "theory" does not have the conventional meaning of an axiomatic system, but refers to the whole of socio-economic science.

Brentano's economic thought was based on a utilitarian philosophy, in which he referred to Schäffle (Brentano, 1908: p. 3). He placed man and his individual and collective wants, and the development of these, at the centre, believing that these necessities must not be understood in a hedonistic way, but should be seen in the context of a social structure, in which altruistic needs and egoistic needs go together. He distinguished between absolute needs and relative needs, the first being the biological functioning of man, the second those which show themselves in social intercourse. In connection with absolute needs, Brentano spoke of the "law of Liebig". He considered these needs to be satisfiable. Relative needs, showing themselves in social intercourse, were considered by him to be unlimited. Using a primitive form of the elasticity concept, he typified absolute needs as "inelastic" and relative needs as "elastic".

An interesting idea in Brentano's utilitarianism is the distinction he made between the active and the inactive satisfaction of wants. The first is consumption which involves a certain effort, for example, a creative activity. In such situations, a high level of satisfaction is often reached with modest means. Passive consumption, which involves very little effort, often results in only a little satisfaction. It is the situation in which one feels unsatisfied unless surrounded by excessive luxury. According to this view, satisfaction of needs is a skill which can be learned. Brentano integrated the principle of marginal utility into his thought and described the phenomenon of perspective declination of future wants. He noticed that satisfaction of a certain need often creates a new one. This gave an organic feature to his utility theory.

Brentano's judgement of cartelizing was positive.

> Why should industrial enterprises not unite to secure their interests just as the workers are doing?[83] (Brentano, 1900, 1910: p. 28.)

---

[82]Studium der Vergangenheit und der Gegenwart, um die zukünftige Entwicklung vorherzusehen und damit der Praxis die Wege zu weisen, ist Aufgabe der Theorie.

[83]Warum sollen sich die Industrieunternehmungen nicht ebenso zur Wahrung ihrer Interessen vereinigen, wie dies die Arbeiter tun?

According to him, the main function of cartels is to level out business cycles. He did not consider it acceptable, however, for them to behave as monopolists, charging prices above the level of competition. He rejected the idea that a certain organization of the economy functions as a propelling force in economic growth. For him it functions only as a condition of development. So he rejected the idea that the expansion of German industry was the result of the tariff reform of 1879, which had aimed at protecting industrial and agrarian production. Brentano attributed the rise of German economy to the progress in research and scientific education in that country. Similar ideas were later put forward by Sombart and Schumpeter.

Economic ethics interested Brentano. He paid attention to the respective influences of Machiavelli's doctrine and Calvin's ethics on the shaping of capitalism. The latter idea, which he put forward in his rectorial address in Munich in 1901, was later developed by Max Weber in an original way. Brentano, who was a practising Catholic, made a plea for a reconsideration of the stand of the church on contraception within marriage. Brentano's "population theory" was a critical elaboration of Malthus' ideas (Brentano, 1909, 1924). An example of the practical orientation of Brentano's thought is the idea that wages are not only determined by the productivity of labour, but that the opposite is also true. Decline of wages might decrease the productivity of labour through affecting living conditions. Brentano (1918: p. 791) advocated *Menschenökonomie*, "human economy", focussed on a development of the working class by institutional economic measures.

Fundamentalists

There are several other interesting writers to be found in Schmoller's school, whose works were written in a reformist spirit. Their publications, however, show less involvement with topical political problems of their day. Works by writers discussed in this section, Held, Inama and Knapp, are of a reflective nature and were primarily aimed at serving as a foundation for political decision-making. Adolf Held died in an accident at the age of 38, before his remarkable study on British industrial development was published. His friend and kindred spirit, George Friedrich Knapp, prepared the work for the press. Nevertheless, I am not going to discuss Knapp immediately after Held, because, to understand Knapp's ideas, it is better first to look at those of Inama-Sternegg.

Held

Adolf Held was born in 1844. His father was a professor of law. He studied in Munich under the Classical-oriented economist, F.B.W. Hermann. He was also a pupil of Engel, who arouse his interest in the social question of those days. After having lectured at Poppelsdorf for several years, he was appointed to a chair in Bonn. He was one of the founders of the *Verein für Socialpolitik*, in which he acted as secretary. Held based his ideas on those of members of the Historical School, especially Roscher and Hildebrand, as well as on those of British Classicals and their German representatives like Rau, Thünen and Hermann. No doubt he was also inspired by Marx. An important part in his life was played by his colleague in Bonn, the socially committed and historically oriented economist, Erwin Nasse, with whom he happily cooperated. Nasse succeeded Schmoller as president of the *Verein*. A remarkable aspect of Held's approach is the normative character of his thought. He disagreed with Roscher on the point of the antithesis between "is" and "should". He believed 'that enlightened "practice" and true theory are no opposites'[84] (Held, 1872: p. 96).

In an article on cooperatives in "Bruno Hildebrand's *Jahrbücher*", Held gave a great deal of information about his methodological ideas. He said that his picture of society is not that of a "mechanism of self-interest", in which man is seen as an isolated individual, neither is it an authoritarian Mercantilist system.

> [F]or we do not ask primarily for wise governmental measures, but for principles which have to govern behaviour of all, and which are orientated towards a common well-being.[85] (Held, 1869: p. 5.)

In a treatise on taxes, he maintained that individual man must always be seen in his relationship to organized society, identified with the "state".

> The individual is not entirely swallowed up by collectivity, which puts either narrow or broad limits to individual action, ...[86] (Held, 1872: p. 33.)

According him, the state is historically determined and should be seen as a realization of the ideas of members of society. This was historicism of idealistic signature, typical of the Historical School. There was no room for the Enlightened idea of *contrat social* in this approach.

Brentano compared present-day unions with medieval guilds, explaining institutions in terms of comparable bodies in the past.

---

[84]... dass aufgeklärte Praxis und wahre Theorie gar keine Gegensätze sind.

[85][D]enn wir fragen nicht vornehmlich nach weisen Regierungsmassregeln, sondern nach Grundsätzen, die das gemeinnützige Handeln Aller beherrschen sollen.

[86]Der Einzelne geht in der Gesammtheit nie vollständig auf; die Gesammtheit setzt der Bewegung des Einzelnen engere oder weitere Schranken.

> Taxes are substitutes for seigneury services of all civilians, and are made possible by the division of labour.[87] (Held, 1872: p. 4.)

He was of the opinion that the division of labour forms the basis for all economic progress (Held, 1881: p. 410).

Although Held rejected an one-sided individualistic reflection of society, he nevertheless considered the Classical approach acceptable, if it was focussed on "the social problem". Results of deductive thought, he said, must be tested against *de facto* social circumstances. His posthumously published work *Zwei Bücher zur socialen Geschichte Englands*, "Two books on British social history", is not only of interest for its contents but also for its methodology. It is a dualistic picture of social development, in which an idealistic and an empirical approach form each other's mirror image. In the first part the development of ideas about the organization of society are discussed; the second is a description of the development of the social order, technology and social relationships. Held believed that there is 'an important inner harmony' *(eine grosse innere Harmonie)* in these developments (Held, 1881: p. 665).

One may ask why it was a German who wrote a standard work on British industrial development, using British parliamentary archives. It is a book that, even after some time, is still a valuable source of information about the Industrial Revolution in Great Britain. Knapp, in his preface to the book, rightly noticed that Held wrote it as a German and for Germans. In the background was the understanding that the British were leading the industrialization process and that the Germans should begin a similar process. This, however, was intended to be realized without committing excesses in the social field.

> England is the true homeland of modern large industry. That is why one can best notice there what is true and what is false in the new ideas, what are the bright sides and what the dark sides of modern relations, the development of which is not yet finished.[88] (Held, 1881: p. 390.)

In his work on Britain's industrial development, Held dealt with the decline of the guild system, the decay of the mercantile system, the advance of capital, the rise of industrial production and the position of the factory workers. He stated that the capitalist production

---

[87]Die Steuer ist der durch die Arbeitstheilung bebotene Ersatz für die persönlichen Staatsdienste aller Bürger.

[88]England ist die eigentliche Heimath der modernen Grossindustrie und darum kann man hier am besten erkennen, was Wahres und was Falsches an den neuen Ideen ist, welche Licht- und Schattenseiten die in ihrer Entwicklung noch keineswegs abgeschlossenen modernen Verhältnisse haben.

mode is considerably older than the industrial way of producing. Industrialization, however, changed the character of capitalism by becoming a dominating feature of society, enforcing class differences. To explain the social implications of technological change, Held gave economic definitions of ideas such as handiwork, cottage industry, primitive manufacture (centralized cottage industry), tool, machine, and factory. He noticed that the size of an ever-growing market depends primarily on a developing infrastructure, and determines the character and location of production. Capitalism stimulates this process on the one hand and takes advantage of it on the other.

Held noticed that as machines took over from muscular strength, production rose more than in proportion to the input of labour. He assumed that, ultimately, workers would take advantage of it. In contrast, he said, this method of production stimulates woman and child labour. In the course of the industrial development studied, workers became ever more dependent; so much that he spoke of white slavery (Held, 1869: p. 13). Apparently this qualification was not out of place. Held challenged Marx's idea that industrial development inevitably leads to a social revolution. He did not consider such a fundamental restructuring of the social order to be desirable either. Nevertheless, he denied that absolute right of ownership is a sacrosanct principle of thinking on social problems. He believed that conditions for "self-help" must be improved. In particular, he had in mind production cooperatives similar to those developed by H. Schulze-Delitzsch and those orientated towards agrarian communities designed by F.W. Raiffeisen. Like Brentano, Held supported trade unions, and like Engel, advocated profit sharing by workers. He was a proponent of a drastic tax reform, outlining a new tax system and defining modern fiscal principles, such as progressive income tax. He presented a concept of national income on the basis of "value added", a concept which could include free time as well as certain productive activities within family households.

Inama-Sternegg

Karl Theodor *von* Inama-Sternegg, economist, social scientist and historian, was born in 1843. He studied in Munich and obtained a chair in "political sciences" at the University of Innsbruck. In the course of his career he turned more and more towards statistics. He became president of the Austrian Commission of Statistics, and extraordinary professor of this branch of science at the University of Vienna. In his enumeration of outstanding members of the *Verein*, Schmoller (1915: p. 39) did not mention Inama. Nevertheless, I consider the latter to have been a member of Schmoller's school, and do not bracket him together with the independent writers, Bücher and Philippovich. Inama's approach shows a strong affinity to that of Schmoller and his intimates.

Inama lectured in "state sciences", an interdisciplinary science that included economics, politics, civil law and sociology, as well as the history of this philosophy. These *Staatswissenschaften* were considered of interest for a picture of society from the point of view of the governing state. This was in line with Lorenz *von* Stein, who had given old Cameralism a more contemporary shape at the beginning of the nineteenth century.

> The state, standing above and outside the classes, was to bring about a reform of society. The ruling interests in society should be subject to the forces of the state and contradictions and conflicts within society were to be solved by the assurance of freedom to every individual, bourgeois or proletarian, through legal equality and increased possessions and education. (G. Salomon *on Stein*, 1934, 1949.)

The essence of Inama's historicism was the idea of the evolution of the state.

> Human life has always had a social character, and every kind of human society bears in it the idea of the state, whether it refers to the lowest form of tribe, or to the highest stage of purposeful political relations, ...[89] (Inama, 1902, 1903: p. 20.)

This historicism had an epistemological aspect. 'The nature of things can only be perceived in their coming into being' *(Das Wesen der Dinge enthüllt sich nur in ihrem Werden)* (Inama, 1881a, 1903: p. 19). Inama's approach had a clear organistic trait which was inspired by Dilthey's philosophy of life and expressed in holistic terms.

> Modern government is founded on the basic idea of the intrinsic unity of social life. All phenomena of this life are the effects of common ultimate causes.[90] (Inama, 1892, 1903: p. 357.)

He noted that it is not only true that men shape society, but also that society determines men. According to him, physical and biological properties of the natural environment play a part in this picture as well.

Inama understood social science as *Verwaltungswissenschaft*, "science of public administration", thus assigning a normative nature to it. However, he did not share the rigorous stand of Cohn and Held on the ethical and political aspects of economic thought. He considered economics as a rather independent branch of social science, focussed on eluci-

---

[89]Denn das menschliche Leben ist zu aller Zeit ein gesellschaftliches gewesen und jede Art der menschlichen Gesellschaft trägt den Staatsgedanken in sich; ob es sich um die niedersten Formen der Horde oder um die höchsten Stufen zielbewuster politischer Verbände handelt.

[90]Die moderne Verwaltung beruht auf dem Grundgedanken der inneren Einheit des gesellschaftlichen Lebens. Alle Aeusserungen dieses Lebens sind Wirkungen gemeinsamer letzter Ursachen.

dating socio-economic development. A normative feature of this thinking was that, like Schmoller, Inama assumed that economics is, in essence, an ethical science. As such it was supposed to formulate the implications of contemporary ethics for the organization of the state.

Inama believed he could settle the methodological dispute called the *Methodenstreit*. He contrasted two paradigms. On the one hand, he saw a system of ideas of an individualistic nature, focussed on phenomena of an individualistic type, like those of the market. On the other hand, he placed a world of thinking in terms of planning, focussed on the organization of society. Although he tried to synthesize these two ideas, the formulations of his solution are not clear in all respects (Inama, 1881a, 1903: p. 10). He held that speculation is the beginning and end of all social science. Between these poles is the field of "historico-statistic research". He referred to verification of hypotheses by way of demonstrable correlation. According to his view, statistics represents the method of induction. He made it clear that statistics is not for the needs of government only, but has to serve society as a whole, in all its individual and social aspects. On the point of "objectivity" of statistics, Inama remarked that this is threatened if the collection and administration of data are entirely fitted into a certain idea of society.

In discussing the monetary aspect of the organization of society, Inama adopted Hildebrand's scheme of stages. He put forward the idea that in the *Naturalwirtschaft* ("natural economy"), money was not an essential element of the economic system, although money and credit were not unknown. However, he said that in the *Geldwirtschaft* ("money economy"), gold and silver coinage allowed the economy more elbow room. From high incomes, large amounts of money could be made available for economic purposes.

> Just as in the natural economy, embarrassment was the mother of credit, so in the money economy, abundance became the father of credit.[91] (Inama, 1881b, 1903: p. 119.)

He noticed that credit is typical of any modern economy, which he accordingly indicated as "credit economy". He noticed that the rich especially take advantage of it. Therefore, the granting of credit was considered a social problem. In the *Kreditwirtschaft*, he suggested that credit cooperatives should solve this problem. They would herald 'the golden age of credit' *(das goldene Zeitalter des Kredits)* (1881b: p. 119).

Finally, mention should be made of Inama's studies on *Agrargeschichte*, "socio-economic history of agriculture". He was not the first member of the Historical School to

---

[91]War die Verlegenheit die Mutter des Kredits in der Naturalwirtschaft, so ist der Ueberfluss der Vater des Kredits in der Geldwirtschaft geworden.

work in this field. Conrad and Nasse, as well as the broadly oriented Roscher, had explored it earlier. All these writers integrated it into a general, multifarious picture of development. In Inama's circle, this branch of study was given independence. The founder was Georg Hanssen, born in Hamburg, in 1809. It was on his ideas that Inama and Knapp were able to build. Inama-Sternegg had a keen eye for physical location factors in agricultural development.

Knapp

I want to round off this survey of Schmoller's school by looking at the versatile author, Knapp. He was one of the founders of the *Verein* and cooperated closely with Brentano. However, he was involved very little in topical political problems, having more affinity with fundamental ones. Georg Friedrich Knapp was born in Giessen in 1842. He studied in Munich, Berlin and Göttingen. His tutors were the economist Hermann, the statistician Engel and the historian Hanssen. He mentioned Karl Helferich as a man who had taught him much practical knowledge in the field of monetary economics. Knapp was appointed director of the Bureau of Statistics in Leipzig, and extraordinary Professor of Statistics and Economics at the University of that town. He then became an ordinary professor in Strasburg. Starting as a statistician, he moved his interest to agrarian historical studies and then to monetary problems, defending his remarkable *staatliche Theorie des Geldes*, "state theory of money", against many critics.

Knapp gave no description of his methodology. However, a number of methodological principles can be perceived in his works. Like that of Stein and Inama, Knapp's approach to economic problems had a juridical dimension. However, this was more integrated into his economic thought than was the case with the other two. Further, it can be noticed that his thought was typically historistic, in the sense that social institutions are seen as the result of an economic development process. The combination of these two methodical features means that he must not only be seen as a member of the Historical School in economics, but also as a representative of the Historical School in jurisprudence, founded by F.C. de Savigny at the beginning of the nineteenth century. Both schools were rooted in the same historistic basic philosophy. It can be said that they met in the person of Knapp.

His picture of development had a strong idealistic streak: it is the common view on organizing society, which is subject to change. This idealism played an important part in Knapp's "monetary theory", in which money derives its value from "the proclamation of government", that was understood as legalizing the ideas of the people. In this way, he said, metal money evolved to money marked and issued by or on behalf of the government.

> Natural man was a metallist. Theoretical man, however, is compelled to become a nominalist.[92] (Knapp, 1905, 1923: p. 8.)

According to his historistic view, an essential characteristic of modern money is "chartered money" or "fiat money", that has been developed from metal coinage. Knapp understood the significance of money of account. He described the creation of money by banks, and noticed the analogy with the issue of bank notes. Yet, he did not succeed in explaining the value of money along these lines, remaining concerned with legal and technical aspects and ignoring quantitative aspects. Unfortunately, he presented his nominal monetary approach as an alternative to a quantitative one, instead of as a complement. This shortcoming was symptomatic for many members of the Historical School, who identified institutional economics and development economics with general economics, losing sight of the merits of the Classical and Neo-classical market models.

Mention should be made of Knapp's historical studies. In 1909, he published a remarkable collection of lectures under the title *Die Landarbeiter in Knechtschaft und Freiheit*, "Farm workers in bondage and freedom". The title refers to the position of the small German farmer, whose predial status evolved to that of a labourer in a liberal economic system. The title has a paradoxical tone, placing the worker between freedom and lack of freedom, concepts which changed in the course of time. Knapp tested the ideal of freedom of both the Enlightenment and Romanticism, concluding that the emancipation of the German agrarian class often resulted in a greater dependency of the farm workers. In 1897 he published a number of lectures under the title *Grundherrschaft und Rittergut*, "Manorial system and manor production". The first term refers to a system of agricultural production in rather independent tenant farms, which was formerly typical of western parts of Germany. The second refers to a system of large-scale production on the estate of the lord, typical of large parts of Prussia. Knapp described the development of manors of the later type into the capitalist agricultural enterprises of the Prussian *Junkers*, "knights".

> Knapp's analysis of such economic systems as the estate economy had an impact on Max Weber, who developed further Knapp's theory that landed estates are a special form of capitalist enterprise with a patriarchic organization of work. (Schweizer, 1968.)

---

[92]Der natürliche Mensch ist Metallist; der theoretische Mensch hingegen ist genötigt Nominalist zu werden.

Chapter 9
HISTORICAL SCHOOL'S "YOUNGEST" REPRESENTATIVES

In the first quarter of the twentieth century, the economists Werner Sombart and Arthur Spiethoff and the sociologist (Max) Weber built their theories, to a large extent, on the ideas of the Historical School. However, I would not consider them part of this school proper, as their ideas were too original and too universally oriented. Nevertheless, their affinity to the school was strong enough for me to denote them "youngest representatives", following Schumpeter (1954: p. 815).

Sombart and Spiethoff

Werner Sombart was born in Ermsleben (Harz) in 1863. His father was Anton Ludwig Sombart, one of the founders of the *Verein*. Werner also became a member, being elected chairman in 1932. He studied law, economics, history and philosophy at the Universities of Pisa, Berlin and Rome. He was appointed a professor at the Technological University at Berlin and later at the University of Berlin. Like Max Weber, Werner Sombart made no distinction between economics and sociology. Although he became famous for his studies on the development of capitalism, his methodological studies also attracted attention. He maintained that social and natural sciences differ in principle. In this, he was not only in line with the neo-Kantians and Max Weber but also with Gustav Schmoller and Wilhelm Dilthey. Nevertheless, it should be said that Sombart integrated natural science wisdom into his system of economic ideas. His idea *Geist der Technik*, "spirit of techniques", can be seen as an attempt to reconcile thought in terms of natural science with his own idealistic conception of economics. This concept can be interpreted as natural science theory applied to technological empiricism, as seen from a typically social science point of view (Sombart, 1928 I: p. 467).

On the point of causality, Sombart's analysis of Western economy was a dynamic one, in the sense that it emphasizes that society is a changing entity, comprising propelling forces of an economic nature. In this picture of development the socio-economic characteristics of the situation change gradually, as does the nature of the "dynamic forces". Yet at all times techniques play a crucial role. In the early stages of the development of Western society, moving forces were incentives in the sphere of capitalistic interests. Sombart mentioned the struggle for practical knowledge, the urge for money and success and the organically oriented production techniques which then existed. He summarized this under the idealistic heading of three sources of *Erfinderwille*: "the urge to invent". In the following stage of development, production techniques escaped from the restrictions of organic nature by using raw materials, by utilizing natural forces, and by looking for adequate production processes in a scientific and a rational way. The modern technological device would be: to know, to be capable of, to introduce (Sombart, 1928 I: pp. 475-78; III: pp. 97, 111).

Sombart's principle methodological work is *Die drei Nationalökonomien*, "Three types of economics", published in 1930. The three types are: the "normative" approach, the "ordering" approach, of both the Classical School and the School of Marginal Utility, and the "understanding" approach, of Sombart himself. He said that most approaches are hybrids. As examples of the three pure types, he mentioned the system of Thomas Aquinas, that of Vilfredo Pareto, and his own system. Within the normative approach he distinguished the "theistic" Scholastics, the "harmonistic" Physiocrats and Utopian Socialists, and the "pantheistic rationalists", like Fichte, Proudhon and Rodbertus. In a certain sense he also reckoned Karl Marx and Classical writers like Adam Smith, Frédérique Bastiat and Frans Oppenheimer to the harmonists. Maintaining that socio-economics must be *Wertfrei*, "value free", Sombart rejected the normative approach for being *Glaubenssysteme*, "systems of belief".

According to Sombart, the ordering approach is based on the rational philosophy of Descartes and the pragmatic philosophy of Francis Bacon, both of whom liberated science from metaphysical ideas. He assumed this approach to have all the characteristics of natural science, the first being the axiomatic principle, the second its orientation on quantification, and the third its mathematical component. He gave John Stuart Mill and Carl Menger as examples. Within this circle of writers, Sombart distinguished "objectivists" (mainly Classicals), "subjectivists" (referring to the marginal utility approach), and "relationists" (referring to general equilibrium analysis). He concluded that the ordering approach is not suitable for "mental sciences", as he considered its epistemological significance to be too small.

I have already made it clear that Sombart's own method allowed no room for value judgements and that it was not supposed to bear the stamp of the natural science method. His approach focussed on *das Verstehen*, "understanding", in the idealistic tradition as shaped by Schmoller. Sombart saw causality in a specifically idealistic way. For him, it referred to relations in the world of ideas of the developing society under discussion. In a study on the economic development of Germany, published in 1903, he discussed the factors which determined this development, assigning a crucial part to the spreading of the liberal spirit, supported by "capitalist interests". Sombart, a historicist *pur sang*, assumed that in social economics all ideas are historical categories.

> If one wants to picture the economy, and to perceive its phenomena in a scientific way, then this can only be conceived of in a social environment which has already come into existence in a historic way, to be understood as a historical picture of a certain shape.[93] (Sombart, 1902, 1916 I: p. 21.)

It is in this citation that the idea of *Gestalt*, "shape", can be seen.

What is remarkable is the part Sombart assigned to the Jews in the creation of Western society. He believed that capitalist mentality originates partly in "the spirit of Judaism". His book on this subject, published in 1911, contains much interesting information. In it he described how Jewish merchants undermined the guild system, offering fashionable ware below determined prices. However, he did not deny that the question remains as to whether liberal elements of Scholastic thought and pragmatic policies of magistrates played a significant part as well. A similar point is his description of the influence of Jewish financiers at the royal courts. Did Jewish bankers introduce the liberal spirit into these circles, or were they invited to help as a result of the liberal considerations of ruling aristocrats?

Technology forms a key element in Sombart's thought. Most of it is found in his three-part work, *Der moderne Kapitalismus*, "Modern capitalism", the first edition of which appeared in 1902. It was explained that, in accordance with the development of a capitalist society, techniques evolved from a partly exogenous element in the economic system to a fully endogenous one; that is, techniques evolved to a branch of science, steered by economic impulses. To express this, I use the terms "techniques" in relation to the early stage of capitalism, and "technology" in connection with later stages. For Sombart, both the exogenous techniques and the endogenous technology are categories of economics. He referred to both concepts in terms of the idea of the *Stil der Technik*: the style of economic activity considered from a technological point of view or, as pointed out before, an idealistic concept of the production technique. According to him, the "technological style" represents a cultural feature of any society (1902, 1928 I: p. 466).

---

[93]Will man Wirtschaft denken und ihre Erscheinungen wissenschaftlich erfassen, so kann man sie nur inmitten einer bereits gewordenen, historischen Umwelt sich vorstellen, also als ein bestimmt gestaltetes geschichtliches Gebilde.

Sombart noted that in the pre-capitalist era and in early stages of capitalism, techniques still lacked an exact scientific foundation. The inventions of fundamental thinkers like Leonardo da Vinci he mentioned as exceptions. In the economically less developed world, inventions arose from the fantasy of people endowed with *donum inventionis*; the inventor was, above all, practically oriented. Sombart put forward the idea that three factors in early capitalism determined inventive activity. First, there was a craving for knowledge, characterized by the "Faustic" feature of the era; this is a cultural characteristic. The second factor, which has more of a specifically economic nature, was the pursuit of money and success in the material sphere. The third factor, formed by the nature of production techniques, was typified as "empiric" and organic. By this he was referring to the process of trial and error in a production practice that was mainly agriculturally oriented. By "organic production" he meant that production techniques are 'under the ban of living nature'. According to him, these three factors are "forces in the sphere of capitalist interests" (I: pp. 466, 472-79).

According to Sombart, the above "forces" in the sphere of production techniques of early capitalism are found in pre-capitalism. Yet in the capitalist era they bring about a development in favour of the "machine principle". In early capitalism, he said, the machine had more the character of "machines of movement", like water mills, that utilize energy of motion. These are machines that replace human and animal power. According to Sombart, such machines fit well into an "organic" production mode. Yet, development would be in favour of "machines of labour", to replace skilled labour (I: p. 484). He described "the new way in production techniques", which "dispensed with the restrictions of living nature". He said that there were three crucial factors in this process: first, the use of raw materials such as metals, second, the use of new sources of energy like coal and petrol, and third, the development of new methods of production. Sombart characterized the New Way of Production as "inorganic". He was of the opinion that in modern technology, practice is based on natural science theory, which precedes and results in practical application, and that this was in line with Leonardo's method. In technology, he said, the theoretical method replaces the intuitive approach of former times (I: p. 467; III: pp. 97, 266).

Sombart suggested that there is a basic characteristic of modern technology that is focussed towards "undeified" nature. In a sense there was an interdependency between this and Max Weber's idea of *Entzauberung der Welt*: "disenchantment of the world". According to Sombart, there is a close relation in modern techniques between the invention and the application in production. This is because, in modern capitalism, although "natural science theory" and "practice" originate in different viewpoints, the two fields of thought are nevertheless systematically orientated towards one another. In this connection, Sombart distinguished between the natural science approach and the rational approach, the latter being the point of departure for economic thought, the compass in the sphere of economic decisions that are based on subjective aims (III: pp. 78-81).

In Sombart's picture of modern technology, natural science is systematized and organized in such a way that stimuli for extending it are built in. Practically oriented technological development is institutionalized, mainly by company research departments and public patent offices, the expansivity of capitalist production warranting sufficient application opportunities. Sombart said that, in capitalist invention culture, the criterion against which inventions are tested is profitability: that what counts as "a good invention is a remunerative invention". He believed this also has a negative aspect, since inventions primarily serve capitalist interests. He said that the entrepreneur forces new products onto the public, even though it is questionable whether these will improve people's conditions (III: pp. 85-95). However, the last words had still not been said. Backhaus *et al.*, in their discussion of "the Althoff system", elaborated the idea of the university as an innovating institution (Backhaus, 1993).

What part do natural resources play in Sombart's reflection on developing economy? In the first instance the answer is that these means of production were drawn into an ever increasing mobility of goods. If the mobility of finished products and semi-manufactured articles appears to be greater than that of raw materials, there is a tendency to establish production plants near the source of these materials. In this connection he referred to Alfred Weber's theory (III: p. 294). Sombart suggested that in the capitalist system, the production factor nature takes on the character of "real capital". This implies nature to be a component of wealth. He showed how in early capitalism large fortunes arose from nature, giving as example the ownership of natural stocks of minerals. Of course, he also pointed to renewable resources like agricultural land. Referring to all natural resources, he distinguished three stages of utilization: laying-out, construction, and development. The first stage was that of planning and founding. The next was that of construction and extension, in which all potentials of the resource are utilized. In the last stage, exploitation reaches its definitive and final form (I: pp. 651*ff*; III: pp. 230*ff*).

Sombart put forward the idea of nature-sparing and labour-sparing technology, describing how some inventions economize on natural resources and others on labour, while some do both. Like Wilhelm Roscher before him, he had an open eye for the phenomena of premature exhaustion in mining and overcropping in agriculture. Further, he noted that an abundant use of natural resources had been an important condition for the development of capitalism. He said that, in the nineteenth century, "capitalism thrust both hands into the treasury of earth" (I: p. 492; III: pp. 261-272). It is possible to say that Sombart "discovered" the sustaining function of raw materials in the process of economic growth. He elucidated the numerous economic opportunities offered by natural resources and the role of technology in utilizing these opportunities. He was conscious of the danger of exhaustion. As such, he may be considered a forerunner of the many present-day economists who focus their attention on these subjects (Krabbe, 1992c).

Many modern economists attempt to reconcile the typical methodological features of economic science on the one hand and natural sciences on the other, by integrating natural science thought into economics. Examples of such economists are Georgescu-Roegen (1971) and Rugina (1986), the latter mentioning a number of other twentieth-century economists who have also done so. This reconciliation was also Sombart's aim. For this he relied on a type of socio-psychology. Jürgen Backhaus gave an outline of Sombart's *Modern capitalism*, characterizing his approach as "comparative economics", giving the latter concept a historistic trait.

> [Sombart's] work consists in establishing the subdiscipline of comparative economics with a historical perspective in order to capture the developmental process leading up to a particular institutional realization. (Backhaus, 1989a: p. 602.)

* *

Arthur Spiethoff was born in Düsseldorf in 1873. He held a university chair first in Prague and then in Bonn. He became known for his idea of "economic styles" and his studies on trade cycles, in which he was influenced by Clément Juglar. Like his contemporary, the American Institutionalist Mitchell, he saw this phenomenon as an aspect of the industrialization process of the economy. Spiethoff's thought had remarkable historistic traits as exemplified by the idea that the character of booms and crises was determined by the stage of development of society.

According to Spiethoff, in economics a distinction should be made between a realistic, historically oriented approach and an approach in terms of "pure theories". "Real types" are formed in the first, "ideal types" in the latter. Real types are pictures of reality. Ideal types, however, are just heuristic devices. Both approaches have repercussions for Spiethoff's idea of *Wirtschaftsstil*, "style of the economy". Both characterize a certain economic situation. An example of a certain style is the "free capitalist market economy".

Spiethoff partly adopted the indications of the various stages from Sombart. In the first stage, business cycles had the character of the type of "speculation crises", of which the "tulip trade" was an example. This was the stage of *Frühkapitalismus*, "early capitalism", in which roundabout production was not yet fully developed. In the second stage, located in the middle of the nineteenth century, cyclic over-investment and over-production occurred. This was because the economy had evolved to *Hochkapitalismus*, "capitalism proper", in which roundabout production was fully grown, and individualism and rationalism were significant features of society. Credit facilities began to play a significant part in this phase of development. Linked to this stage was the third, in which crises were more moderate. This phase was characterized by limited investment opportunities and needs that were satisfied to a rather high degree. The number of economic actors was increased considerably. According to Spiethoff's view, the First World War formed the transition to the fourth stage, characterized by degeneration of the stock of capital and government intervention in economic affairs. In this period the economy changed fundamentally, with drastic consequences for the character of the business cycle. Spiethoff characterized the crisis of the Thirties as a situation in which, even in the preceding boom, over-production was maintained. Another historistic aspect of his approach is that the business cycle is an essential factor in economic development. In this picture, over-production is a causal factor in the social process of capital formation (Spiethoff, 1923; 1933; 1948).

Max Weber

Max Weber, a brother of the economist and sociologist, Alfred Weber, was born in Erfurt in 1864. He studied law, economics, history and philosophy in Heidelberg, Göttingen and Berlin. In 1918, after a period of nervous illness, he was appointed to the University of Vienna. A year later he succeeded Lujo Brentano in his chair at Heidelberg. His vast and many-sided body of work was mainly published after his death in 1920, through the efforts of the sociologist, Johannes Winckelmann, and of Weber's wife, Marianne Schnitger. At the beginning of his scientific career, Weber was a lively participant in the activities of the *Verein für Socialpolitik.* Together with Sombart, he opposed the use of certain value judgements in scientific thought. Over the years he turned more and more to sociological problems.

Weber shared the neo-Kantian idea, put forward by Windelband and Rickert, that the social science method differs essentially from that of natural science. He maintained that these two branches of science utilize two different ideas of causality. He limited himself to the first field of study. According to him, causality is bound to "motives" of acting people. He distinguished purposefully, morally, affectively and traditionally determined motives. His well-known definition of sociology, including economics, was that it is 'a science orientated towards the understanding of social behaviour in an interpretative way, leading to a causal explanation of its course and effects'[94] (Weber, 1921, 1964: pp. 3-7). The central idea in Weber's thought was the interpretation or clarification through *Verstehen*, "un-

[94]... eine Wissenschaft, welche soziales Handeln deutend verstehen und dadurch in seinem Ablauf und seinen Wirkungen ursächlich erklären will.

derstanding". On this point he based his ideas on Wilhelm Dilthey and Karl Jaspers. Weber made it clear that human behaviour is always orientated towards others. He put forward the methodological idea of the pure or ideal type. This *Idealtypus* is supposed to be purified of irrational elements and does not depend on specific empirical forms. Examples are capitalism, family, and craft. He said that ideal types can also be formed of certain social developments. In social sciences, causality has the character of regularity in relations between cause and effect. There is only a "likelihood" or "probability" that certain phenomena will appear. Therefore, in principle, data are subject to statistical analysis. Weber stated that relationships of natural science cannot be understood in these sciences. The data concerned should be considered as given.

Weber posited that science must be *Wertfrei*, "value free". This does not mean, however, that value judgements remained outside the scope of his approach. In fact, his analysis was clearly orientated towards values which are manifest in social intercourse. He stated that, for the researcher to understand social events fully, he should use his own pattern of values. His point was, however, that political and scientific arguments must not be intermingled. Weber maintained that science must be objectively valid. This idea of objectivity does not refer to mathematical models, which for him were simply a means of arriving at knowledge. Objectivity depends rather on whether the method followed can pass criticism. It refers to the merits of the system of ideas used and those of the logical structure of the approach. In Weber's view, objectivity is bound to a certain culture, which is determined by social values. His historicism implied that it is not only men and society that are subject to development, but science and the idea of objectivity, too.

> The qualification of an event as a "socio-economic" phenomenon is not inherent as such in an "objective" way. Rather, it is determined by the direction of our interest, resulting from its specific cultural significance, on the basis of which we approach the event in a specific case.[95] (Weber, 1904, 1968: p. 161.)

Schmoller's successor to his Berlin chair, Heinrich Herkner, opposed the "value free" approaches of Weber and Sombart. Herkner, one of the idealists of the later years, linked ethically oriented social sciences with politics through the idea of the "will". As he put it in Schmoller's spirit:

> Finally, all social development is the result of human willing. ... It is just the point whether science can support its ideals with such convincing arguments as are necessary for determin-

[95]Die Qualität eines Vorganges als "sozial-ökonomischer" Erscheinung ist nun nicht etwas, was ihm als solchem "objektiv" anhaftet. Sie ist vielmehr bedingt durch die Richtung unseres Erkenntnisinteresses, wie sie sich aus der spezifischen Kulturbedeutung ergibt, die wir dem betreffenden Vorgange im einzelnen Fall beilegen.

ing the willingness of a sufficiently large number of people.[96] (Herkner, 1894, 1921 II: pp. 38, 139.)

Walther Lotz, another late idealistically oriented follower of the Historical School movement, agreed with Weber that science and politics must be strictly separated.

> For it cannot be the task of science to consider aprioristic aims as points of departure for the judgement of state organizations. Every politician might foster them in different ways according to his own point of view and ideals.[97] (Lotz, 1917: p. 7.)

Lotz' kindred spirit, Heinrich Dietzel, was of the same opinion. In line with Roscher's is-*versus*-should approach, he put forward the idea that "theoretical" social economics must confine itself to description and explanation. Normative questions should be dealt with in "practical" social economics (Dietzel, 1895: pp. 4, 5, 29, 30).

Weber was an "institutionalist", orientated towards socio-economic development. He distinguished between behaviour characterized as "economizing" and behaviour that is "economically oriented". The former is directed towards objectives in a typically economic field, and the latter towards non-economic objectives. It is, however, also orientated towards 'the provisions of support for utility achievements' *(der Fürsorge für einen Begehr nach Nutzleistungen)* (1921: p. 43). The former aspect of human behaviour is "rationally" oriented, in the individualistic sense of the word; the latter aspect deals with shaping social relations. Weber maintained that regularity in social behaviour is bound to a system of norms, called the "legitime order". This order's legitimacy is derived from tradition, belief and abiding by the law. In this connection he placed the idea of charismatic leadership. *Charisma* is 'the extraordinary devotion to a person's holiness, heroism, or exemplary behaviour, and the order revealed or created by this'[98] (1921: p. 159).

It was particularly Weber's various studies in the field of socio-economic history that became widely known. At the beginning of his career he studied the development of social relations in the eastern part of Germany, a topical subject in the Historical School.

---

[96]Schliesslich ist alle gesellschaftliche Entwicklung doch ein Produkt des menschlichen Willens. ... Es kann also nur darauf ankommen, ob die Wissenschaft ihre Ideale mit so überzeugenden Beweisgründen ausstatten kann, als notwendig ist, um das Wollen einer genügend grossen Zahl von Menschen zu bestimmen.

[97]Denn er kann nicht Aufgabe der Wissenschaft sein, aprioristische Forderungen, die je nach seinem Standpunkt und seinem Ideal jeder Parteimann verschieden in seinem Busen hegen mag, zum Ausgangspunkt der Beurteilung staatlicher Einrichtungen zu machen.

[98]... der ausseralltäglichen Hingabe an die Heiligkeit oder die Heldenkraft oder die Vorbildlichkeit einer Person und der durch sie offenbarten oder geschaffenen Ordnungen.

He concluded that, in the nineteenth century, large landowners in East Germany evolved from feudal lords to capitalist agrarian entrepreneurs. This development disadvantaged the agrarian population, since the Prussian *Junkers* were alienated from their original functions in the agrarian society.

In the field of history Weber's most remarkable study dealt with the influence of Protestant ethics, especially Calvinist ethics, on the "spirit" of capitalism. His thesis was that the doctrine of predestination stimulated believers to behave in a way that testified to their being of the elect. By ceaseless labour man could be certain of a favourable providence of God. According to Weber, the rational ethics and the industrious and thrifty mentality remained after the religious basis had long been forgotten. He gave the utilitarianism of Benjamin Franklin as an example of this. Weber won much approval for this thesis. However, there has been criticism as well. Van Stuijvenberg (1973), who tested it to see if it applied to the Netherlands, concluded that there was no support for it in the Dutch Calvinist literature of that period. In his study on the Protestant ethic, Philip S. Gorski (1993) did not oppose Weber's approach, although he offered a somewhat different interpretation of Calvinism as doctrine, movement and ideology. He stated that Calvinist morality was not only a "work ethic" but also an "ethic of self-discipline", which legitimated the domination of rising political elites. Gorski devoted a section of his article to "building the new Israel: the birth of the Dutch Republic, 1540-1648". It can be said that the value of Weber's idea is primarily to be found in his interesting problem formulation and in his approach, rather than in his generalized conclusions.

Finally, I want to mention the historistic idea of *Entzauberung der Welt* ("disenchantment of the world"), which crops up in various passages. Weber noticed a continuing intellectualization of thought and rationalization of behaviour during the course of time. It is the destiny of modern man to live in a culture in which metaphysical certainties are questioned more and more. Nostalgia for earlier times stamps Weber as a late Romantic, while his realist image of man marks him as one of the founders of present-day thought on "individual and developing society". Recently, Hans Albert supported Weber's "historism", which was bound to Weber's typical concept of "understanding". It is a type of historicism which is based on the "mental sciences" idea.

> [H]istorism emphasizes the individuality, the uniqueness and unrepeatability of social and cultural phenomena. The "historicity" of these phenomena seems to be incompatible with reducing them to laws. (Albert, 1988: p. 576.)

Chapter 10
INSTITUTIONALISM

Historistic and organistic ideas are also found in the American School of Institutionalists, founded by Veblen and, in its first stage, shaped by writers like Commons, Mitchell, (Walton) Hamilton and (John Maurice) Clark. The British "Fabians" had similar ideas, as did Hobson, who was inspired by Veblen. These authors laid the foundation for present-day evolutionary-oriented thought on economic institutions, with names such as Galbraith, (Clarence) Ayres, Gruchy and Myrdal. In Germany, a number of writers followed an almost similar line of thought, directly influenced by the Historical School. Mention is made of Wagner, Dietzel, Herkner and Eucken. Environmentally oriented Institutionalism is mentioned as well. The chapter also refers to the institutional ideas of Schumpeter and Tinbergen. Finally, several present-day ideas which are rather close to the Institutional approach are discussed.

It is not within the scope of this book to give a complete display of historistic and organistic ideas of writers here broadly discussed as Institutionalists. An attempt is made to show how various economists inherited the legacy of old German ideas, which is to characterize the Historical School's echo in the economic thought of later days.

Precursors and founders of twentieth-century Institutionalism

Thornstein Veblen's book *The theory of the leisure class: an economic study of institutions*, published in 1899, shows a remarkable analogy at various points with German writers whose ideas originated in continental Romanticism. This can also be said of his followers' works. Therefore, Allen Gruchy's label "neo-institutional economics" for the thought of later authors in Veblen's school was a fortunate one (Gruchy, 1972, 1974). In the context of this study, however, former members may be included as well. To avoid misunderstanding on this point I use the term "Institutionalism", considering the current of the Historical School as "Pre-Institutionalism". Lazaros Houmanidis called this school *l'Ecole Historico-institutionaliste*, which agrees with my view (Houmanidis, 1994a: p. 102).

There was some influence from the late nineteenth-century Irish historistic writer, John Ingram. This can also be said of the British historistically oriented economist, Cliffe Leslie.

> The most able exponent of the thorough-going historical approach, comparable with that of the German School, was Cliffe Leslie, though his criticism is of the kind often referred to as "unconstructive". (Hutchison, 1962: p. 20.)

Further, in connection with both the Fabian movement and American Institutionalism, mention should be made of John Stuart Mill. In his essay *On liberty*, he posed the question of restricting economic liberty and laid the philosophical basis for "public control" in *laissez faire* economies.

> This [the freedom to purchase elsewhere] is the so-called doctrine of "free trade", which rests on grounds different from, though equally solid with, the principle of individual liberty asserted in this essay. Restrictions on trade, or on production for purposes of trade, are indeed restraints; and all restraint, *qua* restraint, is an evil; but the restraints in question affect only that part of behaviour which society is competent to restrain, and are wrong solely because they do not really produce the results which it is desired to produce by them (Mill, 1859, 1983: p. 164).

The Darwinian root of American Institutionalism should especially be mentioned.

> The Darwinian revolution had affected the thought of all western civilization, yet it was in America that economic thought was reworked in terms of the full meaning of Darwinism. (David Hamilton, 1970: p. 26.)

Institutionalists opened the door for Darwinian ideas by relativizing rationalism and making room for the recognition of the right of existence of "natural inclinations" and other biological aspects of human behaviour.

> It will be universally admitted that instincts are as important as corporeal structure for the welfare of each species, under its present conditions of life. ... No complex instinct can possibly be produced through natural selection, except by the slow and gradual accumulation of numerous, slight, yet profitable, variations. (Darwin, 1859, 1985: p. 236.)

Darwin's influence was quite considerable in Germany, especially on writers like Bücher, Schmoller, Sombart and, in a certain sense, on Carl Menger and his son Karl, who edited the second edition of his father's *Principles*. The line of Historical School thought was continued in the Institutional approach, although Institutionalism was also a continuation of Classical and Marginal Utility economics.

John Bates Clark was among the first group of economists to join the American Economic Association. Another early member was E.R.A. Seligman, who was later to become the editor of the *Encyclopaedia of the social sciences* (1930). He too had studied in Germany. The initiative to establish the American Economic Association came from the desire for economic reform. A.W. Coats noticed that its first members were 'university presidents, reform clergymen, and other public-spirited individuals' (Coats, 1985: p. 1699). To a certain extent this society was a pendant of the *Verein für Socialpolitik.* The first secretary was the influential Professor Richard Ely, who had studied with Karl Knies. Ely's book *An introduction to political economy* (1889) makes it clear that the author was well acquainted with the writers of the Historical School. He pointed out:

> While the doctrine of the Germans is broad and liberal it is at the same time conservative, for it teaches that improved conditions must be a growth, and must take their root in the past. (Ely, 1889, 1891: p. 323.)

However, Ely was also critical of the Historical School. He said that it sometimes tended towards fatalism, justifying the existing situation by using historical arguments (p. 324). In his introduction to the second edition of Ely's textbook, Ingram mentioned Comte and the Historical School as co-founders of the evolutionary-oriented economics of their day.

> It is now universally acknowledged that societies are subject to a process of development, which is itself not arbitrary, but regular; and that no social fact can be really understood apart from its history. (Ingram in Ely, 1891: p. 4.)

Like authors such as Roscher and Schmoller, Ely was fully aware of the significance of geographical circumstances for the economy and natural condition in general. Like, for example, Brentano of the "younger" School, he fostered moderate reformist ideals. Ely advocated an ethically founded approach towards economic problems, and brought the *Methodenstreit* to the attention of American economists. He and Clark the elder should be considered precursors of American Institutionalism.

Although Veblen did not want to adopt Marxist principles nor to accept Marxist discipline in economics, his idea of the "leisure class", which through the ages had led a parasitic life at the expense of the labouring class, is reminiscent of Marx. The same can be said about his idea of "conspicuous consumption", which refers to a phenomenon that, however, is much broader than the useless luxury of "captains of industry".

Like members of the Historical School, Veblen wanted to describe the way in which Western economy had evolved from primitive forms of society. Both views see the economic system as being determined by a complex system of institutional factors. The socio-economic system was considered to be characteristic of a certain stage of economic development. The main link between Veblen and the Historical School was his tutor, John Bates Clark. While studying with Knies in Heidelberg, Clark became acquainted with the historistic approach and the organic concept of society, and integrated these types of "dynamics" into his thought. His pupil, Veblen, and his son, John Maurice Clark, elaborated this element of his thought, each in his own way. Later, John Bates became preoccupied with the idea of economic equilibrium. Veblen, referring to Rodbertus' historical approach, objected to the "mechanical" elements in Clark's dynamics that focussed on capital formation (Veblen, 1908, 1972). Hutchison (1962: pp. 266-67) noticed that Roosevelt's "new deal" idea was based partly on Veblen's thought.

The years in which the A.E.A. and the *Verein* were founded also saw the establishment of the Fabian Society in Great Britain. The society took its name from the Roman, Fabius Cunctator. It consisted of a group of intellectuals interested in social reform. One of the economic-oriented members was Cole, a historian and a socialist economist. Two others were Ashley and Tawney, both scholars of economic history. The former stayed for some time in Germany and was well-informed about the Historical School and sympathized with the ideas of the Socialists of the Chair. The latter's book *Religion and the rise of capitalism* (1926) was inspired by Weber's studies on the subject.

A place must be found among the precursors and founders of Institutionalism for the British economist, John Atkinson Hobson. On the one hand, he was among the stream of Veblen's followers in America and, on the other, that of the German Historical School's variant of the philosophy of life. In his study on the nature of the capitalist system, published in 1894, he referred to Sombart, Brentano and Schulze-Gaevernitz, a late representative of the Historical School. This does not mean that Hobson should not also be seen as a link in the Classical stream of thought.

Many early systems theory ideas are found in Hobson's work.

> So the industrial system has its many suckers in Nature, everywhere drawing out materials and forces to be worked up, partly into consumers' goods, partly into new instruments of production. ... Every one knows, or can find out, how the chief kinds of materials, such as grains, fruits, animals, timber, textiles, coal, clay, metals, are worked up by different trades into the immense variety of finished articles which we use. The regular course of their productive career sometimes calls forth the image of a river, sometimes of a machine, sometimes of an organism. The *organic metaphor* is the most useful, suggesting the likeness of industry to the processes of taking in food, digesting and assimilating it, converting it into working energy and new tissue, and excreting the waste. But none of these images is quite correct. ... None of them takes proper account of one essential fact, viz. that each productive act done to the material in any process requires the co-operation of conscious agents, the owners of the different factors of production that are used. (Hobson, 1911: pp. 43-44; my italics.)

Hobson used the term "industrial organism", a holistic concept, in the context of a set of systems theory ideas. It has a significant evolutionistic dimension.

> [W]e may take Industry as a whole, the Industrial Organism as it exists at any given time, consider the nature and extent of the cohesion existing between its several parts, and, further, resolving these parts into their constituent elements, gain a close understanding of the extent to which differentiation of industrial functions has been carried in the several divisions. (Hobson, 1894, 1926: p. 31.)

In his work on imperialism he put forward the idea that eighteenth-century nationalism developed to colonialism and this to "imperialism", by the way of institutional differentiation (Hobson, 1902, 1938: pp. 3-13).

An exceptional part in the American Political Economy of the last quarter of the nineteenth century was played by Henry George, an autodidact in economics. George should not be considered an Institutionalist proper, since there are significant contrasts between his ideas and those of specific Institutionalists. The latter focussed on socio-economic matters and favoured a certain degree of government intervention. At the centre of George's thought, however, was organic nature. In principle, he favoured *laissez faire*, as far as nature is not under discussion. Nevertheless, there are similarities between George's organicism and that of Institutional thought. Moreover, his influence on American Institutionalism must not be underestimated.

George's main work, *Progress and poverty* (1879), formed a noteworthy link in the train of organically oriented thought in economics. George supported the Physiocrat idea that land is the ultimate source of wealth. He applied Ricardo's rent theory in such a way that the whole of an ever increasing "welfare surplus" falls to the landowner. This led him to the conclusion that all productive land ought to be in the hands of the government, so as to create a proper use for what he considered an unjustified land rent. In the context of this study, George's organistic approach is the most significant.

> Biological processes take a central place in George's scheme of thought. We may even recognize in his writings the modern ideas of an ecological equilibrium and an ecologically sustainable process of production. (Backhaus *et al.*, 1991: p. 494.)

Thus, various specific organically oriented ideas are found in his work. For instance he said:

> Life does not use up the forces that maintain life. ... The human being, physically considered, is but a transient form of matter, a changing mode of motion. The matter remains and the force persists (George, 1979: pp. 133-34).

Significant former Institutionalists

In the first period of American Institutionalism, an important part was played by John Commons. Like father and son Clark, he wanted to integrate the principle of marginal utility into institutional economics. The same was done in Europe by Philippovich. Common's discussion of the collective aspects of economic behaviour was also in line with that of the Historical School. The latter's historicism is found in Common's work.

> Like Veblen, Commons took the economic system to be an evolving process, which had passed through a number of stages of development, and which at the time they were analyzing it was in the stage of the "new industrial order". (Gruchy, 1974: p. 34.)

On these points the ideas of John Maurice Clark are rather similar.

> J.M. Clark followed the pragmatic philosopher John Dewey and the eminent sociologist Charles Horton Cooley in taking society to be an evolving process in which collective action dominates individual action, conflict rather than harmony prevails among social groups and disequilibrium rather than equilibrium is the usual state of affairs. (Gruchy, 1974: p. 54.)

Wesley Mitchell was another authority in the American school. Although he had not studied in Germany, his book *Types of economic theory, from Mercantilism to Institutionalism*, published in 1969, makes it clear that he was well acquainted with continental European literature. He identified the Historical School with Schmoller's. Mitchell noticed unique traits, as well as analogies in successive business cycles. Hutchison (1962: p. 401), comparing him with Spiethoff, noted that there was "a masterly balance" between descriptive and theoretical analyses in both approaches.

An outstanding methodologist in the circle of American Institutionalists was Allan Gruchy. He said:

> In their long-range view of the economic system the neo-Institutionalists substitute the concept of "process" for the concept of "equilibrium". These heterodox economists do not deny that for some analytical purposes the concept of equilibrium is a useful concept ... But in the long run the economic system is an evolving process and not a static equilibrium. This process undergoes a cumulative development in which various factors act and react upon one another in a cumulative process of circular causation. (Gruchy, 1974: p. 293.)

The last sentence in this quotation connects "institutional thought" with the "systems theories", discussed in Chapter 13. A possible example of such a link is the "materials balance" idea, introduced into economics by Kneese, (R.U.) Ayres and d'Arge (1970). An organistic version of this concept is the idea of "industrial metabolism", which is 'the set of physico-chemical transformations that convert raw materials (biomass, fuels, minerals, metals) into manufactured products and structures (i.e. "goods") and wastes', put forward by Ayres and Simonis (1994: p. xi).

As a methodologist, the historian Friedrich Meinecke exerted considerable influence on German socio-economic thought of the first part of the twentieth century. In a way this situation is comparable with Dilthey's engagement with this field of study in the last quarter of the preceding century. Meinecke elaborated on the main questions put forward by the nineteenth-century Historical School. He discussed the problems of causality in social development, the significance of free will, and how methods of the social and the natural sciences are related. Meinecke relativized free will's typical significance to causality and contributed to overcome the methodological duality put forward by neo-Kantians and philosophers of life.

The economists Wagner, Dietzel and Herkner can be considered early German representatives of Institutionalism. Adolf Wagner was a contemporary of Schmoller. A remarkable trait of his approach is that it was essentially organistic, without having any significant historistic dimension. There were no significant ideas of the developing picture of man. His conservative reformist mentality, however, was along the lines of the political ideas of the members of the Historical School and the *Verein*. Similar remarks can be made about Heinrich Dietzel, although he should be placed between Wagner and Brentano, a typical member of the Historical School. He must not be confused with Karl August Dietzel, born in 1829, who had earlier contributed to the idea of the state. Heinrich Dietzel (1895) put forward the concept of both *das Individualprincip*, "the individualist principle", and *das Socialprincip*, "the social principle", as ethical foundations for the organization of society. The first leads to a decentralized system of competition, the second to a centralized system bearing collectivist traits. He did not agree with Schmoller's notion that there is a uniform idea in society about the most desirable institutional structure. The relevant ideas, he said, differ according to, for instance, the various religiously determined views on society. Dietzel believed that social reform and tariff protection are incompatible. He promoted the idea of *Weltwirtschaft*, "world economy".

Schmoller's successor at the University of Berlin was Heinrich Herkner. His thought, like Schmoller's, had a clear normative dimension. As such he opposed Sombart and Weber. Central themes in his approach were the "social question" and the idea of solidarity, with its institutional implications. Unlike Schmoller, he held that it is not the state, but the individual that is the bearer ethics in society (Backhaus and Hanel, 1994: p. 186).

Walter Eucken was a leading German Institutionalist. He was a son of the philosopher Rudolph Eucken and was born in Jena in 1891. Although Walter was educated in the Historical School, he was also influenced by writers of the Austrian School. He was appointed Professor of Economics at the University of Freiburg (Breisgau). Like Roscher earlier, he wanted to keep historistic and organistic thought in balance with deductive-oriented mainstream economics. Eucken believed that a crucial assignment of economics is to "overcome the great antinomy". This antithesis refers to two different approaches to economic empiricism: a specific and historically oriented one *versus* a general and theoretical one (Eucken, 1940, 1941: pp. 18, 215).

> In economics, the tension between observation and reason, concrete and abstract, synthesis and analysis must not be put aside. It should function as a fruitful element. ... It is in these tensions that social economics is situated and it is in this way that it is able to come to know economic life scientifically.[99] (Eucken, 1940, 1941: p. 287.)

Eucken was concerned with the question of whether a "compulsive" character should be assigned to social development. His answer was that there are "tendencies", which do not exclude the freedom of decision in social intercourse. Decisions, however, are conditioned by it. He considered it the task of politicians to support such tendencies (Eucken, 1952: pp. 215-16). He rejected the Historical School idea that in economic development characteristic or typical "stages" can be perceived. Instead of such misleading *Realtypen*, "reality types", he wanted to use *Idealtypen*, "ideal types", which are not bound to time and place, but have universal validity for society. These are principles according to which the economy is organized, as socio-economic situations are subjected to characterization by elements determining the economic order.

Eucken put forward the idea that in modern society, in contrast to nineteenth-century individualism, man's existence is largely determined by the state. This state, in its turn, is influenced by interest groups. He stated:

> Inevitably a new *organic* social ordering comes into existence, with central control of the economic process, in which order leading men have a proper survey of the whole process and are able to steer in a significant way.[100] (Eucken, 1948: p. 125; my italics.)

Typical of Eucken and his followers in the neo-liberal "Freiburg School" founded by him, was thinking in terms of *Ordnungen*, "ordered systems". This approach is also characteris-

---

[99]Die Spannung zwischen Anschauung und Ratio, Konkretem und Abstraktem, Synthese und Analyse darf in der Nationalökonomie nicht beseitigt werden. Sie ist fruchtbar zu machen. ... In diesen Spannungen lebt die Nationalökonomie und gerade dadurch gelingt es ihr, wirtschaftliches Leben wissenschaftlich zu erkennen.

[100]Mit Zwangsläufigkeit würde eine neue organische Sozialordnung entstehen mit zentraler Lenkung des Wirtschaftsprozesses, in der die Männer, welche die Leitung inne hätten, einen Überblick über die Gesamthergänge besässen und sie sinnvoll steuern könnten.

tic of his pupil, the American professor Anghel Rugina (mentioned below) when elaborating the problem of stable *versus* unstable equilibria. Eucken and writers like Wilhelm Röpke laid the foundation for neo-liberal thought in Germany after the Second World War. In this period the reformist spirit of the Historical School had not yet vanished entirely. So, Karl Georg Zinn saw society as a "historically changeable system".

> [T]he state is *obliged* to intervene, and it is only in this way that it legalizes and supports countervailing power to the dominating class of capitalists. ... However, it involves a stabilization (of the economic and socially instable capitalist system), which can also make room for a social process of gradual change.[101] (Zinn, 1980: p. 121; italics in original.)

Later Institutionalists

The contemporary American writer John Kenneth Galbraith should be placed within the Institutional tradition. In the centre of his thought was the developing "industrial state", with its typical ideological and technological dimensions. A characteristic element was that certain institutions, for instance, large firms, play a part in determining economic processes. In this connection he used the term management of specific demand. He considered the modern economy, with its large corporations, a compound of the market system and the planning system.

> By itself the market system ... is broadly stable. ... The planning system, in the absence of state intervention, is inherently unstable. ... The government, through its procurement and in providing for the various needs of the planning system, plays a vital role in advancing the purposes of the planning system. (Galbraith, 1973, 1975: pp. 195, 259.)

In this picture a crucial part is played by the developing "technostructure", which must be understood as a system of economic and socio-economic power. Technological development takes shape in the planning system, in a situation of interdependence.

> In examining the intricate complex of economic change, technology, having an initiative of its own, is the logical point at which to break in. But technology not only causes change, it is a response to change. Though it forces specialization it is also the result of specialization. (Galbraith, 1967, 1974: p. 38.)

Another author in this group of "later Institutionalists" is Clarence E. Ayres, a leading American Institutionalist. A typical trait of his thought is the denial that the economy is

---

[101][D]er Staat ist zu Interventionen *verpflichtet*, und sei es nur dadurch, dass er Gegenmacht-bildungen zur dominierenden Klasse der Kapitaleigner legalisiert und schützt. ... Es handelt sich jedoch um eine Stabilisierung (in das ökonomisch und sozial instabile kapitalistische System), die zugleich einem schrittweisen gesellschaftlichen Veränderungsprozess Raum geben kann.

controlled by independent individualistic rationality only. Complementary to this is his idea of "ceremonial" behaviour, in which a certain analogy can be seen with Max Weber's idea of charism.

> [According to Ayres, ceremonial] behavior patterns develop around imposition and investiture of status. These two aspects of behavior patterns are related, but all behavior has distinct ceremonial and technological aspects. ... Ceremonial patterns are relatively fixed and subject to change only through a break in the continuity of the culture in which they exist. ... It is held by Ayres, as by most institutionalists, that the biological make-up of man does not explain patterns of behavior. In order to understand human behavior, attention must center on culture. (David Hamilton, 1970: p. 54; referring to Ayres, 1944: pp. 89-96.)

Gunnar Myrdal should also be seen as one of the later Institutionalists, though he held a rather independent position. His primary place is in the Swedish scientific tradition with outstanding writers like the economic historian Eli Heckscher and the economist Gustav Cassel. Judging by the references in his work *Mercantilism* (1931, 1962), Heckscher was well acquainted with Historical School literature. In his book *Economic theory and underdeveloped regions*, of 1957, Myrdal explained the main aspects of his method. His approach is essentially socio-economic, in which natural factors are assigned a part.

> In reality there is, of course, no distinction between facts corresponding to our traditional scholastic division of social science into separate disciplines. A realistic analysis of problems can never stop at such lines of division. The distinction between factors that are "economic" and those that are "non-economic" is, indeed, a useless and nonsensical device from the point of view of logic, and should be replaced by a distinction between "relevant" and "irrelevant" factors, or "more relevant" and "less relevant". And this latter dividing line should not be expected to be the same for different problems. (Myrdal, 1957: p. 10.)

In Myrdal's thought an important role is played by the principle of "circular and cumulative causation". In general, he said, there are no dominating forces causing a "stable equilibrium" in the socio-economic system.

> In the normal case a change does not call forth countervailing changes but, instead, supporting changes, which move the system in the same direction as the first change but much further. Because of such circular causation a social process tends to become cumulative and often to gather speed at an accelerating rate. (Myrdal, 1957: p. 13.)

He discussed the philosophical backgrounds to the idea of "harmony of interests", found in economic literature (Myrdal, 1957: p. 136).

A present-day representative of Institutionalism is the Greek economist and economic historian Lazaros Houmanidis. He characterized his approach as "humanitarian economics", a "voluntary"-oriented concept of the socio-economic system. Like other Institutionalists, Houmanidis used the term "evolution". This idea is bound up with the moral development of man. It will be clear that, in a way, this concept is reminiscent of Schmoller's thought. Just as Schmoller and Menger, he restricted the organistic significance of the term (Houmanidis, 1978).

Like Schmoller, Houmanidis criticized the one-sided individualistic point of view of many policy makers, as well as the corresponding typically microscopic approach of economists who follow the marginalist tradition. Houmanidis noticed that, during the time of monopolistic capitalism, moral and economic problems were accompanied by the crisis of the unadulterated individualistic organization which failed to solve the spiritual and material problems of man. This was also something that worried Schmoller and his followers in the "younger" Historical School. According to Houmanidis, the synthesis of the principle of individualism and that of sociality must and will be reached. Historicism is found in Houmanidis, as when he stated that man is the product of history but also a protagonist of it (Krabbe, 1991b: pp. 6-7; 1993-94). It is worth noting Houmanidis' idea of "chronic meditation".

> The explanation of the past and the forecasting for the future are two different ways of chronic meditation, where the former entails the latter. (Houmanidis, 1994b: p. 189.)

An Institutionalist who opened the eyes of many to the limitations of nature was Ciriacy-Wantrup (1952). He brought the subject of "resource conservation" under discussion. The same can be said of Kapp, referred to in Chapter 14. It was Mishan (1967) who made it clear that the institutional context is a factor determining the allocation of means in society. I also want to mention the present-day writer, Peter Söderbaum, who applied institutional thought to environmental problems.

> [N]eoclassical economics is just one perspective and, depending upon the problems faced, some other perspective or perspectives may well be more fruitful. In some cases, and I suggest environmental problems are a good example, the conventional approach may even be part of the problem. (Söderbaum, 1991: p. 32.)

Schumpeter and Tinbergen as Institutionalists

Joseph Schumpeter functioned as a link between German and Anglo-Saxon economics, starting his scientific career in the former and continuing it in the latter. The economy's institutional context was always in his mind, and he paid much attention to it in his works. However, he should not be considered a pure Institutionalist; his institutionalism did not serve as the basis of the whole of his economics. In 1911 Schumpeter's book *Theorie der wirtschaftlichen Entwicklung*, "Theory of economic development", appeared. This book linked up with his general work on economic theory published in 1908, leading to the question of dynamics in economics (Schumpeter, 1911, 1926: pp. 599*ff*). In Schumpeter's basic picture of economic development reference was made to Max Weber's ideas of the rationality of modern thought and his ideal types, to Sombart's ideas of the development of capitalism in Europe, and to Darwin's ideas of development as such. Schumpeter described his basic development picture in terms of economic "life", relating it to gradual modifications of the economic "cycle" (Schumpeter, 1911, 1926: pp. 88*ff*).

Schumpeter's well-known theory of business cycles was placed within this context. A crucial part was played by the "innovating" entrepreneur, applying *neue Kombinationen*, "new 'combinations' of production factors". Most of the ideas used were not new. Nevertheless, Schumpeter's theory was no repetition of Historical School concepts, but a specific synthesis of them. A similar remark can be made about his book *History of economic analysis*, published posthumously in 1954. The book was much more than an encyclopedic work on "mainstream economics". It was also a breakthrough in thinking in terms of economic theory only, by giving full attention to the principles of institutional analysis. As an example of the latter is his treatise on "evolutionism", in which he distinguished between the Hegelian and Marxist approaches, the Historical School's analysis in terms of development stages, the approach of Condorcet and Comte and, finally, the Darwinian variant of Evolutionism (Schumpeter, 1954: pp. 436*ff*).

Jan Tinbergen was primarily an epoch-making economic theoretician with a realistic eye on socio-economic empiricism and a remarkable talent of abstracting on the one hand and a strong ethical commitment to the subjects he studied on the other. With Keynes he was one of the founders of modern macro-economics; with Frisch he was the pioneer of dynamics in economic modelling. In the 1930's he had already received international attention for his mathematical model of America, a study commissioned by the League of Nations. After the Second World War he established the Dutch Central Planning Bureau, which remains active even today. After a visiting professorship at Harvard University, he was appointed to a chair at the Netherlands School of Economics, Rotterdam (now Erasmus University) in 1957. In the time that I studied there, he was teaching "development programming" in an inspiring way. After retiring from "Rotterdam", he taught for a number of years at the University of Leiden, where he focussed on problems of income distribution (Waardenburg, 1994).

It can be said that the socio-economic significance of Tinbergen has two main aspects. On the one hand, he was a disciplined and innovating economist; on the other, he was an enlightened and energetic social reformer, presenting his ideas in a scientific form. The first functioned as the basis for the latter. This gave him a peculiar position. As an econometrician he still has unchallenged authority. However, as an Institutionalist with specific ideas, and as a designer of social reform, while he is admired by many he is only followed by a few. The Royal Netherlands Economic Association established an annual cycle of lectures in 1987, in honour of its famous member. These "Tinbergen lectures" on economic policy, to which outstanding economists were invited, illustrate his significance to economic theory and institutional economics. Contributions have been made by Klein, Malinvaud, Tobin, Kornai, Solow, Feldstein (Knoester and Wellink, eds, 1993). In his works *On the study of economic policy* (1952) and *Economic policy: principles and design* (1956), relating targets and instruments systematically to one another, Tinbergen extended the scope of theoretical economics to the field of economic institutions.

Ideas related to Institutionalism

A century ago, Schmoller and his followers linked psychology and social ethics with economics. A number of modern writers have done so, too. One pioneer in the field of psychology-oriented economics was George Katona. First, he considered individual consumer behaviour, thereby making use of the idea of the human "organism".

> The psychological field contains intervening variables. Between the stimuli and the responses is the *organism*. As the result of past experience there exist habits, attitudes and motives which intervene by influencing how stimuli are perceived and how the *organism* reacts to them. The response then is a function of both the environment and the person. (Katona, 1960, 1972: pp. 240-41; my italics.)

Next, he broadened his scope to include the social group.

> One important aspect of our behavioural environment is group belonging. It is the individual who feels, thinks and acts. But how he feels, thinks and acts is influenced by the group to which he belongs. (Katona, 1960, 1972: p. 241.)

Recently, Cosmides and Tooby discussed the role of "evolutionary psychology" in the analysis of the developing economic process. They maintained that 'well-specified models of the human mind can significantly enhance the scope and specificity of economic theory' (Cosmides and Tooby, 1994: p. 327). Referring to Brian Arthur, the authors Denzau and North (1994), discussed the ideological orientation of economics. They put forward the idea of institutions being "shared mental models", in which ideologies play an important part. According to their view, the process of institutional development is related to the dynamics of these mental models.

When speaking about ideas related to modern Institutionalism, mention should be made of the economic methodologist, Anghel Rugina. His theory of equilibrium *versus* disequilibrium puts forward the idea of 'a rhythmic law of evolution in the development of economic ideas'.

> Up to around 1980 the Keynesian economics and up to 1990 the Marxian economics of disequilibrium seem to have had their time. By the turn of the century, if the cyclical law holds, the successor can not be anything but a new school of economic thought in the direction of a more complete economics of *general stable equilibrium.* (Rugina, 1992: p. 26, italics in original.)

Rugina's approach is of a mondial nature. He also referred to Mikhail Gorbachev.

> Nowadays, we hear and read so much about *perestroika*, a new Russian word which invaded the whole world. Unfortunately, and particularly in the West, we understand the meaning of this word which is "restructuring" applies only to the USSR and other socialist-communist countries. The truth, however, is that restructuring is also needed in the West, in the North and in the South. Humanity indeed is living at a crossroads! The difference is only in degree and direction but basically the problems of instability (disequilibrium), which if we let the analysis go deeper, are the roots of the crisis of our time are everywhere similar in nature. (Rugina, 1990: p. 16, italics in original.)

For any analysis in the socio-economic field, Rugina stressed the need for "consistency of scientific arguments". This, he posited, should be based on the idea of *quinta methodica.*

> Quinta Methodica says that all kinds of problems in economics can be reduced to five categories, exhaustive in the Kantian sense: (1) Economic History; (2) Economic Theory; (3) Economic Ethics; (4) Economic Policy; and (5) History of Economic Thought. (Rugina, 1990: p. 27.)

John O'Brien, a critical authority in Marxian economics, examined Gorbachev's ideas thoroughly.

> Gorbachev's role in the Soviet Union has led him to engage in campaigns against alcoholism, immorality and corruption. In an endeavour to improve the command economy of the USSR, he introduced *perestroika*. In order to allow the people a greater role in governance of their society and open the door to criticism, *glasnost* was introduced as a new feature of life in the Soviet Union. (O'Brien, 1991: p. 25.)

I also want to mention the present-day Institutionalist Kurt Dopfer, whose approach is partly both evolutionary and holistic.

> We call economic institutions ... any correlated behavior of agents that emerges either by self-organization or by policy prescription, and that reoccurs under the same or similar conditions. We may conceive an institution as a "time slice" of a larger evolutionary process. Institutional economics may thus approach the phenomenon of institutions from two sides. It may explain their holistic properties - this being the "time slice" analysis. Institutional economics in this sense is both evolutionary and holistic. (Dopfer, 1991: pp. 535-36.)

In Dopfer's approach "synergism" plays an important part. It was supposed to constitute a "structured whole" in the field of institutions. Over against chaotic human behaviour

Dopfer placed institutional behaviour, characterized by an "order parameter". His analysis is partly based on atomic physics and suggests analogies in the sphere of social actors' behaviour-oriented ideas. Dopfer's crucial question is how ideas as order parameters may "enslave" or "lock in" individual behaviours. His answer falls under the heading of the "morphic power" of ideas. He suggested the existence of a self-referential system, related to class ideology.

> Thorstein Veblen has emphasized the capacity of the upper classes to restate their own "vested interests" in ideological terms. A closure judgment in a mature capitalist society thus is to transform conspicuous consumption into a social norm that is emulated by the lower classes, hence defeating any challenges against conspicuous consumption. (Dopfer, 1991: p. 544.)

Referring to the idea of "productive power" found in the works of Adam Müller and Friedrich List, the economic methodologist Tomas Riha wanted to introduce the concept of "functioning" into economic thought.

> To be an organic part of the whole means to function. To function means to create, to develop, to be alive. To function means to perform for some purpose, to take part in a collective activity undertaken by a number of co-parts, relating to each other. ... All economic phenomena are an interconnected structure of functions in a sense that means function on behalf of ends. (Riha, 1990: p. 53.)

Finally, I want to mention the article *Mr. Sraffa reinterpreted as an ecologist* by Richard England (1986), in which a plea was made for extending the idea of "class struggle" in such a way that it also refers to environmental issues. According to England, workers have to impose production techniques on employers which improve environmental quality. This idea, he said, should be integrated into "radical political economy".

Chapter 11
GEORGESCU-ROEGEN'S "BIOECONOMICS"

Nicholas Georgescu-Roegen was born in Constanza, Romania, in 1906. He studied mathematics, statistics and economics in Bucharest, at the Sorbonne in Paris, and at University College, London. He was Professor of Statistics at the University of Bucharest and visiting fellow at Harvard. Before and during the Second World War he held positions in the Romanian government. After the war he settled down in the United States, where he became Professor of Economics at Vanderbilt University (Dragan and Demetrescu, 1986, 1991: pp. 6-7). Georgescu-Roegen referred to Menger only in connection with the hierarchy of wants and on a few other points. Nevertheless, it is clear that Menger preceded him in various respects. Nicholas Georgescu-Roegen elaborated Carl Menger's thought in a creative and synthetic way, also taking notice of the idea of "ordered systems", put forward by systems-oriented authors like Gustav Schmoller.

His organicism

Georgescu-Roegen's basic idea is that the main distinction in science is between the inorganic sphere and the organic sphere, and not between social science and natural science. The methodological contradiction is between a physical and an organistic epistemology: mechanicism *versus* organicism. He distinguished two levels in the world of economic phenomena: organic and superorganic. The organic domain comprises the typically biological world, the superorganic domain embraces the social world (Krabbe, 1993a).

> Social forms, like biological forms, have ... evolved from other social forms with a flexibility far greater than that of organic evolution. Whatever might be the reason for it, the fact is that the necessity of the laws indisputably weakens as we pass from the inorganic to the organic and from the latter to the superorganic level. (Georgescu-Roegen, [1965] 1976: p. 203.)

Both Menger and Roegen noticed that "organic" systems are characterized by a high level of organization. The idea of the purposefulness of organic systems is also found in the works of both writers. Both were of the opinion that the mechanistic approach complements the organistic one. Georgescu-Roegen, however, integrated both approaches into a unified methodology (Georgescu-Roegen, 1971: pp. 13, 187, 327; Krabbe, 1993a).

Key words in Roegen's approach are "entropy" and "qualitative change".

> The relation between low entropy and economic value is similar to that between economic value and price. An object can have a price only if it has economic value, and it can have economic value only if its entropy is low. But the converse is not true. (Georgescu-Roegen, [1970] 1976: p. 60n.)

He stated that qualitative change is manifested in the development of man and his environment, according to the principle of "exosomatic evolution". This concept is based on the idea that man has a specific property to exploit nature. The species man will become extinct if nature is exhausted, useful low entropy being converted into useless high entropy. Qualitative change, however, is also manifested in partial processes. 'Evolutionary change' Roegen said, 'is inseparable from the Whole'. Nevertheless, it 'cannot be seen except in an isolated, at least quasi-isolated, system'. In institutional problems he complements "analysis" (with its arithmorphic theory) with "dialectics" (Georgescu-Roegen, 1971: p. 203; [1972] 1976: p. 25; [1974] 1976 pp. 236, 244; Krabbe, 1993a).

An important element of Roegen's methodology is the determination of process boundaries. The point of departure was the existence of a "seamless whole" of all phenomena. In this whole an analytical slice must be carved out according to the "natural" boundary of the process. This boundary should be drawn 'where it suits its "purpose" best' ([1965] 1976: pp. 79-80). This is his idea of "parts and wholes". The problem of determining boundaries is also relevant to partial processes. Partial process boundaries, represented by partial analytical boundaries, are characterized by '*duration* and a "geographical" *frontier*, which separates the process from the rest of actuality at all times' ([1971] 1976: p. 40).

Like Carl Menger before him, Nicholas Georgescu-Roegen paid a great deal of attention to causality, putting forward two analytical concepts: geographical frontier, mentioned above, and time. Like Schumpeter earlier, he distinguished between "time" and "Time", mentioning "duration" of processes in terms of the first, and evolution in terms of the second. The latter is what Hutchison (1979: p. 212) meant by "historical time". In connection with the two concepts of time, reference might be made to the *chronoi* and the *kairoi*, respectively, of the classical Greeks. Roegen noticed that analytical economic models should reflect valued "inputs" and "outputs", crossing the analytical boundaries. These include unpriced means, unpriced benefits and waste. The nature of the causality reflected on should be mentioned if the process, or a part of it, is irreversible. It is clear that this approach has particular significance to environmental economics (Georgescu-Roegen, [1974] 1976: pp. 237-51; Krabbe, 1992b and 1993a).

His utility analysis

Georgescu-Roegen transformed Vilfredo Pareto's idea of *ophélimité* in an organistic way. Roegen's idea that wants are partly biologically determined, however, is reminiscent of Menger. The idea of complementarity is found in both Pareto and Menger, in mathematical terms and verbal terms, respectively. Georgescu-Roegen (1966: p. 109) rejected the hedonistic philosophy integrally. For individual welfare, the incomes of other members of society are considered conditional. He inserted altruistic considerations into the utility functions of individuals.

Georgescu-Roegen's welfare theory has three postulates on the idea of hierarchy of wants. The first is the principle of the subordination of wants, in which reference was made to Jevons, Menger and Banfield. There is a scale of wants in which the satisfaction of a certain want 'creates a desire of a higher character' or 'permits the higher want to manifest itself'. This postulate implies the principle of satiable wants. In this connection reference was made to Gossen. Connected with these two postulates is the third, the principle of the growth of wants, 'which is tantamount to the absence of absolute saturation'. The reference here was to Menger and Marshall. Georgescu-Roegen's idea of "saturation points", in indifference maps, is based on these three principles of the hierarchy of wants. Georgescu-Roegen presented an ingenious analysis of the satisfaction of wants by a good which has the capacity to satisfy various needs that are ordered hierarchically.[102] He relativized the idea of ordinal measurement of welfare (Georgescu-Roegen, 1966: pp. 145, 194-98, 200-03; Krabbe, 1992b).

[102]In my doctoral thesis (1974) my own solution for issues like these was to analyse goods in "scarce properties", in the line of K.J. Lancaster, maintaining the idea of shadow prices of properties of economic goods (Krabbe, 1974: p. 114).

Chapter 12
ECONOMIC ASPECTS OF CULTURAL DIVERSIFICATION

In nineteenth-century Germany, nationalist ideas strongly influenced large parts of politics and "state sciences", of which this study is proof. However, there are many types of nationalism. Since the collapse of the Soviet system, the world has been confronted with various manifestations of it. It has become clear that not all of its forms have a positive effect on the stability and efficiency of the institutional system. The effect is negative if nationalism suppresses all criticism of the nation's own habits and customs, and if it enforces antagonism with neighbouring states and minorities within its own borders. However, if it focusses in a critical way on improvement of the culture of its own state and is based on respect for the other man's way of life, the effect is positive.

Because it is a behaviour-determining factor and a motivation in public affairs, nationalism can be seen as an ideology subject to development. It might have a liberal character, though sometimes it is of an anti-liberal type.

> The American nationality was defined by the belief in a set of liberal propositions which, the Americans believed, applied not only to themselves but to all humankind. Similarly, English nationalism as it developed during the eighteenth and nineteenth centuries maintained its roots in the idea of individual liberty. ... Beginning with the middle of the nineteenth century, the history of nationalism on the continent of Europe would be dominated by increasingly anti-liberal, or anti-individualistic, themes. (Mentzel, 1992: pp. 12-13.)

Mises indicated how, in the liberal approach, tensions within nationalism can be decreased. In Yeager's translation the term "statism" is used in this connection.

> Of course, the struggle of nationalities over the state and government cannot disappear completely from polyglot territories. But it will lose sharpness to the extent that the functions of the state are restricted and the freedom of the individual is extended. Whoever wishes peace among peoples must fight *statism*. (Mises, 1983: p. 77; my italics.)

This chapter is devoted to the economic aspects of social behaviour, in its relationship with cultural diversification and nationalist feelings. Most societies are, to some degree, culturally diverse. The question here to be discussed is, what the institutional economic implications of cultural pluralism are. I will approach this problem in a general way, to a large extent abstracting from reality. I discuss what, in principle, the social economic sacrifices and benefits are of cultural isolation on the one hand and cultural interaction on the other. I define cultural pluralism in terms of personal attitudes. On that basis, I consider the implications of pluralism for the market structure, especially for the labour market. Finally, I draw attention to the consequences for the economies of scale and to effects on the distribution of income (Krabbe, 1991a: pp. 126-140).

Cultural pluralism as economic phenomenon. Is "cultural diversification" or "cultural pluralism" of economic interest? Before discussing this question we have to know what pluralism means in this context. In society, groups can be perceived on the basis of various criteria, such as profession, recreational activities, religion, and ethnic or linguistic identity. It makes sense to use a compound criterion that refers to all such factors. In one case, certain of these factors are important, while, in another case, others predominate.

To make an analysis from an economic point of view possible, the criterion should be orientated towards social choice. My idea is that of a selection criterion of three steps in the field of social attitudes of individuals. In the first instance, people are classified according to basic social values, as determined by religion and ideology, and customs. Secondly, there is a refinement of this picture of values: the only ones of interest are those which depend on the fact that they are related to members of one's own group or to "the others". They are "group-oriented values". In the third part of the criterion there is a further refinement. Here, social values are significant only if they have a function in the picture of personal "solidarity" with either one's own group or the group of other men. Economic behaviour influenced by these values is discussed. Naturally, this picture of behavioural values is subject to change during the course of time.

A behavioural analysis based on this selection criterion can shed light on the co-existence of groups with specific cultural identities. In this way, prejudices between members of various social groups will not *a priori* overshadow the analysis. Thus, a well-balanced image can be formed, for example, of the position of foreign workers of particular origins in industrialized countries and that of immigrants from various countries in places like Canada, each group having its own cultural background.

Cultural diversification has an economic aspect. In the first place, each cultural group has a significant consumption pattern. Furthermore, capital and labour markets are divided into sub-markets on the basis of a cultural-based bias towards either supply or demand. Thus, the situation may occur where the quantities traded and the prices reached, wages and interest included, differ according to the cultural identity of the market parties.

Suppose that a society consists of two cultural groups, one well off and the other poor. Suppose further that members of enterprises favour members of their own group when it comes to recruiting executives and staff. In such cases, the existing contrast in wealth between the groups is maintained and possibly strengthened. Cultural pluralism also has an impact on the functioning of the state. If, for instance, the ideas about criteria on the basis of which social relief should be given differ from group to group, this influences the structure and level of social care.

Methodological aspects. Economic problems are mainly approached in terms of an atomistic image of society. Although it is recognized that, to a certain extent, all people are different, in principle all individuals are seen in the same way. In a pluralistic analysis, however, there are at least two groups of individuals, each containing people with a typical behaviour in the socio-economic field. The question is in what way this can be included into economic theory. An obvious solution to an economist is the idea of a "representative" household, in accordance with Marshall's idea of the representative firm. This enables families and firms of specific types to be distinguished. The behavioural features of a stylized household, representing individuals of a certain group in a certain role, are an "average" of the behaviour of the members of the group. Yet this approach is somewhat limited. It ignores the influence of the dispersion of the strength of various individuals and also the interactions within the group.

Another way of looking at society is the "organistic" approach. Here I follow Menger in putting the term between inverted commas, thus expressing the idea that, in economics, no too far-reaching consequences should be attached to this metaphor. This way of thought enables the properties of the group as a whole to be characterized and, further, for statements about the interaction between cultural groups to be formulated. In this connection, I also mention the systems theory, a theoretical framework which allows the incorporation of a mechanistic approach, using atomistic ideas, as well as an organically oriented approach, using holistic ideas. The economy is considered a set of systems within a system.

Poles of isolation and cooperation. The behaviour effects of the above picture of social values can be projected on an axis which depicts the inclination towards cultural isolation on one side and the inclination towards intercultural cooperation on the other. As one tendency becomes stronger, the other becomes weaker. If there is no inclination to isolate, then the society is not a pluralistic one. Otherwise, if there is no inclination to cooperate, there is no united society. I want to look at the economic aspect of the effects in each direction.

The idea that a national society is a melting pot in which all subcultures must merge into a common way of life belongs almost to the past. Nowadays it is recognized that, within the limits of the law and in respect of essential rights, people may live in their own way, both individually and in groups. Implicit in the choice of a specific way of life is an "insular" attitude, a desire to be apart. This attitude can either lean towards the typical values of one's own group against the background of respect for the values of other groups, or it can be orientated towards one's own values, seen as the opposite of those of other groups, whose values are despised. In the first case the isolating inclination of the group is considerably less strong than in the latter.

Cultures and subcultures are not stagnant. Antagonism between groups may vanish. For instance, in most countries social discord between Catholics and Protestants has disappeared, as has the implicit discrimination in the labour, capital and consumer-goods markets. However, new contrasts are being formed, *e.g.* by the arrival of new communities of foreign workers. In any subculture people are constantly being confronted with questions as to how they are supposed to behave towards members of their own group and towards those of other groups. The answer is not an economic one, although it generally has economic facets. It is essential to know what the economic effects are, so that they can be taken into account.

Economic sacrifices caused by cultural isolation. The origins of the social costs of cultural isolation are found in what is, in practice, an insular mentality and an insular behaviour. It is culturally isolating to have a clear vision of the differences between one's own values and those of others, but to shut one's eyes to the common values in religion and ideology. Closely connected to this is the inability to put oneself in the ethical world of the other man, in order to find a consensus that can serve as a basis for economic cooperation. The same effect is found in the idea of "repaying evil with evil", without feeling the need to make the first step towards a better mutual understanding. These forms of isolating behaviour result in the point of view that it is no use giving "the other person" a chance.

In general, it is not possible to quantify the effect of insular behaviour on production costs. What can be done is to indicate what the character of these costs may be and who has to bear them. Some disadvantages of isolation primarily affect the economic welfare of society as a whole. If, when selecting senior staff, a specific cultural qualification is asked for in addition to ability, then the principle "the right person in the right place" may be frustrated. Therefore, the level of production may be lower than would otherwise be the case, either in a quantitative or in a qualitative respect. The same reasoning is true for the factor capital. Since another argument is required beside economic ones, capital may not be allocated to the most productive applications. Furthermore, it is possible that the cultural motive in economic transactions splits markets up into comparatively small segments. In many cases, economic welfare is under pressure from diseconomies of scale.

I also want to draw attention to the economic disadvantages of socially isolating behaviour, in cases where the disadvantages are dispersed over the various groups in a biased way. They are found in a situation in which one cultural group has to bear a heavier load than the others. I have already mentioned the example of a society with both a well-to-do and a poor community. Here the question is whether the household bears the costs of its isolating behaviour itself, or whether the burden is shared by members of the other group. If the cultural contrasts are so strong that a system of transfers of income from the rich to the poor is not feasible, then the welfare of the poor is the most affected. The other side of the story is that intercultural connections can sometimes form the basis for a remarkable joint economic effort by the members of society. Look, for example, at the settlements of Europeans in Canada after the Second World War. Yet this kind of group formation is, in principle, fully compatible with a cooperative attitude towards members of other groups, as mentioned below.

Economic benefits of cultural interaction. In order to gain insights into the economic benefits of cooperating intercultural behaviour, it is useful to define what is meant by this. In this approach, intercultural cooperation is the respecting, understanding, or tolerance of the values of the other groups, and the striving for the accommodation of ethical differences with members of those groups. The adage for this is "give the other person a chance". How will society as a whole benefit? In certain subcultures, the development of specific personal abilities often has a better chance than in other subcultures. In production, intensive intercultural relations make it possible to profit by such specific abilities. Advantage can thus be taken of an improved division of labour and economies of scale. Furthermore, cultural interaction may have a favourable effect on the distribution of income. The opportunities for earning an income and for being able to bear the costs of living are generally greater than in the context of insular behaviour.

* *

In conclusion, it must be said that cultural diversification has a significant economic aspect to it. Given the fact of cultural pluralism, a personal inclination to isolation is in contrast to an inclination to cooperate in a multi-cultural way. The decision on how to act in this field may have an impact on the welfare of society as a whole, as well as on the distribution of wealth within it. This view is compatible with Schmoller's approach, in which society's evolving ethical system determines the economic system. It leads to the conclusion that there are no economic arguments for "insular" social behaviour.

Chapter 13
ECONOMIC SYSTEMS THEORY

The first report by Club of Rome, *The limits to growth* (D.H. Meadows *et al.*), appeared in 1972 and contributed considerably to the opening of the eyes of the world to the seriousness of the present-day's environmental problem. It convinced many scientists of the significance of "systems thinking", in both quantitative and qualitative terms, for solving problems in the field of interactions between economy and natural environment. This way of thinking was mainly mechanistic, which put a stamp on its conclusions. Jay Forrester (1971) supplied the basic model. His son, Nathan Forrester (1973), and D.L. Meadows *et al.* (1974) made it clear that such models can have an organic trait, giving attention to "life cycle" aspects. The Club of Rome's second report had a clear organistic dimension (Mesarovic and Pestel, 1974).

Recently, Henk Folmer and Ekko van Ierland made a plea for a systematic valuation of the environment and a purposeful institutional policy in the environmental field.

> [W]ith a zero price for environmental use, the economic system does not include control mechanisms to check an overuse of the environment and a distortion of the sectoral structure. Hence, an important contribution of economics to a solution to the environmental problem would be the transformation of environmental scarcity to signals which would start off this control mechanism (Folmer *et al.*, 1989: p. 3).

General characteristics

The basis of the Club of Rome model is the so-called DYNAMO approach, found in J.W. Forrester's publications of 1961 and 1986. What is characteristic of this approach are its flow diagrams, dynamic equations, and graphical output.

> A flow diagram is an illustration of the postulated relationships between the elements in a model system. It depicts the model assumptions with a degree of detail midway between the dynamically suggestive but incomplete causal-loop diagram and the detailed, precise DYNAMO equations. ... Complex social systems do not respond immediately and completely to changing conditions and inputs. ... In system dynamics models, a delay is represented by a combination of rates and levels. (D.L. Meadows *et al.*, 1974: pp. 595, 605.)

The combination of diagrams, equations and graphs is also found in Howard Odum's systems ecology. In principle, economic systems and humanity-oriented systems in general are approached in the same way as typically "natural" systems (Odum, 1983). This type of systems theory finds special application in the field of environmental economics, in which economy and ecology meet. Barry Richmond, one of Jay Forrester's followers, developed the STELLA model. Acknowledging the interplay of multiple causal forces, he orientated this model especially towards processes of historical change in the exploitation of land. The main "building blocks" of the model include stocks, flows, converters (to calculate rates of flows), and connectors (transmitting information) (Potash, 1994: p. 36).

Economic systems theory attempts to reconcile the idea of organistic equilibrium with Tinbergen's primarily mechanistic approach. The latter implies that an equilibrium is stable if, after an external disturbance, the original situation is restored by forces of the system itself. If dynamics is not directed towards equilibrium in this way, then there is a repeating cyclical development, or either a gradual deformation of the system or an explosive one (Tinbergen, 1943). In biologically oriented dynamics, the central idea is "evolution", with its aspects of historical modification and organic growth. In dynamics of the Tinbergen and Frisch type, however, a model is considered dynamic if its equations refer to different periods.

A central idea in the systems theory's regulating mechanism is "feedback". By this is meant that a regulating signal is transmitted into the system in one way or another. One effect can be that the system remains in a stationary state. In other cases the impulse is either gradually weakened or reinforced, resulting in different responses of the system. Feedback can also be expressed in organic terms.

> Perhaps the best-known example of negative feedback on a planetary scale is provided in a theory advanced by James Lovelock, an English scientist. Called the *Gaia hypothesis* after the Greek concept for Mother Earth, this view of the world suggests that the earth is a living organism with a complex feedback system that seeks an optimal physical and chemical environment. Deviations from this optimal environment trigger natural, nonhuman response mechanisms that restore the balance. (Tietenberg, 1994: p. 7; italics in original.)

It is in the nature of things that studies on developing economic systems contain historical elements. In this connection, I refer to George Dalton.

> We are learning that each nation's history and political tradition are important in shaping its policy goals, policy instruments and basic economic institutions. (Dalton, 1974, 1975: p. 21.)

Discussing the British "industrial revolution", Dalton mentioned the various components of the process of socio-economic change.

> In its widest meaning the Industrial Revolution is the technological component of what we now call economic development and cultural modernization: a set of mutually reinforcing structural transformations which are revolutionary in the extent to which personal, social and political as well as economic life are made to change. (Dalton, 1974, 1975: p. 51.)

The word "life" in this citation testifies to an organically oriented and evolutionary view.

In 1960 *The stages of economic growth* appeared from the pen of the economic historian, W.W. Rostow, and is reminiscent of the Historical School's *Stufen* approach. The book distinguishes five development stages: the traditional society, the stage of take-off, the drive to maturity, the age of mass-consumption and a stage characterized as "being beyond consumption". The approach is not purely descriptive, but is also a "dynamic theory" of development.

> [S]ocieties have made [decisions] as the choices open to them have been altered by the unfolding process of economic growth; and these broad collective decisions, determined by many factors - deep in history, culture, and the active political process - outside the market-place, have interplayed with the dynamics of market demand, risk-taking, technology and entrepreneurship, to determine the specific contents of the stages of growth for each society. (Rostow, 1960, 1961: p. 15.)

To a certain extent, Rostow's approach fits in with the Institutional current of thought. However, it is also orientated towards dynamic systems theory.

Barry Field (1989) presented a theory of the evolution of property institutions on the basis of the development of transaction costs and property rights under the influence of political and demographic factors. Furthermore, there is also a theory of "societal" systems.

> The Theory of Societal Systems integrates well known sociological, social psychological and economic concepts from the areas of stratification, mobility, social change, status crystallization, symbolic interaction and marginal utility, or at least elements of them. (Hoffmann-Nowotny, 1981: p. 65.)

Geert Hofstede used systems theory concepts to explain the "stabilizing of culture patterns", distinguishing external and internal factors and a process of reinforcement of existing cultural values. He included environmental and technological factors in the picture of culture (Hofstede, 1984: p. 22). Earlier, Pareto had made a fundamental analysis of human culture, distinguishing "residues", related to certain human feelings, beliefs, inclinations, instincts, and other illogically oriented desires, which have a certain permanence, regularity or development, and "derivatives", to be derived logically from the residues. He described the "properties" of residues and derivatives, and indicated their significance to society, presenting a picture of the developing social structure (Pareto, 1935; Eisermann, 1962).

An effective use of the systems theory in economics requires an interdisciplinary approach. Malte Faber and John Proops (1985) urged this, discussing its retrospect and prospect. The authors dealt with the subjects of energy, time, irreversibility, entropy, physical constraints and technological progress.

> [T]here are a wide range of problems, which are of pressing nature, where the economists' and physical scientists' frameworks for analysis are, individually, insufficient for the task. Only by breaking down these conceptual barriers and establishing a wider and more open framework for discourse is progress likely to be made. (Faber and Proops, 1985: p. 612.)

An example of an interdisciplinary approach is Frank den Butter's study on the use of environmental indicators in economics. On the one hand, the indices themselves are of a natural science nature and, on the other, they are correlated with economic magnitudes (den Butter, 1992: pp. 49-75). Jan Renkema and Ada Wossink referred to the idea of interdisciplinarity, stating that Farm Management (a specific branch of agricultural economics) rests on two pillars: (a) sciences of nature, mathematics and statistics, and their applications to agriculture, and (b) social sciences, directed towards human behaviour (Renkema *et al.*, 1993: p. 149).

Organicism in economic systems theory

It should have already become clear that economic systems may have historistic and evolutionary traits, and that there is ample room for organic concepts and constructions within the picture of economic systems theory. In this study, economic systems' organic features deserve special attention. An important part is played by the interaction between economics and ecology, in the field of which the research is, to some extent, 'orientated towards an integrative approach to economics and ecology, *i.e.*, to the design of methods, techniques and tools for a cohesive evaluation, by which values and objectives in both the environmental and the socio-economic area are simultaneously taken into consideration' (Archibugi, Nijkamp and Soeteman, 1989: pp. 2-3). I also refer to Carl Folke's socio-economic idea of "the life-supporting environment", put forward in an essay by the "Eco-Eco Group" (Folke, 1991: pp. 77*ff*).

Systems are characterized by structures of relations. Both the typically economic and the environmental phenomena have features of an organic nature. Sometimes systems are subsystems of a more extensive whole, and consist of subsystems themselves. This is the "system of systems" idea. Peter Nijkamp presented a systems approach to the economy rooted in nature, distinguishing between interactions within subsystems, called *intra*-relations, and interactions between subsystems, called *inter*-relations (Nijkamp, 1979: p. 65).

Ecology deals with mutual interactions of organisms in the context of an adapting physical environment. Herman Daly contributed to the integration of this type of systems theory into economic thought. He used the term "steady-state" in an economic sense. Heijman (1991: p. 38) defined steady-state, as far as renewable resources are concerned, as 'a situation in which human use of nature expressed in physical terms equals natural production'. Between the input and the output of economic processes Daly placed a "throughput" of matter and energy. This throughput should remain between certain limits if a crackdown of the system is to be prevented. In this connection he used the idea of "durability" of stocks of natural resources.

> *Durability* means more than just how long a particular commodity lasts. It also includes the efficiency with which the after-use "corpse" of a commodity can be recycled as an input to be born again as the same of a different commodity. (Daly, 1973 1980: p. 17; italics in original.)

Nijkamp and Soeteman discussed models that are applicable to sustainability policy. They urged the introduction of specific ecologically oriented ideas, mentioning the concepts of "sustainable yield", "carrying capacity" and "resilience".

> *Sustainable yield*: This concept is related to a control strategy for renewable resources in which economic benefit objectives preclude an exhaustion in the long run. It is a well-known strategy in forestry and fishery management models.
> *Carrying capacity*: The concept refers to the level of activities of a certain species that can in the long run be maintained given the regional resources. It is a well-known concept in predator-prey models; see Vincent (1981).
> *Resilience*: This concept refers to the vulnerability or the self-adjustment of an ecosystem; within certain limits a stable growth may occur, but beyond a threshold level a bifurcation may emerge forcing the system to move to a qualitatively different level. In this framework risk assessment models may be helpful; cf. Brooks (1986). (Nijkamp *et al*, 1988: p. 97; emphases in original.)

R.E. Munn mentioned the ecologist C.S. Holling (1986) as the first person to use the idea of resilience in a ecosystem context, arguing that the environment is never in a "steady state".

> Holling introduced the term *resilience* as a measure of the ability of an ecosystem to adapt to a continuously changing environment, being able to absorb external shocks without major structural damage. (Munn, 1989: p. 54; emphasizing in original.)

The work of the biologist L. *von* Bertalanffy has been of considerable importance to evolutionary thought, also in economics. He approached the concept of organic equilibrium or

Table 1: Attributes of mechanical and organic ideal types according to Sutherland

Attributes	*Mechanical ideal type*	*Organic ideal type*
Interface	Usually exists within well-defined, tangible boundaries which may be adjusted endogenously for greater or lesser selectivity with respect to entering or exiting forces.	Highly *open* with respect to environment and exogenous forces. External determinants which affect the system may, therefore, be too far removed (spatially or temporally) to be analytically observable at any point of time.
Structural characteristics:	Generally has its components arrayed in a neat, observable hierarchy such that properties at one level tend to be extrapolations of properties at other levels, with relationships among the various levels being essentially *deterministic*.	Parts are not arrayed in a neat, stable hierarchy but *stochastically*, with the structure and direction of interrelationships generally altering almost constantly in response to localized changes of environmental influences, etc.
Dynamic properties:	Parts are usually highly *constrained*, having only a limited repertoire of responses permitted them; causal trajectories and paths of interaction are generally fixed, controllable and exclusive; driving forces are generally tangible and measurable.	Parts have potential for inaugurating opportunistic or strategic behavior in response to local parameter changes; causal trajectories may be altered locally and interactions may be equifinal; dynamic (driving) forces may be transparent rather than tangible and manipulable.
Normative analytical properties:	*Potentially total:* - observability - measurability - manipulability - predictability	*At least partial:* - empirical inaccessibility - immeasurability - imperfect controllability - unpredictability
Amenability to inference and induction:	Given initial state conditions, future states may be induced with a high probability of accuracy.	Future state conditions cannot be successfully inferred from initial state conditions.

Source: Sutherland (1973; emphases in original)

"steady state" through the idea of *Fliessgleichgewicht*, "flow statics" or "flowing equilibrium". This refers to the idea of a flow of material and energy in a system with a stable structure. The structure of an organic system is maintained by a purposeful steering mechanism (Bertalanffy, 1950). In an article on mechanistic and organistic analogies, Thoben, referring to Bertalanffy, noticed that characteristics of organic systems, as far as they are not derived from those of elements of the system, can be expressed in holistic terms. This includes the *Gestalt* idea, originating in psychology.

> The basic characteristic of the systems approach is that the objects under study are considered as systems, *i.e.* as sets of interconnected elements representing a single whole. (Thoben, 1982: p. 299.)

In his work on the behavioural systems theory, John Sutherland placed the organistic approach alongside the mechanistic (1973). Comparing the characteristics of both, he pointed out the significance and the limitations of organically oriented thought. (See Table 1.)

Kenneth Boulding (1981) advocated an "evolutionary" approach for specific problems in economics, alongside a "mechanistic" one. This analysis focusses on both natural and institutional factors, which determine the development process. Entropy is seen as loss of potential. Boulding's approach agrees with the ecologically oriented economic systems theory, although organic aspects do not play a dominant part. However, the ideas of "organic equilibrium" and "steady-state", mentioned above, fit in with this. Thanks to a "purposeful" steering mechanism, the structure of the system remains. Andries Nentjes and Doede Wiersma discussed Boulding's idea of "spaceship Earth".

> Boulding applied the systems approach to economic development. Systems can be defined as being open or closed for inputs and outputs. ... [He] distinguished three classes of inputs and outputs for economic development: matter, energy and information. ... Because of the finite resources of materials and fossil energy and the limited storage capacity for waste from production and consumption processes, the economic system has to be viewed as a closed system. (Nentjes *et al.*, 1992: p. 147.)

Referring to Malthus' work two centuries earlier, the economic historian Robert Fogel discussed various human life-cycle aspects and other organically oriented factors in economic development and their impact on growth rates.

> Focusing on the thermodynamic and physiological aspects of economic growth calls attention to the long lags that frequently occur between the time that certain investments are made and the time that their benefits occur. (Fogel, 1994: p. 388.)

Furthermore, in his dissertation Willem Heijman mentioned "ecologism" as a paradigm in economics. He said that, on the one hand, the weak point of the evolutionary approach is that it cannot make predictions while, on the other, the advantage of it is that the past can be reconstructed, thus providing a genetic explanation for what exists (Heijman, 1991: p. 31). Finally, I mention that in an organistic approach the question arises what is "sound" and what is not. This question was put by the philosopher Carl Friedrich *von* Weizsäcker, who understood both man and society as organisms.

> "Socially sound" is an individual whose standard of behaviour contributes to the maintenance of the community. More precisely, whose standard of behaviour is a part of the sound behaviour norm of the whole group.[103] (Weizsäcker, 1971, 1982: p. 334.)

---

[103] "Sozial gesund" ist ein Individuum, dessen Verhaltensnorm zur Erhaltung der Gemeinschaft beiträgt; genauer: dessen Verhaltensnorm Teilnorm der gesunden Verhaltensnorm der ganzen Gruppe ist.

Chapter 14
EFFICIENT SUSTAINABILITY: AN INSTITUTIONAL APPROACH

This chapter is an application of institutional principles which are rooted in historistic and organistic thought.[104] In both the Historical School and circles of Institutionalists it was understood that the institutional structure is an important issue in economics. This was also concluded by Johan Torstensson (1994), who investigated the impact on economic growth of well-enforced *versus* not well-enforced property rights. He found that arbitrary seizures of property, taken instead of regular taxes, decelerate growth, and insecure property rights leads to an inefficient allocation of capital. However, the institutional structure itself is also of great importance for achieving efficiency in society.

The world of the economy, controlled by the market, and the world of nature can be seen as antipoles, in which many processes are not tuned to one another and in which economic processes often affect the quality of the environment. This representation of things is realistic in various respects. Yet, environmental policy is being directed towards integrating economic processes into natural ecosystems, as well as to economizing on stocks of natural resources. This policy includes direct prescriptions on the way production and consumption is supposed to take place, which "regulations" are based on the priority given to the preservation of nature. Thus, the relation between economy and nature is not *per se* one of conflict. This relationship can also be seen as one of interaction and mutual dependency, in which the market mechanism functions as an important element of environmental policy. For this, however, a number of institutional conditions must be fulfilled.

The question of economic and environmental policies which are harmoniously tuned towards one another can be approached in different ways. In this chapter the idea of efficiency is central. The point of departure is the static efficiency idea, directed towards typically "economic" magnitudes and related to goods which are traditionally negotiated. The institutional context within which the economic process takes place is, in this initial

---

[104]Chapter 14 is partly based on Krabbe, 1994.

approach, considered to be given. To include processes of the world of nature in the analysis, this elementary efficiency idea should be extended at various points: the dynamization of the static economic model, to which the original efficiency idea refers, the incorporation of the institutional structure into the model and, finally, the integration of components of nature into the economic model. These components of nature then function as "scarce magnitudes", bearing a price. Therefore, I also discuss the issues of elementary, dynamic, institutional, and environmental efficiency. The latter idea characterizes "efficient sustainability", the subject of this chapter. In fact, efficiency and sustainability are different ideas. However, these ideas can be linked to one another if the sustainability idea is conceived of in a holistic way, including all substitution effects, both those in the domain of production and those in the consumption domain.

Efficiency and its dynamization

As economists want to make use of nature in an efficient way, a consideration of the elementary efficiency idea is in order. Efficient behaviour is acting according to the economic principle, already formulated by Wilhelm Roscher, which boils down to achieving the most with a given amount of means or, what comes to the same, to realizing a certain result with the least "scarce" means. In fact, this is a point of departure in economic thought. As such, there has been little discussion about it. Yet, problems arise if questions are asked about how to measure cost elements, on the one hand, and revenue and utility elements, on the other; about what weights should be given to these elements in the operation of aggregation and comparison of costs and benefits. The traditional answer, given in the nineteenth century, is that the quanta of the goods concerned are given by those which are negotiated, and their weights by the prices which come into being on the market. This principle is still accepted, though with the reservation that if specific problems are under investigation, such as the valuation of elements of nature, the procedure of aggregation and comparison should be considerably extended and fundamentally adapted.

The model which the old economists had in mind, at least the Classical-oriented writers, was that of an economy with markets of full competition, in which none of the participants are in a position to influence the price level. Monopolies were considered harmful, frustrating the efficiency principle. Thus, the efficiency idea has long been tied to a specific economic model. Originally it was a model of "natural order", an idea that stemmed from the Enlightenment, which concept was orientated towards the system of the cosmos. Nevertheless, the eighteenth-century Physiocrats also had the ecosystem in mind. In the nineteenth century, ecologically oriented economic thought was found in the German authors discussed in this study. Today it is a topical subject in economics.

In the field of interaction between economy and nature, a number of evolutionary processes take place. Population, production technology and environmental technology (an aspect of the latter), natural stocks and the environment of life in general are all subjects of related processes of development. The model to which the efficiency standard refers ought to be one that can express these dynamics. Therefore, the originally static economic model should be "dynamicized". I have already mentioned the contributions by Tinbergen and Frisch in this field. In this way the efficiency standard becomes a dynamic concept.

Institutional efficiency. An effective government policy is necessary for a proper management of the environment, whether it concerns the exploitation of natural resources by a system of concessions and royalties or the protection of the environment of life. This implies that the institutional context of the market process should be included into the efficiency analysis. Thus, the dynamization of the efficiency idea has an aspect that deserves special attention: institutional development. Referring to Schumpeter, K.F. Zimmermann (1987) used the term "dynamic efficiency" for problems like this. When speaking of "institutional efficiency", I refer to the institutional aspect of this dynamic efficiency.

In a well-organized democratic society, it is one of the aims of "economic structure policy" to maintain and improve a basic system of institutions that is focussed on economic efficiency. Efficiency is not fully defined by "hedonistic" preferences and "natural order" concepts. In my view, it also contains social judgements about the degree of scarcity of natural means of production which are available, not only for the present, but for the future as well. This is particularly true if this policy is focussed on "sustainable development". Economic structure policy forms part of an overall economic policy. With regard to the former, one of the major concerns of politicians is about the basic structure of the system of economic interactions in society, which is an evolving system. Other branches of economic policy are directed towards the correction of deviations from this basic dynamic system, for example, business cycle effects. An additional set of instruments is used to modify such deviations, achieving specific aims which complements those of the system of basic institutions. Thus, I consider only the institutional framework of the economic process as far as it centres on structural "institutional efficiency", placed in the context of sustainability policy.

Institutionally determined efficiency. The institutional message of the Classical economists was *laissez faire*, a term adopted from the eighteenth-century Physiocrats. Present-day transformations of East-European centralized economies into market-oriented systems prove that the message is of classical significance indeed, as it became abundantly clear that the ordering function of the market mechanism cannot be ignored. However, in the

Free World, political elements entered the structure of the "natural" system in the course of time. These elements include social security laws, other measures to maintain the idea of the welfare state, and, more recently, measures for the preservation of nature. Such modifications of the economic system are not thought to affect efficiency in society. In fact, the perception of social efficiency itself is changing. Making the socio-economic system more humane implies a modification of the efficiency idea. This section outlines the structure of a contemporary "efficiency determining basic system".

In my doctoral thesis I elaborated the idea of complementarity between individual wants and the individual's needs for social goods. In this view, social security allowances and other income transfers do not affect social efficiency. I agree that in this field political struggle plays a part. Political interaction, however, takes place within an institutional framework, which is supposed to be acceptable to all. In welfare theory, efficiency is usually characterized by a "Paretian optimum", determined by a system of individual welfare and production functions. This is also within the scope of my analysis. In this study, however, this approach is broader and also includes institutional change, consistent with changing welfare functions. This is referred to in terms of "institutional efficiency".

Efficiency in society can be considered according to various principles. The following approach is a somewhat specific one. I account for the degree of income equality among welfare determining factors, considering it decisive for indicating an *optimum optimorem*, in the sense that a choice is made out of various socio-economic situations, characterized by different distributions of incomes. This type of thinking orders the various attainable situations from a political point of view, according to social preference. On this basis, an optimum income distribution can be determined (Krabbe, 1974).

I connect the efficiency concept with the situation in which social welfare is maximized structurally from an institutional point of view. A situation is considered institutionally efficient if the dominating political conviction is that the structure of efficiency-oriented institutions cannot be improved. Van den Noort (1983), when referring to welfare theory in general and to Tinbergen (1975) specifically, made a plea for a social aims function (Ω) that is operational in economic policy. According to van den Noort, the function should be based on preferences that are manifested in the world of socio-economic policy. My concept of institutional efficiency is along this line of thinking.

Economic policy has consequences for the present as well as for future welfare. A concise way of giving expression to this is by making use of the magnitudes of national income (Y), the degree of income equality (α), and a quality index of nature (N). Then efficiency is given by:

1. $Max\ \Omega = \phi(Y_1,...,Y_t,\ \alpha,\ N_1,...,N_t)$,

where the subscript t refers to the time horizon of public policy. The function ϕ also reflects social time preference, on the basis of certain expectations for population growth. Conditions are given by the quantities of production factors available. However, it must be realized that there is interdependency between these welfare-determining variables. First, in the proximity of the equilibrium value of α, besides an increasing function ϕ, there is the decreasing function ψ:

2. $Y_1 = \psi(\alpha)$

This equation expresses that, within a certain range of values of α, an increase of the degree of income equality may weaken production incentives in the system (Krabbe, 1974). This refers especially to situations in countries like the Netherlands and Sweden in which incomes, to a large degree, are levelled out. In countries with great income inequality the opposite might be true. (So, this approach is focussed on developed countries, not on those which are economically underdeveloped. In the latter case function ψ might increase, expressing that more equality has a positive impact on the level of Y.) Another point is that the actual perception of future income levels ($Y_{t+1},\ldots,Y_t$) contains a degree of uncertainty, related to the direction of the institutional development, which involves gradually changing priorities.

Secondly, besides the direct effect of the quality of nature on welfare, as reflected by function ϕ, there is an indirect effect through production functions:

3. $Y_i = f_i\,(N_i)$,

where functions f_i $(i=1,\ldots,t)$ reflect expectations for population growth, already mentioned, and those for the level and structure of technological development, including capital formation, to be discussed below. By mathematical elimination of α and Y_i in this system of equations, Ω becomes a function of N_i. These indices reflecting the quality of nature are endogenous magnitudes in the institutionally oriented system that is under discussion.

Distinct approaches to judgement of institutional change. The effects of institutional changes are judged *ex ante*, before political measures are taken, as well as *ex post*, determining what the measures brought about. *Ex ante* judgements are based on the present knowledge of the functioning of the economic system. *Ex post* judgements are of significance not only for obtaining additional knowledge of the system, but also for the preparation of further policy measures. Another distinction is the difference between “marginal” and "mutational" institutional change. An example of the former is a small change of a tax rate. In general, effects of marginal measures can be predicted with more certainty than those of mutational changes, particularly if mutations refer to radical changes in the institutional system. Examples of the latter can be borrowed from the construction of the Western welfare state. Many measures had to be amended after it became clear that not all effects were necessarily favourable. Other examples can be found in the present-day transition of Eastern European economies. Thus, the striving for institutional efficiency is a political process. Sometimes the process is characterized by gradual change in a certain direction; at other times by abrupt changes, which may give the development pattern a stochastic feature.

In "mechanistic economics" it is maintained that society is "to be made", in accordance with generally adopted plans. In "organically oriented economics" it is assumed that political plans often result in long-term changes that are not in full accord with rational political intentions. I agree with the idea of the relativity of the mechanistic approach.

Types of efficiency-oriented institutions

For the purpose of this analysis I define "institutions" as factors that influence behaviour in social intercourse. This definition is a pragmatic one, focussed on its effects. It is not supposed to contradict a more detailed description. Institutions which have a function in the economic system are called economic institutions. The set of economic institutions may also be defined as the economic aspect of the set of social institutions. "Institutes", the actors in society, are organizational units in the institutional sphere, sharing responsibility and authority in society. The system of institutes (actors) maintains the system of institutions, and the latter supports the first. For the distinction between institutions and institutes, I refer the reader to Gustav Schmoller. (*Grundriss* I, 1900, 1908: p. 61; see also Chapter 7 of this study). Below I discuss various types of efficiency-oriented institutions, which are subsets of the set of economic institutions in general. I distinguish the following types: those that determine the interaction pattern, prescriptive institutions, behaviour-oriented institutions, market-oriented institutions, and institutions for income transfer.

Institutions determining the interaction structure. In the field of fundamental institutions, determining the economic interaction structure, the main distinction is between production activities and consumption activities. The first I regard as those applying scarce means of production, and the second as consumer behaviour with regard to private and public goods. This distinction is typical of all developed economies. However, the institutional characteristics of households as such, in which production and consumption activities are practised, differ profoundly in various societies. Laws and other regulations, as well as customs, belong to the set of interaction-determining institutions. There are various forms of production, carried on in various types of households, *e.g.* large-scale and small-scale production units, private and government-run households. Consumption takes place in private households as well as in the public sector. The behaviour of producers and consumers, characterized as basic institutes, is influenced by a whole network of institutions. This network is maintained by institutes (actors) that are authorized to do so. Institutions which sustain these authorities should be considered as interaction-determining basic institutions. The following types of institutions also have interaction-determining aspects.

Regulations. The key feature of direct prescriptive institutions, or "regulations", is that government offices dictate what other actors in the system should or should not do. These regulations may affect actors in the system, such as households of certain types. Other institutes in the system can also be influenced by such regulations and can, in turn, influence the behaviour of households. "Prohibitive" regulations form the main type of institution in this category. This means that households are not allowed to do certain things. The impact on welfare is mainly as follows. Prohibitive regulations have a negative impact on welfare by decreasing profits. However, if the measure in question has, *e.g.* a nature-preserving character, then there is also a positive effect, either directly on individual welfare or indirectly through an increasing capacity of the production agent Nature. There may be consequences for income distribution as well, if rents are earned by firms that are less limited in their behaviour than others. Trespassing against prohibitive regulations is usually punishable by fine. If the paying of such fines becomes a morally accepted custom, the fines function as fees (discussed below). It is desirable to legalize such payments, and not to allow infringements of the law to become part of the legal economic system. "Conditional" regulations form a specific type within the category of regulation. The central idea is that the government dictates conditions of economic behaviour, including precautionary measures, such as various forms of care for human and natural resources, for man and the environment. As far as the impact on welfare is concerned, similar observations can be made as for prohibitive regulations.

Behaviour-oriented institutions. Institutions orientated towards economic behaviour are maintained by private as well as public institutes, the "actors" in society. In this area, the keywords are education, information, and the changing of attitudes. The significance of this type of institution for the system under consideration is along the lines of the impact of direct government regulations mentioned. Governments are forced to intervene if, in certain respects, voluntary behaviour fails. Nature-friendly consumers' behaviour can be reinforced by "eco-labelling", to indicate whether goods have been produced by methods which are comparatively not harmful to the environment. However, 'in certain plausible cases, the differentiation of products due to labelling may lead to increased sales of products made by both environment-friendly and environment-unfriendly goods' (Mattoo and Singh, 1994: p. 54).

Thinking of behaviour-oriented institutions, one is confronted with a fundamental difficulty in applied welfare theory. It is paradoxical to consider an improvement of economic behaviour on the basis of social priorities that are supposed to determine the original social welfare function as well as the institutional setting which comes into existence. The resolution of this paradox is to be found in that the political concept of social welfare and its components are subject to gradual change, constantly requiring adaptation of the institutional system.

Market-oriented institutions; price manipulation. Institutions having a direct impact on market behaviour are levies, *e.g.* environmental taxes and subsidies which are applied proportionately to production and sales as well as to the means of production used. Some of these levies and subsidies are related to producers' and consumers' external effects on nature. As far as levies are concerned, it is of interest to know which expenditures are financed by the funds raised. Various forms of "eco-taxes" are examples of market-oriented institutions. Turnover taxes belong to this category as well. Market-oriented institutions are typically orientated towards efficiency in social production.

One of the propagators of tradeable discharge permits is Charles Howe. According to him, in the United States such permits are mostly imposed on top of a regulatory system, as, in general, are also non-transferable eco-taxes of the European type. He rightly noticed that 'both of these key economic instruments are beginning to find appropriate and important niches in environmental planning in both the European Community and the U.S.' (Howe, 1994: p. 166).

Income transfer institutions. Institutions for the transfer of income may not only refer to payments between households, but also to those from the private to the government sphere and *vice versa.* This becomes clear in issues such as the financing of schools, railways, sewage systems, *etc.* Transfers from the private to the government sector may serve not only the financing of the public sector as such, but also facilitate the redistribution of private incomes.

Environmental efficiency

In Chapter 9 I mentioned that in his work, *Der moderne Kapitalismus*, Werner Sombart noticed that in the course of time production took on a scientific character. The further development of scientific knowledge tends to move from the sphere of independent inventors and universities to corporate research departments. He pointed out that, in a culture of capitalist production, inventions are tested with regard to profitability (Sombart, 1902, 1928 III: p. 95). In his book *The social costs of private enterprise*, K.W. Kapp (1950) questioned whether, in a capitalist society, private costs are in line with social costs. Kapp's position is that an environment-friendly technology will not develop as long as "nature goods" are too cheap, both as a resource and a depository for waste. Kapp said that economists should investigate this matter profoundly and that politicians must transform the economic system accordingly. This is what is happening at present. The basic objective of modern economic science and policy is to shape the economic system institutionally in such a way that efficient technologies spontaneously come into existence.

The institutional structure is of particular significance to the economy of nature. It should be made clear that in this context the term nature is not used in the Newtonian sense, referring to a natural order which is supposed to show itself in society. It is the whole of the world's physical and biological elements, the significance of which for man is given by its functions as a set of renewable natural production factors, as a number of depletable natural stocks, and as the environment for life. Nature can be seen as a bundle of components, some of which play an essential role in the process of production and consumption. Whether the scarcities of these natural economic agents are expressed as "prices" and, if this is the case, which factors determine their levels, depends on the system of institutions concerned. These environmental institutions shape the way in which property rights are attached to nature.

In the economic system, the scarcity of material goods, services and production factors are expressed in prices, reflecting marginal utilities, marginal productivities and marginal costs. These prices play a central part in the economic mechanism directed towards efficiency. If the efficiency standard is to be applied to components of nature, then its "prices" must have similar properties. This means that the market mechanism should be simulated. The efficient levels of royalties, land rents, and environmental levies are to be determined in such simulation models. In fact, this system is an optimization model, in which the social economic optimum represents the efficient situation. In the context of striving for a social optimum, sustainability criteria should be in line with the efficiency standard. This is because a situation of environmental efficiency, on the one hand, and a situation in which sustainable production and consumption are affected, on the other, are two incompatible ideas.

Normally, incomes from natural resources and the preservation of nature fall to the community, after deduction of reimbursements for exploration and development. However, the question should be posed for what purposes these funds are applied. The urge for government spending is very strong in modern society. The signal that public funds are exhausted means curbing expenditure. In many cases this succeeds only partly, so that budget deficits result in inflation or in the accumulation of public debts. Under such circumstances there is a strong temptation to draw on public income from nature. However, the policy which generates this flow of income is directed towards a durable use of nature. Therefore, it is obvious that these funds are spent to benefit nature, either directly or indirectly. An example of indirect spending is the financing of a decrease of the costs of labour, which calls forth a process of substituting nature by labour in their functions as factors of production.[105]

Time preference in sustainability criteria

According to my view, sustainability criteria can be expressed in terms of the rates of nature-preserving technological development, depletion of exhaustible resources, population growth, and time preference. The greater the social time preference, the greater also the demand for technological progress, for the conservation of natural resources, and for birth control. Comparing the spontaneous impact of the economy on the environment and on stocks of natural resources with the political ideal of sustainability, I consider that the actual interest rate might not sufficiently reflect the comparatively low social "time preference" for nature preservation. I attempt to explain that this discrepancy is to be eliminated in the institutional sphere, including a modification of the spontaneous price structure. Towards this end, factor substitution, in the context of institutional and technological renewal, is at the heart of the nature-preserving model.

Time preference is the preference for consumption in the present rather than consumption in the future, based on "perspective declination" of future wants. It is the main factor, alongside the demand for capital, related to its productivity, that determines interest rates. As well as reflecting an essential aspect of monetary policy, the actual level of interest also reflects the time preferences of actors in the economic system under specific circumstances and, as such, the *de facto* time preference of the economic system as a whole. Time preferences of members of society for sustainable production, however, could be considerably below this level.

According to Hotelling's rule, a determining factor in the process of utilizing natural resources is the level of interest. Yet, the rate of depletion that is considered desirable in

[105]Substitution effects are also discussed in the next chapter and the appendix to this study.

preservation policy might be substantially below that of the spontaneous depletion of natural resources in a system of *laissez faire*. Thus, in general, a low interest rate is favourable for the preservation of natural resources. However, an artificial lowering of the rate of interest will not solve the problem, since interest rates affect various parts of the economic system differently. This implies that making interest rates fully subservient to preservation policy would deregulate the economy, because socio-economic aims such as monetary equilibrium and employment would receive insufficient attention. Therefore, nature-benign technology should be mainly achieved through institutional changes. I already made it clear that this policy has two main dimensions: direct regulations for producers and consumers and modification of the price structure, "price manipulation". The latter modification means that production factors and products which, from a social point of view are scarcer than is spontaneously expressed in its prices through uncontrolled *laissez faire*, become comparatively more expensive through institutional impacts on the price structure.

The term sustainability expresses a judgement about certain patterns of economic development. This implies realistic prognoses about technological progress and, on that basis, determining a "normative discount rate" for future needs. This norm should be developed in the political process of a community of people who accept responsibility for the future of mankind. In valuing nature, a crucial part is played by expectations of the intensity and character of technological development. The substitution of components of nature that gradually become scarcer by components that will be less scarce form an important element in this picture, although there exists much uncertainty about substitution opportunities in the future.

A criterion for sustainability can be formulated on the basis of these ideas. For this purpose, I subdivide nature into depletable production factors (n_d), renewable production factors (n_r), and direct environment of life (n_e). Furthermore, I distinguish between the rates of time preference (f), the depletion of natural stocks (d), the technological progress that is preserving depletable nature (h_d), and the technological progress that is economizing renewable nature (h_r).

Leaving n_d and n_e out of consideration, the production function is:

4. $y = y_r(n_r)$,

or in linear form,

5. $y = \alpha\ n_r$,

in which r refers to "renewable nature", supposed to be the only production factor. In this case the sustainability criterion takes the form:

6. $$\int_0^\infty \alpha\,(e^{it} - 1)n_r\,dt \geq 0 \quad (i = h_r - f)\,,\quad or$$

7. $$h_r - f \geq 0$$

If n_e is included, which means that the environment of life is also taken into account, then social welfare (w) is:

8. $$w = \phi(y, n_e) \quad \Rightarrow \quad w = \psi(n_r, n_e)$$

The rate of degeneration (k) of the direct environment of life is rarely subject to compensation. Let the maximum degeneration rate (k^*) considered to be acceptable be equal to the minimum rate that is feasible. Then the sustainability criterion is:

9. $$h_r - f \geq v\,k^*,$$

where the parameter v represents the weight of environmental degradation in the social welfare function. This means that technological progress must outweigh the sum of time preference and a term reflecting the degeneration of the environment of life.
If n_r is not included, and $y = \beta\, n_d$, the criterion is:

10. $$\int_0^\infty \beta\, d\,(e^{jt} - 1)n_d\,dt \geq v\,k* \quad (j = h_d - d - f)\,,\quad or$$

11. $$h_d - d - f \geq v\,k^*$$

This is valid if “exhaustible nature” is supposed to be the only production factor. In this situation technological progress must also outweigh the depletion of nature, as well as the terms like those mentioned in Equation 9.

Finally, I want to consider the case where all aspects of nature are relevant. The rate of population growth (g) and its weight (z) in the welfare function are also included. If the production and the welfare functions are linearized, the sustainability criterion then is:

$$12.\quad \int_0^\infty (e^{it} - 1)n_r\, dt + a \int_0^\infty d\,(e^{jt} - 1)n_d\, dt \geq v\, k* + z\, g\,,$$

$$(a > 0)\quad (i = h_r - f\,;\; j = h_d - d - f)\,,$$

with the magnitudes f, d and h being in hundredths of a percent (10^{-4}). Unfortunately, this equation cannot be expressed as simply as Equations 7 and 11. The left term of Equation 12 is a "compound" of Equations 9 and 11.

The crucial political question is whether nature-preserving technological development will offset the effects of time preference, depletion of nature, and population growth (Krabbe, 1992b; 1993b).

Environmental economic engineering

Engineering can be defined as the developing of production processes, to which end tools and products in general are designed and new organizational structures introduced. In engineering, creativity and sciences play crucial parts. One of these sciences is economics. In the designing process economic behaviour also intuitively takes place. The development of production processes and the design of products require the application of means of production not available in unlimited quantities. These are human resources and components of nature of various kinds, and products in which such original production factors are incorporated. From a technological point of view, production factors can mostly be applied in varying proportions. From an economic point of view, however, it is which design will be applied that is important: the one that most favours cost-benefit proportion being preferred. To determine this proportion, it is necessary to attach a price to production factors. Thus, an important part in engineering is played by the price ratios of the various means of production, reflecting the scarcity ratios of the production factors which are applied.

In designing a product, the prices of the various goods involved have a specific function. This refers not only to prices of goods, including services, which serve as means of production, but also to products and services that play a part in the utilization of the product designed. An illustration of this is found in car design, where wages and the prices of raw materials and intermediate products must be known. Yet, the design should also be tuned to the price of petrol, to insurance tariffs and such like. Therefore, within the scope of engineering are "product analysis" and "product development". Product analysis has a specifically economic aspect, based on the idea that, in many cases, products can be considered bundles of scarce properties. Carl Menger had already stressed that properties of goods are of crucial importance in economics. He noticed that wants must be seen in their relation to properties of scarce things: private and public goods. The next step was set by Kelvin Lancaster (1966), who maintained the idea of shadow prices of properties of economic goods.

When thinking in terms of scarce properties, the following theoretical problem arises in the context of product development. It is possible to vary a certain property of a heterogenous good, by considering a set of variants of the good. However, in many cases it is not possible to determine the effect on the production cost of the product concerned under the *ceteris paribus* condition for the other properties of the heterogenous good, since there is often complementarity of a technological nature between various product properties. So the designer has to ask what combination of properties best fits into the relevant preference structure, given the prices of the various variants of the heterogenous good. The idea of a good being a bundle of scarce properties can also be applied to social goods such as components of the natural environment (Krabbe, 1974).

A basic question of engineering concerns the interests that are to be served. In the car example, there are not only the typical interests of a "representative user", but also those of other participants in the traffic. The interests of people whose welfare is affected by environmental effects play a part as well. Specific interests are protected by legal regulations and "price manipulation". This means that, in fact, government agencies participate in the engineering process. This shows that the social process of engineering is a complicated one, with different designers focussing on specific properties of products and specific characteristics of the process of production and consumption. It can be said that, in the private sector, engineering takes place within the context of a system of laws. However, this does not mean that the private contribution to design is only orientated towards the hedonist interests of buyers of the products concerned. The interests of other members of society, if not already protected by government measures, also play a part.

Engineering, in its global sense, is orientated towards the whole of the production process. In both the private and the government sphere, many actors make a contribution to a particular design. These actors are coordinated by the market mechanism, functioning within an evolving institutional framework. Every actor has its own responsibility, for which it executes various tasks. The scope of a certain participation in an engineering project is given by a specific task.

Economic cybernetics

Analysing the character and the functioning of the efficiency-oriented system, one must keep in mind that in the "chaos" of economic data, various systems can be perceived. The model under discussion not only represents a theory about decisions of economic actors under given circumstances, but attention is also directed towards the various types of conditions under which decision making takes place. This is the question which has also been raised by Gustav Schmoller (*Grundriss* I) and, recently, by the late Nicholas Georgescu-Roegen (1971).

The centre of the efficiency-oriented system is formed by a system of decision-making by economic actors. This decision system refers to the formation and application of means of production being the basic allocation system; it contains within itself a system of institutions and a system of actors that maintain it. The set of economic actors consists not only of consumption and production households, but also of actors that indirectly contribute to the allocation of the factors of production. Basic institutions are the consumption and production households' striving for efficiency, from their specific points of view, under given circumstances. This basic behaviour is affected by other institutions. Institutions are realizations of (sometimes conflicting) aims of economic actors. Thus, the system of efficiency-oriented institutions rests on a system of preferences of all economic actors involved. However, these preferences are related to circumstances, *e.g.* the levels, structures and developments of technology, population and natural resources, including environmental quality. Therefore, the decision system concerned needs to contain sets of data in these areas. On the crucial question in economics of how to analyse this complex of phenomena, the last word has not yet been spoken. Yet some points are clear enough. It is in line with economic tradition to approach the economic decision system with the help of welfare theory, including property rights theory. Thinking primarily in these terms, one can state that the influence of institutional change manifests itself in the modification of decision functions of economic actors, and in extending existing optimization units by special functional relationships and additional constraints.

The use of human and natural resources is, on the one hand, a necessary condition for production. On the other hand, degradation of capacities of natural resources is the result of the process of production and consumption. Thus, institutions are related to resources along two lines. Furthermore, it must be realized that, in a sense, man himself is also part of "nature". Depending on the type of subsystem under consideration, thought is of a specific kind. Logic has either a welfare-economic character, a politico-ethical one, a biology-oriented one, or a physics-oriented one. Therefore, the social aims function (Equation 1) presented in the first section of this essay should be understood empirically. It expresses economic actors' ideas of efficiency, exercised through the institutional system under specific environmental circumstances. These ideas may differ from actor to actor; the weight of any idea depends on the structure of the system and the actor's place in it. In the system various types of interdependency can be perceived. Interdependency in the rational or ethical sphere is such that actors condition each other's decisions. Causalities in rational or ethical sphere is such that actors condition each other's decisions. Causalities in the sphere of nature, however, play a part as well. So, institutions are rooted in the rational sphere, and also in the biological and physical spheres. Although the economic cybernetic system contains a clear biological component, as a whole it should not be considered an organism. However, there are similarities with organic systems. Both types of systems are characterized by interdependencies, and by a certain purposefulness, to which various system elements contribute. Therefore, the use of organically oriented terms, such as "evolution", must not be rejected on *a priori* grounds.

Thus, it can be maintained that, in social intercourse, efficiency is the result of a political process in which various types of institutions play a part. In a system of *laissez faire* the rate of interest might have a negative impact on nature. This should be corrected through various institutional measures affecting producers' and consumers' decision patterns. For this purpose, sustainability criteria can be formulated, indicating that technological development must offset time preference, the depletion of nature, and population growth. The above cybernetic model of institutional controlling of the economic system reflects environmental aspects of European and of North American economies' institutional frameworks that have evolved over the last few decades.

Chapter 15
PERSPECTIVES OF ORGANISTIC THOUGHT

Economic development can be outlined in various ways, according to how it is analysed. This particularly applies to the process of industrialization of the Western world. So, two contrasting ideas of development can be put forward. Economic science arose from the philosophy of the Enlightenment, a way of thinking that has left a lasting stamp on economic thought. This has the advantage that explanations of the functioning of nature put forward by physicists can easily be assimilated into the pattern of economic thinking. A disadvantage is that economic thought can easily function as a sounding board for aprioristic optimism about economic development in the future. This is because welfare optimism, being a long-standing characteristic of economics, is rooted in Enlightened thought. In the latter philosophy, a continuing interweaving of "reason" in the thinking about the organization of society, is the propelling force in social development.

This train of thought contains the idea that the spectacular economic development of the past centuries was merely the result of the human spirit, which, building on the inventions of previous generations, was capable of ever greater achievements. According to this view, the use of raw materials is a facet of the relation between man and nature, enabling man to utilize nature ever more intensively. Once a natural resource is exhausted, attention is directed to other possibilities of nature, which always comes up with new solutions in the light of increasing knowledge. Why should one worry about living conditions in the future, with so many proofs of ever-increasing technological and organizational ingenuity?

There is also another approach. Nineteenth-century Romanticism functioned as a matrix to ways of economic thinking in which, following in the footsteps of the Physiocrats and Malthus, not human ability but the bounty of nature is primarily considered to be the source of welfare. In the Historical School preservationist utilization of nature was a significant topic. The following view on the process of industrialization can be placed against this background. Man forms part of a natural system, which gives him a special ability to provide for himself. He has a propensity to use his abilities in such a way that nature deteriorates under the influence of production. In former times, large parts of the earth became infertile, due to over-exploitation (deforestation and salinization). In industrial production a similar process of depletion of natural resources takes place, although on a much larger scale. In order to allow a small part of the world population an unprecedentedly high standard of life, large amounts of natural stocks have to be used up. Yet these sources ought to benefit other people and future generations, who have to bear the burden of the pollution of the environment. Who would not worry about the future with so many proofs of mismanagement? (Krabbe, 1989: pp. 33-34.)

Let us look at these two views, of which the first testifies to a mechanistic way of thought and the second bears traits of an "organical" approach. Both approaches have the right to exist, and scientific and political discussions can be based upon both of them. The significance of organically oriented thought, however, is not restricted to providing an alternative to mechanistic thought, in such a way that the one view is complementary to the other. It is necessary to make a contribution towards bridging the gap between the two approaches.

Historicism and organicism were by no means the monopoly of Historical School members and Institutionalists. The historically oriented approach was, for example, also part of Classical thought. Historical contributions by Adam Smith and James Mill, to mention two writers, were characterized by Hutchison (1979: pp. 8, 37) as 'descriptive and historical material' and 'the historical narrative', respectively. The two currents met in Alfred Marshall, who studied Historical School ideas.

> The Austro-German *Methodenstreit* was to continue for decades. But in England history and analysis went their separate ways. ... Certainly Marshall tried to take seriously the lessons of [it] in his *Industry and Trade*, but this important aspect of his work was largely neglected and abandoned by his successors. (Hutchison, 1978, 1979: p. 79; italics in original.)

In his early work on postulates of economic theory, Hutchison discussed predictability and causality in economics. However, in his explanation he used the idea of life without referring to any organically oriented law of development.

> As a matter of fact, all economic life, like all life, depends on a certain degree of successful predictability. ... We certainly do not volunteer here to give any other meaning to concepts like "the causes of a trade depression" than, simply, "certain events immediately preceding or accompanying a trade depression". (Hutchison, 1938, 1965: pp. 69, 72.)

John Hicks discussed the principle of causality in the context of induction on an empirical basis.

> We do indeed have plenty of examples of empirical relations ... [I]t is assumed in [correlation] estimates that if we found a perfect fit, over an indefinitely large number of instances,

> we should have perfect confidence in it. It is granted that in practice the number of instances that can be presented is finite, not indefinitely large; so that we can never have a quite perfect confidence. But if the number of instances is large, we are supposed to have a near-perfect confidence; ... But should we be so persuaded? (Hicks, 1979: pp. 28-9.)

His opinion on this question was that "empirical and logical implication should be brought together".

Historicism and organicism can be seen as attempts to step over the boundaries of methodological individualism. The limitations of the individualistic approach in scientific as well as in political problems are expressed in the term "prisoners' dilemma": how should you act if you do not know what your fellow individual who is involved in your affairs is going to do. An attempt to overcome individualism in economics is found in the Richard T. Ely Lecture given by Kenneth Arrow.

> I do conclude that social variables, not attached to particular individuals, are essential in studying the economy or any other social system and that, in particular, knowledge and technical information have an irremovably social component, of increasing importance over time. (Arrow, 1994: p. 8.)

It must be recognized that most decisions taken by an actor in the economic system are determined, to a certain degree, by his ultimate aims and his behavioural principles, which are, in turn, culturally determined. Another answer to the question of the prisoners' dilemma is political. For instance, a question might be why an individual should decide not to pollute if there is no certainty that other people will do the same. The solution is that the government creates a system that functions as a coordination mechanism, in the form of education, information, (direct) regulations, levies and subsidies.

In this connection I want to consider the principle of free trade. I made it clear that the idea of *laissez faire* is an economic philosophical concept that arose from Physiocratism. The concept was bound to the Enlightenment idea of the "natural order", on the one hand, and biologically determined production, on the other. In nineteenth-century Classical economics, the biological dimension of the concept shrank drastically. Yet it did not vanish entirely, as the ideas of Malthus, Ricardo and Thünen testify. In mainstream economics, however, the idea of the natural order took on an esoteric character, expressed in the idea of the "natural" rate of growth. Unlike Physiocratic thought, this natural rate of growth of Enlightenment origin conflicts with present-day ecologically oriented economists' concepts of a natural (sustainable) growth.

As clarified before, *laissez faire* was criticized by nineteenth-century German philosophers such as Fichte, then by adherents of the Historical School and, in the first part of the twentieth century, by adherents of American Institutionalism and by the New Deal movement. In Europe, the idea was criticized by Keynes and Tinbergen. Their criticism focussed on the negative aspects of the impact of *laissez faire* on the welfare of the man in the street. Later, the hazardous impact of free economic forces on nature was also considered. In the 1970s the Club of Rome and, in its footsteps, a number of environmentalists launched a further attack on *laissez faire*.

Nowadays, however, in some way the pendulum is swinging back. In both East and West the conviction is gaining ground that, in the past, essential principles of *laissez faire* were wrongly neglected, both in theory and policy. Today, economists and politicians are searching for ways of stimulating desirable incentives by the pricing system. *Laissez faire*, understood in a new, partly "organic" way, is no longer seen as being in conflict with the realization of social welfare and preservation of nature, but rather as an indispensable aid in reaching these goals. The centre of the institutional problem in economics is to analyse the institutional structure of the pricing system (Krabbe, 1990: pp. 51-2).

General equilibrium and the organistic approach

An essential element in the process of economic growth is factor substitution, which is also central to "organistic" analysis. What is at issue are the repercussions of the process of depletion of natural stocks and the consequences of the pollution process, on the one hand, and the implications of the various forms of technological development, on the other. As a consequence, price ratios alter according to changing scarcity situations. In this picture, an important part is played by capital formation under the principle of "induced technology". The latter idea implies that, to a certain degree, the character of technology is determined by the structure of factor prices and factor shares in production (Kennedy, 1964; Binswanger, 1974; McCain, 1974). This idea includes "induced institutional change". (Binswanger and Ruttan, 1978; see also the Appendix to this study.)

The idea that technological change is directed towards an increase in the application of factors that are becoming comparatively cheaper like, for example, labour is expressed by the following two functions, characterizing a long-term production function.

1*a*. $$E_L = f_L\left(\frac{P_L}{P_N}\right)$$

$$1b. \quad E_N = f_N\left(\frac{P_L}{P_N}\right)$$

In these functions E_L and E_N are production elasticities of the factors labour and nature, respectively, and P_L and P_N are the price levels of these production factors. Functions f_L and f_N are decreasing (Equation 1a) and increasing (Equation 1b), respectively.

The substitutability between the production factors labour (L) and nature (N) is given by the equation:

$$2a. \quad \frac{L}{N} = \mu\left(\frac{P_N}{P_L}\right)^{\sigma}$$

In this formula, σ is the substitution elasticity and μ is a positive constant, related to the "distribution parameter" of the production function concerned. Note that μ, the "technology - price ratio factor", reflects the ratio in which production factors are applied if factor prices are defined in such a way that the price ratio concerned is unity. If marginal factor productivities are equal to factor prices, Equation 2a can be transformed into:

$$2b. \quad \mu = \frac{E_L}{E_N}\left(\frac{P_L}{P_N}\right)^{\sigma-1}$$

Insertion of Equations 1a and 1b in Equation 2b gives:

$$3. \quad \mu = \frac{f_L}{f_N}\left(\frac{P_L}{P_N}\right)^{\sigma-1}$$

In this context substitution elasticity is a magnitude reflecting the ways technological solutions are found. In general, this parameter has a greater value if the reaction time is longer.

Changing price ratios form part of government policy which is focussed on *e.g.* preservation and development of resources. In such a policy, price ratios are "artificially" modified (through price manipulation) since, in order to induce an environmental benign technology, the production factor nature must be comparatively expensive, while the factor labour must be as cheap as possible. So, in a properly institutionalized market economy, induced technology contributes to efficiency in production (Krabbe, 1992a: pp. 15-20).

In a dynamicized general equilibrium model, intertemporal causality must be expressed clearly. This should be done in such a way as to increase pressure of production on the capacities of land, as well as to gradually exploit finite natural resources, so that all depletion aspects are clearly exposed. Many steps have already been taken along the path towards institutional analysis and dynamization of the model of general equilibrium. This field of analysis, however, has not yet been exhausted. Therefore, we should continue to go along this road, for which organically oriented ideas can serve as a "compass" and a source of inspiration. It is not easy to indicate precisely where the border lies between a historico-evolutionary approach with holistic traits and a detailed deterministic analysis. If "predictability" is taken as a criterion, it is possible to say that further research will widen the latter's domain at the expense of the former's. The border is where "prediction" comes to an end and "speculation" about the future begins. Speculative scenarios should be based on understanding of the past and proper intuition on the point of development opportunities.

Applicability of organically oriented ideas

Traditionally, organically oriented production is the central idea of agricultural economics. This not only involves processes bound to the seasons, but also those which take many years to evolve. One example is the optimizing on basis of a "logistic" growth function. In environmental and resource economics such concepts play a crucial role. Another issue is the idea that the economic system itself can be conceived of as an organism. The warning given by both Menger and Schmoller that the significance of the analogy is limited is still relevant. Nevertheless, this approach enables the insight into the development of the whole of societal institutions to be improved. Further, a historical study which is also based on biologically oriented ideas can give an insight into the degree of uncertainty inherent in mechanistic economic extrapolations, particularly if long-term developments are subject to investigation. A test for a proper application of the organic metaphor is that results are complementary to and not antagonistic towards mechanistic conclusions.

Chapter 16
EPILOGUE

Finally, I want to consider what the basic ideas of my history-of-thought-oriented study are. I want to pose the question of the "significance" of this study. Publications of former writers should be seen in the context of the philosophies of their day, of the socio-economic paradigms which were valid then, and of the topical social economic problems of the era, such as the urge for economic development and the need for social security. As such, these works possess their own significance. However, there is more to be said about the background of studies on the history of economic thought. Further to my remarks in Chapter 3, on the *prima facie* subject of the Historical School, I want to point out that approaches of the past, and the economic problems from then, are related to the modern method which should be followed, and the present-day problems which must be coped with. This gives an extra dimension to the subject matter. To a certain extent earlier scientific and political problems coincide with present topical problems in the same fields. Of course, present-day scientific and political pictures, with their emphasis on natural environment and resources, have a unique aspect also. New problems require new solutions, which should be more convincing than those inherited from the past.

In economic literature, negative references to the "Historical School" can be found. These are mostly meant to support a plea about what economics should be; what is supposed to be in contrast to the way members of the school approached the various subjects. The main examples are the stance modern writers take against including normative considerations in economic thought, the belief that economic development takes place according to causal laws, and the advocation of protection by import duties and the undervaluating of free trade. I do not object to that, if the examples are rightly chosen and the argumentation is correct. However, it must be understood that not all writers of the school were of the same opinion, and that such ideas can often also be found outside the school. Nevertheless, I certainly object if this leads to the conclusion that the Historical School was no good at all. It should not be forgotten that the School anticipated various aspects of modern economics, like the Institutional and Keynesian approaches. In my eyes the School's most significant contribution was in the field of historistic and organistic thought, to which this study is devoted.

Appendix
LONG-TERM FACTOR SUBSTITUTION

Factor substitution is a main consideration in natural resource and environmental policies, and therefore it is a principal point in environmental economics. In this Appendix I discuss the role played by factor substitution in a long-term model of general equilibrium, and, further, what the historistic and organistic aspects of the model are. The "Technology - Price-ratio Factor" (TPF), mentioned in Chapter 15, is here elaborated. I confine myself to an outline of the model.[106] First, I discuss the properties of a Pigouvian-oriented model of general economic equilibrium with substitution characteristics. Next, I look at the role of induced technology, and finally, at its historistic and organistic traits. In this connection I point out that, like his tutor A. Marshall, A.C. Pigou can be placed in the traditions of both the Classical economists and those of the Historical School.

Elementary model. My point of departure is a model of perfect competition, which can be characterized as follows. It contains:

(a) an additive function of social utility *(Y)* of the Pigou type, in which social welfare is the sum of the (*cardinal*) welfares of the various members of society, expressed in income terms (reflecting quantities and prices of goods consumed), aggregating the incomes y_i $(i = 1,...,n)$ of each of the n members of society,
$Y = y_1+...+y_n$;[107]

(b) n sets of equations, reflecting the behaviour of the n utility maximizing consumption households, each set containing an individual utility function u_i in real terms of

[106]In my study *The idea of environmental welfare economics* (1990) I made an attempt to develop this idea. The model presented, however, was rather global, and I did not succeed in solving all problems of model building that arose.

[107]This social welfare function can be seen as a specific form of an increasing social welfare function of individual welfares (Krabbe, 1974: pp 59-60). A condition of this Pigouvian-oriented approach is that the income distribution is optimal (see variable α in Equations 1 and 2 of Chapter 14).

goods x_a $(a = 1,\ldots,r)$, and a (linear) income formation function of production factors q_c offered at equilibrium prices p_{qc} $(c = 1,\ldots,s)$;

(c) r sets of equations, reflecting the behaviour of r profit maximizing firms, each set containing a specific production function in real terms, referring to their typical products x_a and s production factors used, and a (linear) revenue function of goods produced and sold at equilibrium prices p_{xa} $(a = 1,\ldots,r)$;

(d) a number of equations determining the functioning of the various consumption and production households and markets of products and production factors, and those determining the total supply of production factors (q_o).

All equations of the above model are in the additive form. For the social utility function (a), the n individual utility functions, mentioned under (b), and the r production functions, mentioned under (c), are assumed to be homogenous of degree one. Thus, the model is abstracted from economies of scale. Parameters of production functions and those of utility functions represent production elasticities and, analogously, "utility elasticities", respectively. In this elementary model these parameters have an exogenous character. Parameters of the model determine prices (p_{xa} and p_{qo}) and quantities (x_a and q_o) of products and production factors in the situation of general equilibrium, in which social welfare and individual welfares are optimal, and net profits are eliminated. Social welfare is expressed by the total value of goods produced and consumed. This elementary model is to be formulated in such a way that the value of all substitution elasticities is *1*, so that the model as a whole has the characteristics of a Cobb-Douglas approach. The system is solvable, in principle. In this approach capital formation is kept beyond consideration. I indicate this model as **X**.

Basic model. The above elementary model can be made suitable for also reflecting other substitution elasticities except 1. To do this, model **X** is extended by a section **S**, in such a way that the production and utility elasticities mentioned above are converted into endogenous magnitudes. This is explained in the additional section **S**, for which a set of equations similar to the type of Equations 2 of Chapter 15 is used.

2*a*. $$\frac{L}{N} = \mu \left(\frac{P_N}{P_L}\right)^{\sigma}$$

or:

2b. $$\mu = \frac{E_L}{E_N}\left(\frac{P_L}{P_N}\right)^{\sigma-1}$$

In model **XS** the substitution elasticities between production factors q_c $(c = 1,...,s)$ in the production sphere, to be indicated as σ_{qcd} (c and $d = 1,...,s$), and goods x_a $(a = 1,...,r)$ in the consumption sphere, to be indicated as σ_{xab} (a and $b = 1,...,r$), are exogenous. In the model are s production elasticities (E_{qc}) and r "utility elasticities" (E_{xa}). The substitution elasticities should be determined empirically. One condition for solving the model is that it is structured in such a way that there are as many substitution elasticities (σ_{qcd} and σ_{xab}, respectively) as there are production and utility elasticities (E_{qc} and E_{xa}, respectively). If this is not done, the model is either over- or under-determined. When dealing with substitution elasticities of certain values, one should bear in mind that specific *ceteris paribus* conditions might affect these values (Blackorby and Russell, 1989).

A methodical aspect of the above operation is the function of the parameters μ, the TPFs mentioned. There are s magnitudes μ_{qcd} in the production sphere and r magnitudes μ_{xab} in the consumption sphere. In the latter context the term "Utility - Price-ratio Factor" (UPF) is more appropriate. (Similar numbers count for prices and substitution elasticities in either the production or the consumption sphere.) The ratios μ are determined empirically, according to Equation 2a in which, however, L and N do not refer to "labour and nature", but to the quantities used of two specific economic goods in either a production function (L and N refer to q_c and q_d; c and $d = 1,...,s$) or an individual utility function (L and N refer to x_a and x_b ; a and $b = 1,...r$). Thus, in this context Equations 2b means, in the production sphere:

2b.a. $$\mu_{qcd} = \frac{E_{qc}}{E_{qd}}\left(\frac{p_{qc}}{p_{qd}}\right)^{\sigma_{qcd}-1}$$

and, in the consumption sphere:

2b.b. $$\mu_{xab} = \frac{E_{xa}}{E_{xb}}\left(\frac{p_{xa}}{p_{xb}}\right)^{\sigma_{xab}-1}$$

A practical aspect of the solution procedure is that empirical determination of the magnitudes μ is only possible if workable assumptions can be made about the price structure. So prices and allocated quantities are explained simultaneously with an empirical determination of the TPFs and UPFs. The model **XS** can also be used in a different way, by considering substitution elasticities endogenously, and production and utility elasticities exogenously. Also then prices and allocated quantities are explained simultaneously with magnitudes μ. However, it must be remembered that only those substitution elasticities that fit into the model can be explained. Welfare theory, which is in the tradition of Walras and Pareto, is rightly appreciated for its axiomatic perfection. For specific problems, however, more pragmatic and empirically oriented approaches can also be used. The above model might serve as an example.

Induced technology. Capital plays a crucial part in modern production. This Appendix includes capital formation, referring to what was said about "induced technology" in Chapter 15. It also includes institutional impacts on structural price ratios which are supposed to express relative scarcities, valued from a social point of view. Marginal factor productivities and time preferences are of crucial importance in determining the size and texture of capital. The state of the technology applied, related to specific production circumstances, is given by the productivities of the original factors labour and nature and the derived factor capital. In situations that tend to equilibrium, marginal factor productivities tend to factor prices, and time preferences to interests. Thus, the volume and structure of the factor capital can be seen as a component of applicable technology.

Technology has an "induced" character; it is determined by scarcity ratios, manifesting itself in factor prices. It is known that substitution elasticities between factors of production are greater in the long term than in the short term. This is because technology adapts itself better to changing price ratios when the adaptation period is longer. Changing marginal factor productivities are the main determinants in this long-term process of substitution, because technological change is directed towards applying more of those factors which become comparatively cheaper due to increases in their marginal productivities. The consequence of this for the above model is that values of parameters of production functions depend upon the reaction period. Within certain limits, the latter effect is also to be expected for the parameters of consumption functions (Krabbe, 1992a: pp. 19-20). A central problem of structural economic policy is how to create conditions for efficient technologies. The institutional structure ought to be such that production factors that are considered scarce from a social point of view (say, certain components of nature) are not priced too low.

Historistic and organistic aspects. Although the model described above is capable of dynamization in the "mechanistic" sense of the term, there are also historistic and organically oriented aspects to it. So, on the point of the weights man assigns to his various priorities, his ideas are subject to change. This brings with it an element of uncertainty in the determination of the social optimum in which future circumstances play a part.

Further, in the sphere of production, since technology is not fully determined by economic factors, substitution elasticities are given by the topical technology applied, and are as such partly unpredictable. The economic system functions as a selection mechanism, by which the most suitable technology is chosen. In this selection process, factor productivity considerations are of dominating importance, only a minor role being played by substitution opportunities proper. Thus, values of substitution elasticities in new technologies form another element of uncertainty in the picture of development.

References

Albert, H., 'Hermeneutics and economics: a criticism of hermeneutical thinking in the social sciences', *Kyklos* Vol. 41 (1988): pp. 573-602.

Althusser, L., *Politics and history: Montesquieu, Rousseau, Hegel and Marx*. NLB, London (1959) 1972.

Archibugi, F., P. Nijkamp and F.J. Soeteman, The challenge of sustainable development. In: F. Archibugi and P. Nijkamp (eds), *Economy and ecology: towards sustainable development*. Kluwer Academic Publishers, Dordrecht 1989.

Aron, R., *Les étapes de la pensée sociologique: Montesquieu, Comte, Marx, Tocqueville, Durkheim, Pareto, Weber*. Gallimard, Paris 1967.

Arrow, K.J., 'Methodological individualism and social knowledge' (Richard T. Ely lecture), *American Economic Review* Vol. 84 (1994) Number 2: pp. 1-9.

Ayres, C.E., *The theory of economic progress*. University of North Carolina Press, Chapel Hill 1944.

Ayres, R.U. and U.E. Simonis, *Industrial metabolism: restructuring for sustainable development*. United Nations University Press, Tokyo 1994.

Backhaus, J.G., 'Sombart's Modern capitalism', *Kyklos* Vol. 42 (1989a): pp. 599-611.

_____, Schmollers *Grundriss der allgemeinen Volkswirtschaftslehre*: ein aktueller Klassiker. In: H.C. Recktenwald *et al.* (eds), *Vademecum zu einem Klassiker der historischen Methode in der ökonomischen Wissenschaft*. Verlag Wirtschaft und Finanzen, Düsseldorf 1989b.

_____, Wilhelm Roschers "Geschichte der National-Oekonomik in Deutschland": ein Standardwerk der Dogmengeschichte. In: B. Schefold (ed.), *Vademecum zu einem Klassiker der deutschen Dogmengeschichte*. Verlag Wirtschaft und Finanzen, Düsseldorf 1992.

_____, (ed.), 'The economics of science policy: an analysis of the Althoff system', *Journal of Economic Studies* Vol. 20 (1993) Number 4/5.

Backhaus, J.G. and J. Hanel, *Die Nachfolge: ein Versuch über Heinrich Herkner, den Volkswirt*. Metropolis, Marburg 1994.

Backhaus, J.G. and J.J. Krabbe, 'Henry George's contribution to modern environmental policy: Part I', *American Journal of Economics and Sociology* Vol. 50 (1991): pp. 485-501; 'Part II' in Vol. 51: pp. 115-127.

Barnard, F.M., 'National culture and political legitimacy: Herder and Rousseau', *Journal of the History of Ideas* Vol. 44 (1983) Number 2: pp. 231-253.

Bergstrom, T.C. and O. Stark, 'How altruism can prevail in an evolutionary environment', *American Economic Review* Vol. 83 (1993) Number 2: pp. 149-155.

Berns, E.E., 'Value and time in Menger's *Grundsätze*', *Journal of Economic Studies* Vol. 16 (1989) Number 2: pp. 84-108.

Bertalanffy, L., 'The theory of open systems in physics and biology', *Science* Vol. 3 (1950): pp. 23-29.

Binswanger, H.P., 'The measurement of technical change biases with many factors of production', *American Economic Review* Vol. 64 (1974): pp. 964-76.

Binswanger, H.P. and V.W. Ruttan (eds.), *Induced innovation: technology, institutions and development*. Johns Hopkins University Press, Baltimore 1978.

Blackorby, C. and R.R. Russell, 'Will the real elasticity of substitution please stand up? (A comparison of the Allen/Uzawa and Morishima elasticities)', *American Economic Review* Vol. 79 (1989): pp. 882-888.

Böhm-Bawerk, E., *Positive Theorie des Kapitales*, erster Band. In: *idem, Kapital und Kapitalzins* (II), fourth edition. Gustav Fischer, Jena (1888) 1921.

Boulding, K.E., *Evolutionary economics*. Sage Publications, London 1981.

Brentano, L., *Das Freihandelsargument*, second edition. Buchverlag der 'Hilfe', Berlin (1900) 1910.

_____, 'Versuch einer Theorie der Bedürfnisse', *Sitzungsberichte der Königlich Bayerischen Akademie der Wissenschaften*. Munich 1908.

_____, Die Bevölkerungslehre. In: *idem, Konkrete Grundbedingungen der Volkswirtschaft*. Felix Meiner, Leipzig (1909) 1924.

_____, 'Arbeitslohn und Arbeitszeit nach dem Kriege', *Die neue Rundschau* 24. Fischer, Berlin 1918.

_____, *Der wirtschaftende Mensch in der Geschichte*. Felix Meiner, Leipzig 1923.

_____, Die Volkswirtschaft und ihre konkreten Grundbedingungen. In: *idem, Konkrete Grundbedingungen der Volkswirtschaft*. Felix Meiner, Leipzig 1924.

Brinkmann, C., W.G.F. Roscher. In: E. v. Beckerath *et al.* (eds), *Handwörterbuch der Sozialwissenschaften*. Fischer, 1956.

Brooks, H., The typology of surprises in technology, institutions and development. In: W.C. Clark and R.E. Munn (eds), *Sustainable development of the biosphere*. Cambridge University Press, Cambridge 1986.

Bücher, K., *Die Entstehung der Volkswirtschaft*, erste Sammlung [I]. Laupp, Tübingen (1893) 1922.

_____, *Die Entstehung der Volkswirtschaft*, zweite Sammlung [II]. Laupp, Tübingen (1893) 1925.

_____, *Arbeit und Rhythmus*, third edition. Teubner, Leipzig (1896) 1902.

_____, Volkswirtschaftliche Entwicklungsstufen. In: K. Bücher, J. Schumpeter, F. von Wieser, *Grundriss der Sozialökonomik*, I. Abteilung: Wirtschaft und Wirtschaftswissenschaft. Mohr, Tübingen 1914.

Butter, F. den, The mirror of cleanliness: on the construction and use of an environmental index. In: J.J. Krabbe and W.J.M. Heijman, *National income and nature: externalities, growth and steady state*. Kluwer Academic Publishers, Dordrecht 1992.

Ciriacy-Wantrup, S.V., *Resource conservation: economics and politics*. University of California Press, Berkeley, Los Angeles 1952.

Coats, A.W., 'The American Economic Association and the economics profession', *Journal of Economic Literature* Vol. 23 (1985): pp. 1697-1727.

_____, 'What can we accomplish with historical approaches in an advanced discipline such as economics? in: J.G. Backhaus (ed.), Essays on Gustav Schmoller', *History of Economic Ideas* Vol. 1 (1993) Number 3 and Vol. 2 (1994) Number 1: pp. 227-65.

Cohn, G., *Grundlegung der Nationalökonomie*. In: *idem*, *System der Nationalökonomie*, erster Band. Ferdinand Enke, Stuttgart 1885.

_____, *Zur Politik des deutschen Finanz-, Verkehrs- und Verwaltungswesens, Reden und Aufsätze*. Ferdinand Enke, Stuttgart 1905.

Conrad, J., *Grundriss zum Studium der politischen Oekonomie*, erster Teil: *Nationalökonomie*, third edition. Gustav Fischer, Jena (1896) 1900.

_____, *Grundriss zum Studium der politischen Oekonomie*, vierte Teil: *Statistik*, second edition. Gustav Fischer, Jena (1896) 1902.

_____, *Leitfaden zum Studium der Volkswirtschaftspolitik*, fifth edition. Gustav Fischer, Jena (1901) 1914.

Cosmides, L. and J. Tooby, 'Better than rational: evolutionary psychology and the Invisible hand'. *American Economic Review* Vol. 84 (1994) Number 2: pp. 327-332.

Dalton, G., *Economic systems and society, capitalism, communism and the Third World*. Penguin Education, Penguin Books, Harmondsworth (1974) 1975.

Daly, H.E., Introduction to the steady-state economy. In: H.E. Daly (ed.), *Economics, ecology, ethics: essays toward a steady-state economy*. Freeman, San Francisco (1973) 1980.

_____, Elements of environmental macroeconomics. In: R. Constanza (ed.), *Ecological economics*. Columbia University Press, New York, 1991: pp. 32-46.

_____, Introduction to essays towards a Steady State Economy. In: H. Daly and K. Townsend (eds), *Valuing the Earth*. MIT Press, Cambridge, Massachusetts 1993: pp. 11-47.

Darwin, C., *The origin of species, by means of natural selection*. Penguin Books, Harmondsworth (1859) 1985.

Denzau, A.T., and D.C. North, 'Shared mental models: ideologies and institutions', *Kyklos* Vol. 47 (1994): pp. 3-31.

Dietzel, H., Theoretische Socialökonomik. In: A. Buchenberger, K. Bücher, H. Dietzel, *Lehr- und Handbuch der politischen Oekonomie*. Winter, Leipzig 1895.

Dopfer, K., 'Towards a theory of economic institutions: synergy and path dependency', *Journal of Economic Issues* Vol. 25 (1991) Number 2: pp. 535-550.

Dragan, J. C., and M.C. Demetrescu, *Entropy and bioeconomics: the new paradigm of Nicholas Georgescu-Roegen*, second edition. Nagard, Rome (1986) 1991.

Dupont (de Nemours), P.S., *Physiocratie ou constitution naturelle du gouvernement le plus avantageux au genre humain*. "Leyden" and Merlin, Paris 1768.

Eisermann, G., *Vilfredo Paretos System der allgemeinen Soziologie*. Ferdinand Enke, Stuttgart 1962.

Ely, R.T., *An introduction to political economy*. Swan Sonnenschein, London, and Hunt and Eaton, New York (1889) 1891.

England, R.W., 'Production, distribution, and environmental quality: Mr. Sraffa reinterpreted as an ecologist', *Kyklos* Vol. 39 (1986): pp. 230-244.

Eucken, W., *Die Grundlagen der Nationalökonomie*, second edition. Fischer, Jena (1940) 1941.

_____, Die soziale Frage. In: *Synopsis* (Festgaben Alfred Weber). Lambert Schneider, Heidelberg 1948.

_____, *Grundsätze der Wirtschaftspolitik.* Published by E. Eucken and K. Hensel. Francke, Bern, and Mohr, Tübingen 1952.

Faber, M., and J.L.R. Proops, 'Interdisciplinary research between economists and physical scientists: retrospect and prospect', *Kyklos* Vol. 38 (1985): pp. 599-616.

Fichte, J.G., *Der geschlossne Handelsstaat.* Felix Meiner, Leipzig (1800) 1910.

Field, B.C., 'The evolution of property rights', *Kyklos* Vol. 42 (1989): pp. 319-345.

Fogel, R.W., 'Economic growth, population theory, and physiology: the bearing of long-term processes on the making of economic policy', *American Economic Review* Vol. 84 (1994) Number 3: pp. 369-395.

Folke, C., Socio-economic dependence on the life-supporting environment. In: C. Folke and T. Kåberger (eds), *Linking the natural environment and the economy: essays from the Eco-Eco Group*. Kluwer Academic Publishers, Dordrecht 1991.

Folmer, H., and E.C. van Ierland, Valuation methods and policy making in environmental economics: relevance and scope. In: H. Folmer and E.C. van Ierland, *Valuation methods and policy making in environmental economics*. Elsevier, Amsterdam 1989.

Forrester, J.W., *Industrial dynamics*. M.I.T. Press, Cambridge, Massachusetts 1961.

_____, *Principles of systems*. Wright-Allen, Cambridge, Massachusetts 1968.

_____, *World dynamics*. Wright-Allen, Cambridge, Massachusetts 1971.

Forrester, N.B., *The life cycle of economic development*. Wright-Allen, Cambridge, Massachusetts 1973.

Galbraith, J.K., *The new industrial state*. Penguin Books (Pelican Books), Harmondsworth (1967) 1974.

_____, *Economics and the public purpose*. Penguin Books (Pelican Books), Harmondsworth (1973) 1975.

George, H., *Progress and poverty*. Schalkenbach Foundation, New York (1879) 1979.

Georgescu-Roegen, N., *Analytical economic issues and problems*. Harvard University Press, Cambridge, Massachusetts 1966.

_____, The entropy law and the economic problem (1970). In: idem, *Energy and economic myths: institutional and analytical economic essays*. Pergamon, New York 1976.

_____, *The Entropy Law and the economic process*. Harvard University Press, Cambridge, Massachusetts 1971.

_____, *Energy and economic myths: institutional and analytical economic essays*. Pergamon, New York 1976.

Gide, C and C. Rist, *Histoire des doctrines économiques*, third edition. Recueil Sirey, Paris (1909) 1920.

Gide, C and C. Rist, *History of economic doctrines*, translated by R. Richards, second English edition. Heath, Boston (1909) 1947.

Giouras, A., *Arbeitsteilung und Normativität: zur Rekonstruktion der Historischen Sozialtheorie Gustav Schmollers*. Haag & Herchen, Frankfurt 1994.

Gorski, P.S., 'The Protestant ethic revisited: disciplinary revolution and state formation in Holland and Prussia', *American Journal of Sociology* Vol. 99 (1993) Number 2: pp. 265-316.

Goudzwaard, B., *Ongeprijsde schaarste*. Van Stockum, The Hague 1970.

Gowdy, J.M., 'The social context of natural capital: the social limits to sustainable development', *International Journal of Social Economics* Vol. 21 (1994) Number 8: pp. 43-55.

Gruchy, A.G., *Contemporary economic thought: the contribution of neo-institutional economics*, second printing. Augustus Kelley, Clifton, New Jersey (1972) 1974.

Hamilton, D., *Evolutionary economics: a study of change in economic thought*. University of New Mexico Press, Albuquerque 1970.

Hayek, F.A., Eugen Philippovich von Philippsberg. In: E.R.A. Seligman *et al.* (eds), *Encyclopaedia of the Social Sciences*. MacMillan (1933) 1949.

Heckscher, E.F., *Mercantilism*, revised edition by E.F. Söderlund. George Allen and Unwin, London, and MacMillan, New York (1931) 1962.

Heertje, A., *Economie en technische ontwikkeling*. Stenfert Kroese, Leiden 1973.

Hegel, G.W.F., *Phaenomenologie des Geistes*. In: *G.W.F. Hegel's Werke* (edited by Ph. Marheineke *et al.*), zweiter Band. Duncker & Humblot, Berlin (1807) 1841.

Heijman, W.J.M., *Depletable resources and the economy*. Wageningen Economic Studies (Number 21). Pudoc, Wageningen 1991.

Held, A., *Die ländlichen Darlehenskassenvereine in der Rheinprovinz und ihre Beziehungen zur Arbeiterfrage*. Mauke, Jena 1869. Also in Bruno Hildebrand's *Jahrbücher* Vol. 13 (1869) (Numbers 1 and 2).

_____, *Die Einkommenssteuer*. Marcus, Bonn 1872.

_____, *Zwei Bücher zur socialen Geschichte Englands*. Edited by G.F. Knapp. Duncker & Humblot, Leipzig 1881.

Herkner, H., *Die Arbeiterfrage*, seventh edition. Vereinigung wissenschaftlicher Verleger, Berlin and Leipzig (1894) 1921.

Hicks, J., *Causality in economics*. Basil Blackwell, Oxford 1979.

Hildebrand, B., *Die Nationalökonomie der Gegenwart und Zukunft*. Literarische Anstalt, Frankfurt 1848.

_____, 'Naturalwirthschaft, Geldwirthschaft und Creditwirthschaft', *Jahrbücher für Nationalökonomie und Statistik* Vol. 2 (1864) (Mauke, Jena): pp. 1-24.

_____, 'Die wissenschaftliche Aufgabe der Statistik', *Jahrbücher für Nationalökonomie und Statistik* Vol. 6 (1866): pp. 1-11.

Hobson, J.A., *The evolution of modern capitalism: a study of machine production*, fourth edition. George Allen & Unwin, London, and MacMillan, New York (1894) 1926.

_____, *Imperialism*, third edition. George Allen & Unwin, London (1902) 1938.

_____, *The science of wealth*. Williams & Norgate, London 1911.

Hoffmann-Nowotny, H.J., A sociological approach towards a general theory of migration. In: M.M. Kritz *et al.* (eds), *Global trends in migration*. Center for Migration Studies, Staten Island, New York 1981.

Hofstede, G., *Culture's consequences: international differences in work-related values*, abridged edition. Sage Publications, Beverly Hills 1984.

Holling, C.S., The resilience of terrestial ecosystem. In: W.C. Clark and R.E. Munn (eds), *Sustainable development of the biosphere*. Cambridge University Press, Cambridge 1986.

Houmanidis, L.T., Humanitarian economics. *Spoudai* Vol. 28 (1978) Number 2: pp. 3-38.

_____, *Le salaire ouvrier depuis les classiques jusqu'a nos jours*, édition augmentée. Synchroni Ekdotiki, Athens 1994a.

_____, *Humanitarian economics: a new perspective of social economics.* Synchroni Ekdotiki, Athens 1994b.

Howe, C.W., 'Taxes *versus* tradable discharge permits: a review in the light of the U.S. and European experience', *Environmental and Resource Economics* Vol. 4 (1994): pp. 151-169.

Hume, D., *Enquiries concerning the human understanding and concerning the principles of morals*. Clarendon Press, Oxford (1777) 1970.

Hutchison, T.W., *The significance and basic postulates of economic theory*, reprint. Augustus Kelley, New York (1938) 1965.

_____, *A review of economic doctrines 1870-1929*. Clarendon Press, Oxford (1953) 1962.

_____, *The politics and philosophy of economics: Marxians, Keynesians and Austrians*. Basil Blackwell, Oxford 1981.

_____, *On revolutions and progress in economic knowledge*. Cambridge University Press, Cambridge and London (1978) 1979.

Inama-Sternegg, K.T., Vom Wesen und den Wegen der Sozialwissenschaft. In: *idem*, *Staatswissenschaftliche Abhandlungen*. Duncker & Humblot, Leipzig (1881a) 1903. (Also published in *Statistische Monatschrift*)

_____, Das Zeitalter des Kredits. In: *idem*, *Staatswissenschaftliche Abhandlungen*. Duncker & Humblot, Leipzig (1881b) 1903. (Also published in *Deutsche Rundschau* Vol. 7)

_____, Arbeitsstatistik. In: *idem*, *Staatswissenschaftliche Abhandlungen*. Duncker & Humblot, Leipzig (1892) 1903. (Also published in *Statistische Monatschrift*)

_____, Allgemeine Gedanken über soziale Politik. In: *idem*, Staatswissenschaftliche Abhandlungen. Duncker & Humblot, Leipzig (1902) 1903. (Also published in *Zeitschrift für Volkswirtschaft, Sozialpolitik und Verwaltung* Vol. 11)

Jevons, W.S., *On the coal question*. MacMillan, London 1866.

Kapp, K.W., *The social costs of private enterprise*. Harvard University Press, Cambridge, Massachusetts 1950.

Katona, G., Attitudes and expectations. Reprinted excerpts from *The powerful consumer*. In: A.S.C. Ehrenberg *et al.* (eds), *Consumer behaviour*. Penguin Education, Penguin Books, Harmondsworth (1960) 1972.

Kennedy, C., 'Induced bias in innovation and the theory of distribution', *Economic Journal* Vol. 74 (1964): pp. 541-7.

Knapp, G.F., *Grundherrschaft und Rittergut*, Vorträge. Duncker & Humblot, Leipzig 1897.

_____, *Staatliche Theorie des Geldes*, fourth edition. Duncker & Humblot, Munich (1905) 1923.

_____, *Die Landarbeiter in Knechtschaft und Freiheit*, Vorträge. Duncker & Humblot, Leipzig 1909.

_____, Lujo Brentano im Jahre 1872. In: *Lujo Brentano; Kundgebungen zu seinem 70. Geburtstag*. Ueberreicht von der Münchener Volkswirtschaftlichen Gesellschaft. Duncker & Humblot, Munich and Leipzig, 1915.

Kneese, A.V., R.U. Ayres and R.C. d'Arge, *Economics and the environment: a materials balance approach*. Resources of the Future, Washington 1970.

Knies, K., *Die politische Oekonomie vom Standpunkte der geschichtlichen Methode*. Schwetschke, Braunschweig 1853.

_____, *Geld und Credit*. Hans Buske, Leipzig (1873-85) 1931.

Knoester, A., and A.H.E.M. Wellink (eds), *Tinbergen Lectures on economic policy*. North-Holland Publishers, Amsterdam 1993.

Krabbe, J.J., *Individueel en collectief nut* (PhD dissertation). Mededelingen Landbouwuniversiteit, Wageningen 1974.

_____, *Historisme in economisch denken*. Van Gorcum, Assen 1983.

_____, 'Organistic theory in economics: the contribution of the Historical School', *International Journal of Social Economics* Vol. 14 (1987) Number 3/4/5, pp. 105-117.

_____, 'Menger's valuation of nature: an atomistic and "organistic" approach', *Journal of Economic Studies* Vol. 15 (1988) Number 3/4: pp. 55-63.

_____, *The idea of environmental welfare economics*. Wageningen Economic Studies Number 12. Pudoc, Wageningen 1989.

_____, 'Environmental welfare economics: implications for technology, wages and incomes', *International Journal of Social Economics* Vol. 17 (1990) Number 1: pp. 49-58.

_____, Cultural diversification in economics: a consideration. In: *Economic history and economic theory* [*Festschrift* in honour of Lazaros T. Houmanidis]. University of Piraeus, Piraeus (Greece) 1991a).

_____, 'Schmoller's evolutionary economics', *Archives of Economic History* Vol. 1 (1991b) Number 2: pp. 5-17.

_____, Nature in Pigouvian oriented economics. In J.J. Krabbe and W.J.M. Heijman (eds), *National income and nature: externalities, growth and steady state*. Kluwer Academic Publishers, Dordrecht 1992a.

_____, Quantifying sustainability: the entropy approach. In: W.J.M. Heijman and J.J. Krabbe (eds), *Issues of environmental economic policy*. Wageningen Economic Studies Vol. 24, Pudoc, Wageningen 1992b.

_____, 'Nature and technology as economic categories: Sombart in the mainstream' *International Journal of New Ideas* Vol. 1 (1992c) Number 2: pp. 108-113. (Also in J. Backhaus (ed.), *Werner Sombart (1863-1941): social scientist*. Metropolis Verlag, Marburg 1993)

_____, 'New Organicism: sketch of the development of organismic thought in economics', *American Journal of Economics and Sociology* Vol. 52 (1993a): pp. 155-66.

_____, 'A "Physiocratic" approach to sustainability, *International Journal of Social Economics* Vol. 20 (1993b) Number 9: pp. 15-21.

_____, 'Schmoller on economics and the environment: the economy as a system of systems, in: J.G. Backhaus (ed.), Essays on Gustav Schmoller', *History of Economic Ideas* Vol. 1 (1993b) Number 3 and Vol. 2 (1994) Number 1: pp. 397-413.

_____, Institutional conditions for efficient sustainable development: implementing low social time preference. In: S. Karsten (ed.), *The U.S. economy in the light of justice, solidarity, subsidiarity, and complementarity*. Studies in the Social Sciences Vol. 32. West Georgia College, Carrollton 1994.

_____, 'Roscher's organistic legacy', *Journal of Economic Studies* Vol. 22 (1995) Numbers 3/4/5: pp. 159-170.

Kuhn, T.S., The structure of scientific revolutions. In: O. Neurath *et al.* (eds), *International Encyclopedia of Unified Science*. The University of Chicago Press, Chicago, 1962.

Lancaster, K.J., 'A new approach to consumer theory', *Journal of Political Economy* Vol. 74 (1966): pp. 132-157.

List, F., *Outlines of American political economy*. In: M.E. Hirst, *Life of Friedrich List and selections from his writings*. Reprints of Economic Classics. Augustus Kelley, New York (1827) (1909) 1965.

_____, *Das nationale System der politischen Oekonomie*, sixth edition. Cotta, Stuttgart (1841) 1877.

Lotz, W., Finanzwissenschaft. In: H. Marquardsen *et al.* (eds), *Handbuch des oeffentlichen Rechts der Gegenwart*. Mohr, Tübingen 1917.

Marshall, A., *Principles of Economics*, eighth edition. MacMillan, London (1890) 1925.

Mattoo, A. and H.V. Singh, 'Eco-labelling: policy considerations', *Kyklos* Vol. 47 (1994): pp. 53-65.

McCain, R.A., 'Induced bias in technical innovation, including product innovation, in a model of economic growth, *Economic Journal* Vol. 84 (1974): pp. 959-66.

Meadows, D.H. *et al.*, *The limits to growth: a report for the Club of Rome's project on the predicament of mankind*. Universe Books, New York 1972.

Meadows, D.L. *et al.*, *Dynamics of growth in a finite world*. Wright-Allen, Cambridge, Massachusetts 1974.

Menger, C., *Grundsätze der Volkswirthschaftslehre*. Braumüller, Vienna 1871.

_____, *Principles of economics* [*Grundsätze*, first edition, 1871], translated and edited by J. Dingwall and B.F. Hoselitz. The Free Press, Glencoe, Illinois 1950.

_____, *Untersuchungen über die Methode der Socialwissenschaften, und der politischen Oekonomie insbesondere*. Duncker & Humblot, Leipzig 1883 (Series of Reprints London School of Economics, Number 18, 1933).

_____, *Investigations into the method of the social sciences with special reference to economics* [*Untersuchungen*, 1883], edited by L. Schneider, translated by F.J. Nock. New York University Press, New York (1963) 1985.

_____, *Die Irrtümer des Historismus in der deutschen Nationalökonomie*. Scientia Verlag, Aalen (Vienna, 1884) 1966.

Mentzel, P., 'Nationalism', *Humane Studies Review* Vol. 8 (1992) Number 1: pp. 1-16.

Mesarovic M. and E. Pestel, *Menschheit am Wendepunkt / Mankind at the turning point*. Agon Elsevier, New York 1974.

Milford, K., Menger's methodology. In: B.C. Caldwell (ed.), *Carl Menger and his legacy in economics*. (Annual supplement to *History of Political Economy* Vol. 22.) Duke University Press, Durham 1990.

Mill, J.S., *On liberty*. Penguin English Library, Penguin Books, Harmondsworth (1859) 1983.

Mises, L., *Nation, state and economy*, translated by L.B. Yeager. New York University Press, New York and London 1983.

Mishan, E.J., 'Pareto optimality and the law', *Oxford Economic Papers* Vol. 19 (1967): 256-287.

Mitchell, W.C., *Types of economic theory, from Mercantilism to Institutionalism*. Edited by J. Dorfman. Augustus Kelley, New York 1969.

Montesquieu, C. de Secondat de, *De l'esprit des lois*. Garnier-Flammarion, Paris (1748) 1979.

Munn, R.E., Towards sustainable development: an environmental perspective. In: F. Archibugi and P. Nijkamp (eds), *Economy and ecology: towards sustainable development*. Kluwer Academic Publishers, Dordrecht 1989.

Myrdal, G., *Economic theory and under-developed regions*. Duckworth, London 1957. (Also published as *Rich lands and poor*. Harper & Row, New York 1957.)

Nentjes, A., and D. Wiersma, On economic growth, technology and the environment. In: J.J. Krabbe and W.J.M. Heijman, *National income and nature: externalities, growth and steady state*. Kluwer Academic Publishers, Dordrecht 1992.

Nijkamp, P., *Naar een prijzenswaardig milieu?!* Van Gorcum, Assen 1979.

Nijkamp, P. and F. Soeteman, 'Ecologically sustainable economic development: key issues for strategic environmental manegement, in: J.J. Krabbe (ed.), Principles of environmental policy', *International Journal of Social Economics* Vol. 15 (1988) Number 3/4: pp. 88-101.

Noort, P.C. van den, Het vraagstuk van de optimale beleidskeuze voor de Europese landbouw. In: A.A.P. van Drunen *et al.* (eds), *Economie en landbouw*. Vuga, The Hague 1983.

O'Brien, J.C., 'The eternal path to communism: from Marx via Lenin and Stalin to Solzhenitsyn and Gorbachev', *International Journal of Social Economics* Vol. 18 (1991) Number 5/6/7: pp. 10-31.

Odum, H.T., *Systems ecology: an introduction*. John Wiley, New York 1983.

Pareto, V., *The mind and society: a treatise on general sociology*, translated by A. Bongiorno and A. Livingstone (two volumes). Dover Publications, New York (1935) 1963.

Philippovich, E., *Grundriss der politischen Oekonomie*, erster Band: *Allgemeine Volkswirtschaftslehre*, eighteenth edition [I]. Mohr, Tübingen (1893) 1923a.

_____, *Grundriss der politischen Oekonomie*, zweiter Band: *Volkswirtschaftspolitik*, erster Teil, fifteenth edition [II]. Mohr, Tübingen (1893) 1923b.

_____, La politique agraire. In: Bonnet (ed.), *Bibliothèque internationale d'économie politique*. Girard, Paris (1904).

_____, 'Die wissenschaftliche Behandlung des Transportswesens', *Zeitschrift für Volkswirtschaft, Sozialpolitik und Verwaltung* Vol. 14 (Braumüller, Vienna and Leipzig 1905).

_____, *Die Entwicklung der wirtschaftspolitischen Ideen im 19. Jahrhundert*. Mohr, Tübingen 1910.

_____, Entwicklungsgang der wirtschafts- und sozialpolitischen Systeme und Ideale. In: K. Bücher *et al.* (eds), *Grundriss der Sozialökonomik*; I. Abteilung: Historische und theoretische Grundlagen; I. Teil: *Wirtschaft und Wirtschaftswissenschaft*, second edition. Mohr, Tübingen (1914) 1924.

Popper, K.R., *The poverty of historicism*. Routledge & Kegan Paul, London 1957.

Potash, P.J., 'Systems thinking, dynamic modeling, and teaching history in the classroom', *Historical Methods* Vol. 27 (1994) Number 1: pp. 25-39.

Renkema J.A. and G.A.A. Wossink, Het taakveld van de agrarische bedrijfseconomie in beweging. In: W.J.M. Heijman and J.A.C. van Ophem, *De toekomst is verleden tijd*. Eburon, Delft, and LUW, Wageningen 1993.

Rickman, H.P., *W. Dilthey, selected writings*. Cambridge University Press, Cambridge 1976.

Riha, T.J.F., 'The dehumanisation of economic science: in search of the appropriate methodology', *International Journal of Social Economics* Vol. 14 (1990) Number 12: pp. 47-63.

Roscher, W., Zur Lehre von den Absatzkrisen. In: *idem, Ansichten der Volkswirthschaft aus dem geschichtlichen Standpunkte*, zweiter Band, third edition. Winter, Leipzig and Heidelberg (1849) 1878.

_____, *Die Grundlagen der Nationalökonomie*. In: *idem, System der Volkswirthschaft*, erster Band, seventh edition, Cotta, Stuttgart (1854) 1868.

_____, *Nationalökonomik des Ackerbaues und der verwandten Urproductionen*. In: *idem, System der Volkswirthschaft*, zweiter Band, eleventh edition. Cotta, Stuttgart (1859) 1885.

_____, Ein neuer Versuch, die Volkswirthschaftslehre zu katholisiren. In: *idem, Ansichten der Volkswirthschaft aus dem geschichtlichen Standpunkte*, erster Band, third edition. Winter, Leipzig and Heidelberg (1863) 1878.

_____, 'Die romantische Schule der Nationalökonomik in Deutschland', *Berichte der Kön. Sächs. Gesellschaft der Wissenschaften*, 1867.

Rostow, W.W., *The stages of economic growth: a non-communist manifesto*. Cambridge University Press, London and New York 1960

Rugina, A.N., 'Principia Oeconomica: new and old foundations of economic analysis', *International Journal of Social Economics* Vol. 13 (1986) Number 7/8.

_____, 'The problem of restructuring modern capitalism: the road to a unified science of positive and social economics', *International Journal of Social Economics* Vol. 17 (1990) Number 1: pp. 16-48.

_____, 'Is there any better alternative for the East and West? Toward a third revolution in economic, social and political thinking', *International Journal of New Ideas* Vol. 1 (1992) Number 1: pp. 17-37.

Salomon, G., Lorenz von Stein. In: E.R.A. Seligman *et al.* (eds), *Encyclopaedia of the Social Sciences*. MacMillan (1934) 1949.

Samuelson, P.A., 'Altruism as a problem involving group versus individual selection in economics and biology', *American Economic Review* Vol. 83 (1993) Number 2: pp. 143-148.

Sax, E., *Das Wesen und die Aufgaben der Nationalökonomie*. Alfred Hölder, Vienna 1884.

Say, J.B., *Traité d'économie politique*, sixième édition. Guillaumin, Paris (1803) 1841.

Schefold, B., Schmoller als Theoretiker. In: H.C. Recktenwald *et al.* (eds), *Vademecum zu einem Klassiker der historischen Methode in der ökonomischen Wissenschaft*. Verlag Wirtschaft und Finanzen, Düsseldorf 1989.

Schmidt, K.H., 'Schmoller's structure and process analysis: technological change and the labour problem, in: J.G. Backhaus (ed.), Essays on Gustav Schmoller', *History of Economic Ideas* Vol. 1 (1993) Number 3 and Vol. 2 (1994) Number 1: pp. 379-95.

Schmoller, G., 'Zur Methodologie der Staats- und Sozialwissenschaften', *Jahrbuch für Gesetzgebung, Verwaltung und Volkswirtschaft im deutschen Reiche* Vol. 7 (1883): 239-58.

_____, *Wechselnde Theorien und feststehende Wahrheiten* (lecture). Büxenstein, Berlin 1897.

_____, *Grundriss der allgemeinen Volkswirtschaftslehre*, erster Teil, siebentes bis zehntes Tausend. Duncker & Humblot, Leipzig (1900) 1908.

_____, *Grundriss der allgemeinen Volkswirtschaftslehre*, zweiter Teil, dreizehntes bis fünfzehntes Tausend. Duncker & Humblot, Munich (1900) 1923.

_____, Lujo Brentano zum siebzigsten Geburtstage. In: *Lujo Brentano: Kundgebungen zu seinem 70. Geburtstag*. Ueberreicht von der Münchener Volkswirtschaftlichen Gesellschaft. Duncker & Humblot, Munich and Leipzig 1915.

Schumpeter, J.A., *Das Wesen und der Hauptinhalt der theoretischen Nationalökonomie*. Duncker & Humblot, Leipzig 1908.

_____, *Theorie der wirtschaftlichen Entwicklung*, second edition. Duncker & Humblot, Munich and Leipzig (1911) 1926.

_____, *History of economic analysis*, fourth printing. George Allen & Unwin, London (1954) 1961.

Schweizer, A., Georg Friedrich Knapp. In: D.L. Sills (ed.), *International Encyclopedia of the Social Sciences*. MacMillan 1968.

Seligman, E.R.A., Gustav Cohn. In: E.R.A. Seligman *et al.* (eds), *Encyclopaedia of the Social Sciences*. MacMillan (1930) 1949.

Senn, P.R., 'Gustav von Schmoller in English: how has he fared?, in: J.G. Backhaus (ed.), Essays on Gustav Schmoller', *History of Economic Ideas* Vol. 1 (1993) Number 3 and Vol. 2 (1994) Number 1: pp. 267-329.

Shearmur, J., From Hayek to Menger: biology, subjectivism, and welfare. In: B.C. Caldwell (ed.), *Carl Menger and his legacy in economics*. (Annual supplement to *History of Political Economy* Vol. 22.) Duke University Press, Durham 1990.

Simon, H.A., 'Altruism in economics', *American Economic Review* Vol. 83 (1993) Number 2: pp. 156-161.

Simonde de Sismondi, J.C.L., *Nouveaux principes d'économie politique, ou De la richesse dans ses rapports avec la population*. Calmann-Lévy, Paris (1819) 1971.

Smith, A., *An inquiry into the nature and causes of the wealth of nations*. Everyman's Library 412 and 413, London and New York (1776) 1910.

Söderbaum, P., Actors, roles, and networks: an institutional perspective to environmental problems. In: C. Folke and T. Kåberger (eds), *Linking the natural environment and the economy: essays from the Eco-eco group*. Kluwer Academic Publishers, Dordrecht 1991.

Solow, R.M., 'Economic history and economics', *American Economic Review* Vol. 75 (1985) Number 2: pp. 328-331.

Sombart, W., *Der moderne Kapitalismus*, erster und dritter Band. Duncker & Humblot, Munich and Leipzig (1902) 1916 and 1928.

_____, *Die deutsche Volkswirtschaft im neunzehnten Jahrhundert und im Anfang 20. Jahrhunderts*, fourth edition. Georg Bondi, Berlin (1903) 1919.

_____, *Die Juden und das Wirtschaftsleben*, zwölftes und dreizehntes Tausend. Duncker & Humblot, Munich and Leipzig (1911) 1922.

_____, *Die drei Nationalökonomien; Geschichte und System der Lehre von der Wirtschaft*. Duncker & Humblot. Munich and Leipzig 1930.

Spann, O., *Die Haupttheorien der Volkswirtschaftslehre*, eighteenth edition. Quelle & Meyer, Leipzig (1910) 1928.

Spiegel, H.W., *The growth of economic thought*. Duke University Press, Durham, North Carolina 1971.

Spiethoff, A., *Die wirtschaftlichen Wechsellagen; Aufschwung, Krise, Stockung*. Mohr, Tübingen and Polygrafischer Verlag, Zürich (1923) 1955.

_____, Die Allgemeine Volkswirtschaftslehre als geschichtliche Theorie. Die Wirtschaftsstile. In: A. Spiethoff (ed.), *Festgabe für Werner Sombart*. Duncker & Humblot, Munich 1933.

_____, Anschauliche und reine volkswirtschaftliche Theorie und ihr Verhältnis zueinander. In: E. Salin (ed.), *Festgabe für Alfred Weber*. Schneider, Heidelberg 1948.

Steuart, J., *The works, political, metaphisical & chronological, of Sir James Steuart*. Reprints of Economic Classics. Augustus Kelly, New York (1767) (1805) 1967.

Streissler, E.W., The influence of German economics on the work of Menger and Marshall. In: B.C. Caldwell (ed.), *Carl Menger and his legacy in economics*. (Annual supplement to *History of Political Economy* Vol. 22.) Duke University Press, Durham 1990.

Stuijvenberg, J.H. van, "De" these van Weber: een poging tot interpretatie. In: *Economie dezer dagen*. Universitaire Pers, Rotterdam 1973.

Sutherland, J.W., *A General Systems Philosophy for the Social and Behavioral Sciences*. Braziller, New York 1973.

Tawney, R.H., *Religion and the rise of capitalism*. Harcourt, Bruce & Co., New York 1926.

Thoben, H., 'Mechanistic and organistic analogies in economics reconsidered', *Kyklos* Vol. 35 (1982): pp. 292-306.

Thurlings, T.L.M., *Turgot en zijn tijdgenoten*. Mededelingen Landbouwhogeschool, Number 78-11, Wageningen 1978.

Tietenberg, T.H., *Environmental economics and policy*. Harper Collins, New York 1994.

Tinbergen, J., *Economische bewegingsleer*. Noord-Hollandsche Uitgevers, Amsterdam 1943.

_____, *On the theory of economic policy*. North-Holland Publishers, Amsterdam 1952.

_____, *Economic policy: principles and design*. North-Holland Publishers, Amsterdam 1956.

Torstensson, J., 'Property rights and economic growth', *Kyklos* Vol. 47 (1994): pp. 231-244.

Veblen, T., *The theory of the leisure class: an economic study of institutions*, new edition. Modern Library, New York (1899) 1934.

_____, Professor Clark's economics. Reprinted excerpts. In: E.K. Hunt *et al.* (ed.), *A critique of economic theory*. Penguin Education, Penguin Books, Harmondsworth (1908) 1972.

Vincent, T.L., 'Vulnerability of a Prey-Predator Model under harvesting, in: T.L. Vincent and J.M. Showvonsh (eds), Renewable resource management', *Lecture Notes in Biomathematics* Vol. 40 (1981).

Waardenburg, J.G., Professor Jan Tinbergen 1903-1994. *Desiderius* (Journal Erasmus University, Rotterdam) Vol. 7 (1994) Number 3: pp.2-6.

Weber, M., Die "Objektivität" sozialwissenschaftlicher und sozialpolitischer Erkenntniss. In: *idem*, *Gesammelte Aufsätze zur Wissenschaftslehre*. Edited by J. Winckelman, third edition. Mohr, Tübingen (1904) 1968.

_____, Die protestantische Ethik und der Geist des Kapitalismus. In: *idem*, *Gesammelte Aufsätze zur Religionssoziologie* I, fourth edition. Mohr, Tübingen (1904/5) 1947.

_____, Der Sinn der "Wertfreiheit" der soziologischen und ökonomischen Wissenschaften. In: *idem*, *Gesammelte Aufsätze zur Wissenschaftslehre*. Edited by J. Winckelman, third edition. Mohr, Tübingen (1917) 1968.

_____, Wissenschaft als Beruf. In: *idem, Gesammelte Aufsätze zur Wissenschaftslehre*. Edited by J. Winckelman, third edition. Mohr, Tübingen (1919) 1968.

_____, *Wirtschaft und Gesellschaft: Grundriss der verstehenden Soziologie*. Edited by J. Winckelman. Kiepenheuer & Witsch, Cologne and Berlin (1921) 1964.

Weizsäcker, C.F., *Die Einheit der Natur*. Deutscher Taschenbuch Verlag, Munich and Vienna (1971) 1982.

Wieser, F., *Der natürliche Werth*. Alfred Hölder, Vienna 1889.

Wright, H.R.C., 'Schmoller and economic history: then and now, in: J.G. Backhaus (ed.), Essays on Gustav Schmoller', *History of Economic Ideas* Vol. 1 (1993) Number 3 and Vol. 2 (1994) Number 1: pp. 101-16.

Zimmermann, K.F., 'Trade and dynamic efficiency', *Kyklos* Vol. 40 (1987): pp. 73-87.

Zinn, K.G., *Die Selbstzerstörung der Wachstumsgesellschaft*. Rowohlt, Reinbek bei Hamburg 1980.

Zuidema, J.R., 'Carl Menger, author of a research programme', *Journal of Economic Studies* Vol. 15 (1988) Number 3/4: pp. 13-35.

Zuidema, R.P., *Produktie, kapitaal en produktiviteit*. Bohn, Haarlem 1970.

Index

The Author

Jacob Jan Krabbe was born at Hoogeveen, a provincial town in the Netherlands, on February 11th, 1928. After completing his secondary education in 1947, he spent a couple of years in the then new Republic of Indonesia, where he worked in banking and trade. Back in the Netherlands, he studied economics at the Nederlandsche Economische Hoogeschool in Rotterdam, now Erasmus University. During his study Krabbe paid a great deal of attention to the theoretical ideas of Professor L.M. Koyck and to Professor J. Tinbergen's view on development programming.

After graduating in 1963, Jaap Krabbe was appointed to the staff of Wageningen Agricultural University, first as assistant, later as senior lecturer and finally as associate professor. He taught economic theory, environmental economics and theory of economic thought. During a few years of reorientation, he acted as head of the Department of General Economics. He also set up a cooperation programme between Wageningen Agricultural University and the Agricultural University Debrecen, in Hungary. His last position was that of visiting professor of economics at the Mediterranean Agronomic Institute of Chania (Crete), Greece. At present, he devotes most of his time to writing on economics.

In 1974 Krabbe published his PhD dissertation entitled *Utility, considered individually and collectively*, in which he incorporated some organistic ideas into welfare theory. His first work on historicism appeared in 1983, followed by a series of articles on environmental and resource economics and on the history of economic thought.

MIX
Papier aus verantwortungsvollen Quellen
Paper from responsible sources
FSC® C105338

If you have any concerns about our products,
you can contact us on
ProductSafety@springernature.com

In case Publisher is established outside the EU,
the EU authorized representative is:
Springer Nature Customer Service Center GmbH
Europaplatz 3, 69115 Heidelberg, Germany

Printed by Libri Plureos GmbH
in Hamburg, Germany